GW00372093

A Bishop Could Not Do Otherwise

Compiled and edited by Míceál O'Neill, O.Carm

A Bishop Could Not Do Otherwise

The life and witness of Bishop Donal Lamont
(1911–2003)

the columba press

First published in 2013 by
the columba press
55A Spruce Avenue,
Stillorgan Industrial Park,
Blackrock, Co. Dublin

Cover by Red Rattle Design
Origination by The Columba Press
Printed by CPI Antony Rowe

ISBN 978 1 78218 067 8

Purchased People first published in 1959 by Catholic Mission Press, Gwelo.

Speech from the Dock first published in 1977 by Kevin Mayhew Publishers in association with the Catholic Institute for International Relations.

The maps on pp 62–3 are based on those which appeared in the original 1977 publication of *Speech from the Dock* and have been illustrated by Eve Anna Farrell.

Contents

Introduction

Ten years have passed since the death of Bishop Donal Lamont, on 14 August 2003. Just when it might have seemed that he had faded from memory we offer this book as a tribute to his life, work and witness, especially in Zimbabwe where he served as a missionary from 1946 to 1982.

The idea for this publication came from a joint initiative of the Carmelite provinces in Spain and the University of Comillas of Madrid, on the centenary of Bishop Lamont's birth in 1911, to publish a Spanish translation of his very important pastoral letter, *Purchased People,* along with his *Speech from the Dock,* enriched by two conferences, one by Fr Fernando Millán Romeral, O.Carm., present Prior General of the Carmelite Order, and Professor Carmen Márquez Beunza, of the University of Comillas.

This present volume is the translation of that work. It includes a reprint of *Purchased People* (1959) and *Speech from the Dock* 1977, the latter with kind permission of Mayhew and McCrimmond Publishers.

Fernando Millán's article offers a biography of Bishop Lamont, with a theological analysis of *Purchased People* and the bishop's contribution to the Second Vatican Council. Professor Beunza, for her part, looks at the bishop and diocese of Umtali in the context of the development of the Church in Africa, using as the title of her article, Lamont's episcopal motto, *Ut placeam Deo.*

The foreword is written by Mrs Mary McAleese, former President of Ireland, who shares Lamont's Northern Irish origins and is a long-time admirer of the human rights champion from Zimbabwe.

The title chosen for this book, *A Bishop Could Not Do Otherwise,* reflects a very strong feature of Lamont's character. Whether it was in Ireland, Zimbabwe or Rome, Lamont was driven by a deep moral imperative that had to do with his life as a follower of Christ and as a bishop of the Catholic Church.

This volume is important not only as a tribute to the life and witness of Bishop Donal Lamont, but because both his stand on human rights in Zimbabwe and his plea for a more inspiring document on the mission of the Church from the Second Vatican Council must be considered as two important contributions to the defence of the human person and the integrity of the Catholic Church.

Míceál O'Neill, O.Carm.

Foreword

Who could ever hope to do justice in a few words to Donal Lamont or to his legacy? God gave him a long life and Donal still managed to pack it full of enough drama for fifty lives. He hailed from Ballycastle in the far north of Ulster and as a boy was to know first-hand the misery of his brother and sister Catholics who, after Ireland's partition, found themselves in a State whose political and spiritual leaders saw nothing incongruous in describing it with pleasure as a 'Protestant State for a Protestant people.' The thirst for equality and justice became his unquenchable lifelong companion. The well of courage that he drew from never ran dry no matter how difficult life became for him. Indeed life did become extremely difficult, though not in his beloved Ireland but in far off Africa where he went as a Carmelite missionary priest in 1946 some years after his studies in both Dublin and Rome.

If the territory then known as Rhodesia was vastly different from the Emerald Isle, its history as a colony whose impoverished people were dominated by an oppressive regime was very familiar to Donal. He knew this story intimately and took little time in making common cause with black Africans and thus became a figure of hate among the ruling white elite. 'Far from your policies defending Christianity and Western civilisation, as you claim,' he told Ian Smith, 'they mock the law of Christ …'

As the first Bishop of Umtali he stood with those who fought for their freedom and lost his as a consequence, sentenced to ten years imprisonment for taking the only moral stand that was possible at the time. He was deported to Ireland in 1977 without serving his sentence but his pastoral letter of 1959, *Purchased People,* in defence of Zimbabwe's black people had eventually galvanised the leaders of the Catholic Church to champion their cause and set the scene for a historic regime change. Donal was nominated for the Nobel Peace Prize in 1978. In that same year Kenya included his image in a series of postage stamps to mark the Year of Anti-Apartheid. He returned, as a hero, to the newly-independent Zimbabwe in 1980, at the invitation of Robert Mugabe. He soon recognised that the time had come for him to resign as bishop and leave the opening for the appointment of a Zimbabwean as bishop of what was now called Mutare.

Donal never seemed to mind being a voice crying in the wilderness. Over a decade earlier his fiery speech at the Second Vatican Council earned him a standing ovation. Pushing the Council fathers to use their own initiative and go far beyond the dull, unremarkable pre-council positions of the Curia, he told them that the missionary bishops had come looking for Pentecostal fire but were being given 'a penny candle'; they had asked for modern weapons to conquer the world for Christ but were being 'presented with bows and arrows'. It was to be the most remarkable intervention by any Irish bishop and it not only earned him the admiration of Paul VI but saved the Council from simply rubber-stamping the Curia's pre-packed documents. At the Synod of Bishops in Rome in 1971 he suggested that 'suitable married men' should be ordained when unmarried priests were in short supply. Needless to say, his ideas got a somewhat cold reception. No matter, Donal knew how to live with criticism and how to live in loving fraternity with his critics. His was the Church of thinkers, of lively discussion and debate, of pushing out into the deep unafraid.

Donal had a long and fulfilling retirement in his beloved Terenure College. When he died on 14 August 2003 he was, at his request, buried in his brown Carmelite habit and not in his episcopal robes. To the end he was faithful to his vocation as a Carmelite, as a courageous follower of Christ and of the truth, a man of great intellectual and spiritual gifts, a great priest and a formidable bishop. Like I said at the beginning, I could never hope to do justice to this man who was guided by the angels. As he was and always will be my very special hero and inspiration I hope this volume will open up his life anew and allow a fresh evaluation of Donal Lamont's remarkable contribution to the history of Zimbabwe and the history of the contemporary Catholic Church in Africa and throughout the world. His legacy deserves it and we deserve the memory of his legacy. His generous heart, out of the blue, wrote me personal letters of encouragement and I am so happy to be able to give something back to him by being associated with this lovely publication.

Mary McAleese

List of Contributors

DONAL LAMONT, born 1911 in Northern Ireland and became a Carmelite friar in 1930. He began his missionary work in Zimbabwe in 1946, was ordained the Bishop of Umtali in 1957 and was tried in 1976 for not reporting the activity of outlaws. He was deported from Zimbabwe in 1978. He died in Dublin in 2003.

CARMEN MÁRQUEZ BEUNZA graduated in Law at the Universidad de Valencia, and in Theology at the Universidad Pontificia Comillas in Madrid. Since 2002 she has been a professor of the Theology Faculty at the Universidad Pontificia Comillas where she lectures in Christianity, Social Ethics, Evangelisation and Culture.

MARY MCALEESE, Doctor in Law, former Pro-Vice Chancellor of Queens University in Belfast, President of Ireland from 1997 to 2011, the period in which an end was brought to the conflict in Northern Ireland, now studying in Rome.

MICEAL O'NEILL, O.CARM, currently Prior of the Carmelite International Centre of St Albert in Rome.

FERNANDO MILLÁN ROMERAL, O.CARM., former professor of Dogmatic Theology at the Universidad Pontificia Comillas in Madrid, now Prior General of the Carmelite Order.

TIM SHEEHY, staff member of the Catholic Institute of International Relations (now Progressio). In 1987, after having been deported from Rhodesia, in gratitude for the support he had received from CIIR, Bishop Lamont invited Tim Sheehy to witness him receiving an Honorary Degree from Notre Dame University along with the recently elected President Jimmy Carter and human rights champions Cardinal Paul Arns from Brazil, and Cardinal Stephen Kim from Korea.

EILEEN SUDWORTH, staff member of the Catholic Institute of International Relations (now Progressio), along with Tim Sheehy, worked closely with Bishop Lamont during the period he was most active as Chair of the Rhodesian Catholic Commission Justice and Peace (CCJP). Eileen was sent to Rhodesia covertly in 1975 to meet with the bishop in order to smuggle out of the country for release in London a critical report on the war, *The Man in the Middle*, which could not be published locally.

Purchased People

PASTORAL INSTRUCTION OF THE RIGHT REV. DONAL
RAYMOND LAMONT, O.CARM., BISHOP OF UMTALI,
TO THE CATHOLICS OF THAT DIOCESE

Note from Original Text

Although throughout this instruction I have referred mainly to the two numerically important races, i.e. Africans and Europeans, it is to be understood that what has been said in regard to racial discrimination applies to all other races or groups of people. Racial discrimination of its very nature is an evil thing and cannot be sufficiently condemned.

The unhappy events of the past months and the conflicting opinions which have resulted from them, urge me as your Bishop, to direct to you, the Faithful of the Diocese of Umtali, the following instruction:

Teaching Authority of Bishops

At what was probably the most critical moment of His life, when Our Divine Lord stood in judgement before Pilate, the representative of the greatest civil power on earth, He described His teaching mission in these words: 'For this was I born and for this came I into the world, that I should give testimony to the truth' (Jn 18:37). That same mission He later confided to His Apostles, telling them: 'As the Father hath sent me, I also send you' (Jn 20:21). Finally, His last command to them before His ascension, was that they should go and teach all nations, in the confidence that He would be with them always, guiding, instructing and comforting them, till the world itself should cease to be (Mt 27:19).

The Bishops of the Church united under the leadership of the successor of St Peter, are themselves corporately the successors of the Apostolic College and inherit its authority. They must teach, govern in things spiritual, and administer the patrimony of sanctification committed to them by the Author of all sanctity Himself. They must feed their flocks with the word of truth, preaching it in season and out of season, reproving, entreating, rebuking, in all patience, and doctrine (2 Tim 4:2).

In the fulfilment of his teaching office, a Bishop must always bear in mind that the message confided to him is not his to modify or dilute, or least of all, to silence. 'That which I tell you in the dark, speak ye in the light: and that which you hear in the ear, preach ye upon the housetops. And fear ye not them that kill the body and are not able to kill the soul: but rather fear him that can destroy both soul and body in hell' (Mt 10:27ss). No wonder the terrifying words of St Paul re-echo in the heart of every Bishop from the day of his appointment: 'For if I preach the Gospel, it is no glory to me, for a necessity lieth upon me: for woe is unto me if I preach not the gospel!' (1 Cor 9:16). Preach the Bishop must; not permitting himself to be silenced by merely human fears or temporal considerations; not watering down his message for the sake of spurious peace, or loss of friendship with any worldly authority, or possibility of being deliberately misinterpreted by wicked men. 'Every one that shall confess me before men, I will also confess him before my Father Who is in heaven. But he that shall deny me before men, I will also deny him before my Father Who is in heaven' (Mt 10:32–3).

It would constitute the most dreadful apostasy were a Bishop to fail in the teaching mission entrusted to him, seeking to come to terms with the spirit of worldliness, taking secularism and materialism for granted, and attempting coexistence with a Godless world. Terrible beyond all describing would it be, if so forgetting his apostolic heritage he were to forget also the supranational quality of the Church, its divine promise of indefectibility, its nature as the Mystical Body of Christ, its timelessness, its divinely guaranteed permanence, its dowry of suffering and persecution, and allow it to become the willing servant of any political party or of other temporal power.

No, the Church, through her Bishops, must speak no matter what the fears, what the opposition, what the criticism. Unless she does, the notion of Almighty God's having anything to do in the affairs of nations and of individuals may be lost and the ideal of a social order based on the Christian principles of justice and charity may be abandoned as an unrealistic, impractical and visionary illusion.

There are some who sturdily resent the miraculous existence of the Church; more who refuse to recognise it; others who would confine all church activity to the sacristy, demanding of the Church the subservience of silence in all public affairs. Yet, oddly enough, it is precisely such people who most bitterly and vociferously condemn the Church for failing to influence profoundly our modern life.

States may persistently disregard or repudiate the rights of the spiritual power, rejecting its tutelage and claiming in their blindness *absolute* sovereignty; but whether they like it or not, the Church must insist on her imprescriptible right to intervene in temporal matters, insofar as these affect the spiritual order of salvation, e.g. the denouncing or avoiding of sin, the preservation of the order established by God, or the maintenance of her own liberty.

At this moment in the history of our country, when the future is being moulded for a multiracial community, when the spirit of the nation is yet young, and when the majority of its people are receiving for the first time the basic truths of Christianity and attempting to reconcile them with the secularist belief and behaviour which they see all about them, it is more than ever necessary that I, your Bishop, should as far as is in my power, proclaim for you the teaching of the Church in all its extent and profoundity, but especially in regard to those matters which immediately affect the relationship of one race of people to another.

The Fundamental Problem

The great problem which here and now confronts the Church in Southern Rhodesia, and indeed in the whole of Central Africa, is not simply that of solving racial difficulties or of reconciling the political aspirations of varied ethnic or national groups. The conflicts which these provide are but manifestations of a much more deeply rooted and dangerous evil. What is really at the heart of the trouble is that God has been banished politely from public life, His eternal law has been quietly set aside, hesitant lip service is paid to Him only, and thoughtless men attempt to order society without taking the Maker's rules into account.

No less evil is the belief, so prevalent in many places, that Our Divine Lord is in some way to be dissociated and distinguished from His Church; that He is, at most, a mere historical figure long separated from the world, that He has no care for men, except insofar as long ago He gave to mankind an admittedly admirable code of behaviour, which however 'impractical and idealistic' it may be, nevertheless represents high ethical standards. The living Christ, today present in His Church, fulfilling His promise ever to be with it, speaking through His Vicar on earth, teaching with unerring voice imperishable truths – all this has been forgotten, derided, or politely disregarded, and as a consequence, fickle men with no immutable principles to assist them, make expediency their law and their beliefs become as variable as the wind. Our civilisation, forgetting the historic religious beliefs on which it is founded and mesmerised by the brilliance of its scientific and technical achievements, has rejected the moral force which science is unable to supply, and can only end in chaos if it does not return to traditional Christianity.

It is difficult to exaggerate the extent and gravity of the dangers to society once it rejects religion, because man's religion and that of society itself, represents his basic attitude to life and his notion of what all things are. It is the great dynamic of social life and the source of all true cultural progress. Once religion goes from public life, society loses its vitality and social decay sets in; law itself becomes a lawless thing; legal positivism takes the place of divine ordinance; public men forget that they are responsible to God for their official actions and confusion becomes inevitable.

It would seem that such a sad condition of affairs threatens to exist here in Southern Rhodesia, and that if it be not summarily and seriously rejected, there can be no hope of real cooperation between the different racial groups in this potentially great land. Men must so learn the truths of Christianity that they shall be doers of the word and not hearers only (Jas 1:22). The moral idealism of the Christian must be strengthened or revivified. His faith in the practical possibility of Christian living must be restored, because Our Divine Lord's doctrine of justice and charity can alone provide the basis for mutual understanding and ultimate peace. That doctrine has in other ages proved successful in reconciling the varied social conditions of men, has civilised barbarous races, has made clear how master and servant can live in the peace of the one great Christian family. That doctrine has lost nothing of its original power for good, and if put into daily practice, can accomplish as much today as it did in ages past.

The Family of Nations

One of the chief causes of conflict between nations and races is that once they have ceased to be God-conscious, they not only forget their common origin in creation, but they lose also the vision of God's Fatherhood of men and the notion of the family quality of the nations themselves. That nation should war against nation, race struggle against race, is then accepted as a natural thing, and something to be expected, and not rather as humiliating and unnatural as would be open dissension between members of one family. The idea of family responsibility among the nations has been neglected. That one nation should be bound either in justice or in charity, or by both, to assist its brother nation in need, lifting it up from poverty or degradation, sharing its material or cultural wealth with its poorer or unprivileged family relative, *because of the family relationship in God* – all this has long ago been forgotten by the generality of men, and must be taught anew.

Not only this, but in the Christian ethos, man has a further and more individual obligation towards his fellows, because the heart of Our Divine Lord's teaching is the revelation of the paternity of God of an altogether special kind. It is not only a collective paternity such as was acknowledged by the Chosen Race, but an intimate and personal relationship, in virtue of which each of us may call God 'Our Father', and are brothers in Christ, one to another. All this has been accomplished by 'the one Mediator of God and men, the Man, Christ Jesus, Who gave Himself as redemption for all' (1 Tim 2:5), and thus gathered us up in adopted sonship in such a mysterious way that the Apostle Paul could say: 'You are now the body of Christ and members of it' (1 Cor 12:27) and could urge that there be no want of unity between us, but that we should be 'mutually careful one for the other' (1 Cor 25).

This personal yet social and community character of redeemed man, our membership one with another in the Mystical Body of Christ, we must ever keep before us if we would order our lives in peace; for Our Divine Lord did not come on earth merely to reveal methods of obtaining a better understanding between man and man, considered separately one from the other, no more than He came merely to enunciate principles of decent behaviour, or to establish His Church as an extrinsic aid or court of appeal in moments of difficulty. No. He came to complete our family relationship with our Heavenly Father in the living family which is the Church.

The Dignity of the Human Person

This belief in our common membership of God's family of men, involves a daily and vivid realisation of the natural dignity of the human person; because, remember this, the doctrine of the Brotherhood of Man under the Fatherhood of God, is not simply a silly sentimental idea, but a plain fact based on reason. And this fact alone should be sufficient in itself to increase our regard for one another, even if we had not the more noble and compelling motives of Christianity to encourage us. Just think of it: so earthbound in vision and materialistic in aim have men become, that they have ceased to marvel at the miracle which man of his very nature is. A renewing and vitalising sense of wonder and regard for the natural dignity of every human person, irrespective of his condition in life, must be thoroughly developed in each of us, if we are to live in a real world and not in a world of fantasy created by our own irrational prejudices. Justice demands it. Truth requires it. Peace can come from it.

No wonder men have little regard for one another when they have even lost all sense of their own natural perfection! The more delicate and intricate a piece of mere machinery, the more we care for it and esteem it. How much more regard should be given to man *as man*, the maker of such things, whose form and faculty are of such excellence that he bridges the gap between the limitless world of spirit and that of sense, and by his Creator's will, reduces the unintelligible chaos of the world to reason and order!

Here in Central Africa, we need, first of all, just this: an appreciation of the natural dignity of man in his quality of rational and free being.

But this is only a beginning. Of immeasurably greater importance is it that the light of Faith should fill our eyes, and that we should learn to look on ourselves and on our neighbours every one, as the friends of Our Divine Lord. This above all, gives men their real dignity, because since Calvary and the

Resurrection, they know that they are no longer made for this world and no longer fit into it; that they are no more mere creatures, but by Baptism the adopted sons of God, brothers of Christ and heirs of Heaven. Such is our greatness, so boundless the love of our Creator for us, that we are in the words of the Prince of the Apostles 'a chosen generation, a kingly priesthood, a holy nation, a purchased people' (1 Pet 2:9).

Should not reason and justice and every noble instinct of civilised man, and particularly of every Christian man, rebel at the thought of despising or branding with a stigma of inferiority, our neighbour with whom we share so much in common? In this regard, we cannot do better than to quote the words of our late Holy Father, Pope Pius XII. Writing of the unity of the human race, he says: 'We see it as one in its common origin from the hand of a Creator: "one God and Father of us all, who is above all and reaches through all and dwells in all of us" (Eph 4:6).' We see it as one in its composition, involving the union of a body with an immortal and spiritual soul; as one in the proximate end which is assigned to all of us, and in the common duties we are called upon to perform in this life. We see it as one sharing a common habitation, this world of ours, whose resources every man has a natural right to enjoy, insofar as they are needed for his preservation and his self-development. We see it as one in the possession of a common supernatural end, God Himself, to which we must direct all our actions, and in the means He has given to all of us in common, enabling us to reach that end at last.

The Apostle of the Gentiles proves the unity of the human family from those links which bind us to Him Who is the image of the invisible God, Jesus Christ, in Whom 'all things were made' (Col 1:16). He proves it from the fact of our common Redemption; telling us how Christ, through His bitter Passion, restored us to God's friendship, as it has been ours at first, and reconciled God to men: 'there is only one God, and only one mediator between God and men, the man Christ Jesus' (1 Tim 2:5).

And He, that same negotiator of all our peace and salvation, when He was preparing to make the supreme sacrifice of Himself, uttered in the silence of the Cenacle some words which were designed to draw the bond of friendship closer between God and the human race; words which, echoing down the centuries from those sacred lips of His, spur on our hearts, unloving as they are and soiled with hatreds, to heroic deeds of charity, 'This is my commandment, that you should love one another as I have loved you' (Jn 15:12).

Yet in spite of this, in spite of this divine commandment, such is the tragedy of the world's forgetfulness of God, that men look down on, and treat with contempt, and persecute, and deny ordinary justice to their fellow men, and continue to call themselves Christians. How far have we fallen from the primitive practice of the Church which made the heathens cry out in admiration: 'Behold these Christians, how they love one another!'

Rejection of the Natural Law

It is not surprising that having turned away from God, men should then have rejected His Eternal Law and its manifestation in human nature, which we call Natural Law. Until this one universal standard of morality is put back in its place of honour, all human legislation must be rendered nugatory. Bereft of its guidance, both private life and the condition of society itself become chaotic because all other laws for man's conduct must first accord with this primal law and any positive ordinance which offends against it cannot be regarded as binding in conscience. Wherever the genius of law seeks out its origins, there it will find Natural Law. There can be no justice, no true freedom without it, for freedom consists in being ruled with justice. And since justice is only possible by observing the Natural Law, all so-called laws which reject it as a basis are bound to fail. As a modern philosopher puts it, 'The Natural Law always buries its undertakers.'

Arising from this neglect of the Natural Law and the consequent ignorance of the kind of being man is, come equally disastrous errors regarding human rights, and a failure to distinguish between those rights which are fundamental and those which are contingent or secondary. Nothing but confusion prevails in this realm of thought here in Central Africa, with the result that grave injustices are inflicted and prolonged on whole groups of people, family life is disrupted, the liberty of the individual is needlessly constrained, uninstructed masses are confused about what is their duty and what is their due, and legislators themselves, with no very clear idea of the essential nature of man or of his destiny, and with no unalterable principles to guide them, enact measures so ill-considered and immature, that they make a mockery of justice itself.

It will be useful to our purpose to remember that rights are the result of obligation. In the realm of human conduct, this means that since man must live according to the nature which God has given him, he must not be deprived of those facilities which are essential to this end. Such facilities, or rights as we may call them, are fundamental or primary. As social conditions change, and according to the political milieu in which he lives, other so-called rights may enter in, e.g. in the democratic system, the right to vote. This, however, is not truly a fundamental right at all, but at the most, a secondary or contingent one.

Failure to anchor positive legislation on to Natural Law, to realise the source of natural rights, and to distinguish between their degrees, can do irreparable harm to any society, and can destroy any possibility of peaceful coexistence between people of different cultures or of varying degrees of culture or of different racial origins. And this is so, because morality is a higher norm than the positive law of man, since it consists in preserving the hierarchy of being established by the Creator. It involves as of necessity, the giving to the human person all that belongs to him by right so that he may develop his natural genius; and it also includes the due recognition of the complementary character of Family, State and Church, under the supreme dominion of God Who is the Author of each. From this it follows, that an immoral state of affairs exists when nationalism or race or economics or any other similar thing becomes the dominant norm of behaviour, and is placed above man, considered as an individual or as a group.

The Clash of Nationalisms

The problem of the relations between peoples of different civil-isations or of unequal degrees of civilisation, is of the gravest moment to the Church, since Christianity is primarily a missionary religion. It is a practical problem too, in a more than ordinary sense, here in Southern Rhodesia, where the African people, hitherto used to another form of social organisation and to the simplest material standard of living, lacking science, literature, and the art of mechanical devices, are confronted with a totally new order of things, altogether centuries in advance of anything they ever previously knew.

This meeting of two races so greatly differing in their degrees of development, and in the condition of ruler and ruled, could not but bring in its train problems of the most profound complexity. The normal difficulties involved in working out a peaceful way of living between them would provide trouble enough for the most skilled legislators; but these problems whose solution has frequently been, and in recent times, more diligently sought, have been heightened and intensified, not only by disregard of the principles inherent in Natural Law, but also by the sudden appearance of the unbridled nationalism of race, as represented by groups of extremist Africans and no less extremist Europeans.

It must be said that reports of the conflict between the races have been greatly exaggerated both within the country and abroad. In practice, there is, thanks be to God, a very remarkable degree of harmony in the everyday relationships between the African and the European. The recent appeal to extremism and to the use of force on the part of some Africans, is probably not of local origin, for it is something quite alien to this patient and peace-loving people. Moreover, it is unrepresentative both of the masses themselves and of the more advanced and responsible elements among them. It is an importation, a manifestation of a wider movement which has already appeared in other parts of the continent, and which may conveniently be termed Pan-Africanism. Its basis is the desire of the awakening African people to take over government from the European colonial powers, and to achieve independence everywhere in the continent. Whether this desire is itself a natural growth or whether it has been inspired and sponsored by external agencies, has, as we have suggested, not yet been clearly established. But the fact of the appearance and development of a new national spirit among many of the African people, hitherto apparently indifferent to its appeal, is something which cannot be denied.

Nationalism True and False

In order to obtain some clarity in the matter, it will be useful to keep in mind the real distinction which exists between the State and the Nation. They are not synonymous terms, but are distinguished by the end to which each is adapted. The purpose or end of the State is the establishment and preservation of order, for the benefit of the community; that of the Nation, is the development of a people's national personality.

Again, we should not confuse national life in the proper sense, with nationalistic politics. The former, as Pope Pius XII said in his Christmas Message of 1954, is 'the right and prized possession of a nation, which may and should be promoted; the other, as a germ infinitely harmful, will never be sufficiently repelled. The nationalist state is the seed of rivalries and the fomenter of discord'.

If nationalism as it manifests itself here among the African people, means the desire of that people to participate fully in the life and in the development of their country; if it means a will to hold on to the things which they believe to have a traditional and cultural value and which are not contrary to the Moral Law; if it means a refusal to be stripped of their ancient character and turned out in mass production, de-characterised and presented to the world as ersatz Europeans; or if it means a sincere and simple wish to be regarded by all and to be treated by the State as equal citizens, and not as second-class citizens, then obviously such aspirations are beyond reproach and the Church must support them.

If, on the other hand, nationalism – African or any other – means simply xenophobia, hatred of anything foreign, or if it means the permanent domination of one race over another *at any cost*, the Church cannot ever approve of it. There is much evidence to show that Pan-Africanism is of this kind and that the African National Congress is infected by such errors. Both these movements show little interest in preserving the true and positive values of African culture and society; instead, they encourage race hatred and are segregationist in essence. Such nationalism, or any other which is based simply on race or colour, must be condemned, because it denies the common origin of man, his solidarity in nature and in redemption, and because it disregards the fact of the family quality of the nations themselves.

Nevertheless, it must not be forgotten either, that the desire of a national group to be free from subjection to a foreign ruler, is a most legitimate one, provided that it can be achieved without any violation of justice; for justice forbids rebellion against duly constituted authority which has not forfeited its mandate by a grave abuse of its power. Of such laudable wish for freedom, Pope Pius XII said in his memorable encyclical *Fidei Donum*: 'Would that a just and progressive political freedom be not denied to those people who aspire to it, and that no obstacle be set in the way.'

Extreme Means of Redress

In this regard it should be remembered that any organised attempt to overthrow a legally constituted government can only be justified by the presence of the three following conditions:

1. If there be on the part of the government, grave and prolonged violation of the rights of the subject.
2. If all constitutional methods of obtaining redress have been seriously tried and have failed.
3. If there be a reasonable prospect of success and of setting up an objectively better government; because unless there be, the common good demands that civil war be averted.

Rights of Indigenous Primitive People

Just as rebellion against duly constituted authority is forbidden unless these conditions are fulfilled, so too it should be borne in mind that it is not only foolish but equally wrong for a colonising Power to neglect the legitimate aspirations of the subject people. No matter what the social condition of those people may have been; irrespective of their ignorance of the sciences and the arts; even though they may have had the lowest standards of private and public morality, these people still have the fundamental character of men, and still possess the rights which come to them from the Natural Law. They have a natural right to life, to freedom of movement, to the development of their faculties, to association with their fellows, and to all those other things which are essential to human living. Moreover, even though as far as growth in civilisation is concerned, they may be regarded as 'children', they still have, just as minors can have, *'dominium'*, rights of ownership. From this it follows that any violent seizure of territory which was at the time inhabited and cultivated by a native tribe and subject to the authority of its rulers, constitutes unjust aggression. Furthermore, any exploitation of the country, of such a kind as would destroy or impoverish it or lead to the establishment of exclusive privileges for the newcomer to the detriment of the indigenous people, or which would entail a humiliating or injurious alienation of sovereignty, is equally without moral justification.

Prescriptive Right of Colonial Power

Again, even in the case of unjust conquest by a usurping Power, if the new rulers do in fact fulfil the functions of government and administration; and if through custom and lapse of time and the tacit consent of the governed, their so-called authority remains unquestioned, the principle of prescription may be applied and although the new rulers have objectively no true claim to the allegiance of the people, rebellion even against that imperfect authority is still unjustifiable, unless the conditions for it, as already described, are simultaneously fulfilled.

Nationality not Paramount

Nevertheless, although the rights inherent in nationality are real, the claims of nationality are not paramount. The different nations are all members of the one human family of God, and while each has the right to freedom and to its individual development, this right must be coordinated with and subordinated to the rights of the other nations. The claims of a universal human society must be preferred to those of any one nation, just as the greater good is to be preferred to the particular. In other words, the fact of the family quality of the nations must ever be borne in mind.

Benevolent Colonialism

It should be particularly borne in mind by colonising Powers, because if their primary intention be not to destroy the existing society of the indigenous people, but to prepare them for self-government; and if they aim to bring the benefits of their own civilisation to an unprivileged people in an undeveloped country; and if in the administration of justice they are truly impartial and constantly remember that their power is tutelary, and that they act towards the indigenous people as elder brothers in the human family, they can even perform a great work of charity by so colonising. Nor should it be forgotten, that as from nature, men still have the right of acquisition by the first corner, to territory which is either unclaimed and full of potential wealth or sparsely inhabited by nomadic tribes who have no intention of remaining there permanently; and men still have the right, as from nature, to travel and trade and settle, and to have a share in those good things of the earth which are not already the property of others.

Where the occupation of such unclaimed and undeveloped countries is legitimate, as in the manner described, the occupying Power is thereafter justified in introducing laws calculated to raise the standards, social, political, and intellectual, of the native people. But it must ever bear in mind that such reforms must be directed to the good of the governed, and it must try to harmonise their rights with the legitimate needs of the newcomers, and never seek to benefit these latter to the detriment of the former. Again, it must not introduce anything which disrupts tribal life, without putting anything better in its place. On the contrary, it must respect the national character, the native language, and every tradition which is not in conflict with the Moral Law. Finally, it must bear in mind that all innovations must be directed to preparing the indigenous people for the responsibilities consequent on their taking full part in the government of the country. Such preparation cannot be accomplished overnight; it may even take some generations, depending in great measure on the natural disposition of the people; but with charity, justice, and Christian education, it can confidently be hoped for.

African Change of Outlook

If we are to achieve permanent conditions of peace in this country, not only must the principles which we have here enunciated, be promptly and universally applied, but as a necessary concomitant, the attitudes of both European and African must undergo radical change.

The African, for instance, must recognise in realistic humility, that however high his thoughts may aspire to complete independence, he is as yet equipped neither academically nor technically nor economically, to assume complete control of what is rapidly becoming a highly complex and industrialised country. He must face the fact, that his European neighbour would appear to have at least prescriptive rights here, that he intends to remain, and that his presence is, for the moment at any rate, essential to the development of the country's enormous potential. He must remember too, that in spite of the inequalities which operate against him, he is undoubtedly much better off here than he would be under any other of the colonial systems known in Africa, and that he certainly has infinitely more freedom now than he could ever hope to have under Communism – the devil he does *not* know. He must recognise the truly marvellous advances which have been accomplished for his benefit by a succession of well-meaning governments; the very substantial sums spent annually on education, housing, land conservation, health services, communications, and the like. He must not lose confidence, but firmly believe that by the use of constitutional

means, and with the assistance of growing numbers of sympa-
thetic and influential Europeans in Rhodesia, he will even more
quickly than he imagines obtain full social, political, and
economic opportunity. He must beware of unscrupulous
agitators, rejecting their lies and exaggerations, and learn to think
for himself, and to think of the future of his children, so that for
these at least, he may demand and obtain, not superfluities, but
the essential things, especially a thoroughly Christian education,
which will fit them for responsibility and thus enable them to
play a full part in the government of their country. He must
recognise that though we all have the same human nature, we
have not all the same natural talents, nor the same background;
that even among Europeans there are very different social strata
and degrees of intellectual capacity and conditions of wealth.
Finally, he must bear in mind that the Church, guardian and
defender of the weak and the unprivileged, will always support
him in his legitimate grievances, will never attempt to de-
nationalise him, but will make him a better African by making
him a thorough Christian. If his Faith be great enough, he will
come to recognise God's plan for him and will see, even in the
colonialism which has not been too kind to him, the unsuspecting
instrument of Providence, bringing him into the one great family
which is the Church, and making possible for him the eternal
happiness of Heaven.

European Change of Outlook

An equally comprehensive change of outlook must take place
with the European too. Just as in the case of the African, into
whom acrimony is instilled by a minority of articulate extremists,
so too among the Europeans, the majority of whom are moderate
and hopeful of muddling through to racial harmony, a by no
means representative but vocal minority is responsible for much
of the ill-feeling that there is. This minority, basing its cause on
the plea that control of the country must always remain in the
hands of civilised persons, perverts that excellent sentiment into
meaning that one race of people, their own, shall dominate for all
time and at any cost. It refuses even to consider the possibility of

the African's being capable of intellectual progress or his being in any way capable of responsibility. In a frenzy of fear, such people speak of the Africans as being sub-human. Blind to historical possibility, they deny that they had ever properly settled in Rhodesia before the coming of the white man. Provocative in the extreme, their attitude towards the African is that of the coward and the bully – the bully with a bad conscience. Nor are they alone. Even more to be pitied are the more educated intransigents, whose defeatist, stockade mentality manifests the despair of an effete generation whom self-interest has blinded to all understanding of justice or tolerance.

Were the Almighty to punish such bigots by changing their racial characteristics, so that in colouring and in feature they should come to resemble the race which they despise and would hold in subjection, they would then quickly agree to forfeit their peculiarly presumed position of privilege. But the Almighty does not need such exceptional displays of His power. He does not need to change either skin or physiognomy. He knows too well that racial hatred bears within it the very sword that makes a slave of the oppressor, and time is on His side.

The treasured belief that they are a courageous, confident, virile, fair-minded, and adventurous people must surely be dismissed as an illusion, if the Europeans of this country are not prepared or are incapable of moderating their outlook, to meet the challenge of a changing world in which the barriers of space and time have so rapidly been broken down that men of different nations and of different racial origins are brought more quickly and closely together than ever before.

Function of the State

And as with the individual, so too in these trying times it is exceedingly important that the State examine carefully its function, and thence recognise its limitations. It has no real claim to *absolute* autonomy, nor can it in justice sponsor or serve the interests of one particular race or group of people to the detriment of another. It must serve the common good, by recognising and promoting the hierarchy of being established by the Creator, giving to every human person his natural dignity and his inalienable rights, remembering the unity in nature and in ultimate destiny of the whole human family. Only when this common work of justice is accomplished and when people of all races enjoy the same essential equality of opportunity, can we reasonably hope for lasting harmony in this multiracial community.

Removal of Restrictions

We are still far from such an ideal condition of affairs, though a pleasing change in public opinion is already noticeable and some unnecessary restrictions have been abolished. In regard to these, however, it would appear that a false order of priorities has been chosen and the real grievances overlooked. Relatively few Africans, for example, are really interested in being permitted to buy European drink or to dine in the best hotels; a surprisingly small number have shown any great interest in exercising the franchise; the majority had possibly become inured to our offensive 'Europeans Only' signs in public buildings; few, under present conditions, can be absorbed into the Civil Service; and not many will consider themselves to have achieved full equality before the law or to have attained the essential rights of first-class citizens, by being given the privilege of risking their hard-earned wages in the purchase of lottery tickets. Though these are indeed concessions, they are superfluities, not the essential things on which true social stability can be built.

The Real Need

What the African wants, what any rational being would want, is simply sustenance both for body and soul – in other words, land and educational opportunity – and a general recognition, in fact and not in theory only, that he is as much a citizen of this country as are people of any other race and that his rights are equal to theirs.

He wants land from which to produce the food which will keep him and his family in existence, and he wants, as every normal parent wants, facilities for the education of his children, so that he may do better by them than he has done by himself. He has a right to expect these things, but that which has been given him has been doled out with seeming reluctance and in insufficient measure. Try as he may to avoid the issue, anyone who really knows the African and who seriously examines the cause of the present discontent, will always return to these essential needs, land and education.

Land and Land-Hunger

In time, someone may possibly produce an authoritative historical study of the manner in which the most fertile areas and the major portion of the land of Southern Rhodesia came into the possession of the governing minority. Lacking such information, it is not possible to pass judgement on the morality of the achievement. However, although it is frequently stated that the Land Apportionment Act was introduced to protect the African and to prevent his being rendered completely landless, there must surely exist in many minds, doubts about the honesty of acquiring so much land so easily from a primitive and un-suspecting people. Apart from this, if the notion of the tutelary rights of a colonial Power enters in, it opens the moral issue even wider still.

It seems to have been clearly established, however, that had the newcomers not thus effectively occupied the country, its productivity would by this time have been seriously imperilled and the indigenous population decimated by famine, because of their lack of skills in husbandry, their neglect of soil preservation and their inherited nomadic instincts. This fact would indeed give much moral justification to the present unequal distribution of land in this country.

In spite of this, it should ever be borne in mind that no subject people has long remained contented where it suffered from land-hunger. History proves with relentless uniformity that land-hunger has always been the most effective motivating force in nationalist movements for independence, and there is no reason to suspect that its aptitude has changed or has been forgotten today.

Can you in conscience blame the African, if, eking out a tenuous existence from poor soil in an overcrowded Reserve, he is swayed by subversive propaganda, when close beside him there lie hundreds of thousands of acres of fertile soil which he may not cultivate nor occupy nor graze, because although it lies unused and unattended, it belongs to some individual or group of individuals who perhaps do not even live in the country, but who hold the land in the hope of profit from speculation? It will readily be understood, of course, that in adducing this example, I have no intention of denying the doctrine of private ownership which is paramount in the teaching of the Church. It will be understood too that I do not believe that it is necessary that every African should be a land-owner, and that I have not forgotten the inestimable service done to the country by the majority of European farmers who in great part feed the nation, and whose work is essential if the nation is to survive. Nevertheless, it is absolutely necessary that serious and prompt attention be given by the responsible authorities to solving the problem of land-hunger among the majority.

Recent legislation which aims at securing for Africans stability of ownership in regard to land, is most welcome but the provisions of that legislation are totally inadequate and they involve unnecessary economic hardships for great numbers of the people. More generous measures must be contemplated and put into effect. This would entail something in the nature of a social revolution, but it could be achieved peaceably; whereas without such action, the alternative could be revolution of another order, disastrous for all. The matter assumes a new urgency when it is remembered that Southern Rhodesia cannot long remain in political isolation unaffected by the influences at work in many other parts of the continent, and that the African people are rapidly increasing in numbers.

With regard to this question of the natural growth of the African population, it will not be amiss to remark here that even the Africans view with disgust and with a good deal of what might be called 'political' suspicion, the iniquitous propaganda which has appeared in various Locations and Reserves, and the various semi-official and specious counsels given them, urging them to restrict their families by unnatural practices, so that they may obtain a more comfortable existence and fit into the areas allocated to them. One cannot but reflect on the truly awful similarity which exists between the present moral condition of our country and that of great nations which have perished in the past from the very same evils which are prevalent here. The lessons of history, it seems, will never be taken to heart. Mighty empires in every stage of history have fallen into decay by just such rejection of the Moral Law as we have in Southern Rhodesia today. Yet here in this young country, otherwise so rich in promise for the centuries to come, men choose hedonism rather than heroism, and foolishly hope for survival while our daily Press reports in frightening profusion, a record of unnatural vice, easy divorce, and drunkenness which would put professedly pagan nations to shame.

Segregation and Morality

Closely connected with the difficult problem of land is the question of segregation, and in this regard it is useful to remember that unless the common good require it, and unless this can be proved conclusively, there is absolutely no moral justification whatsoever for laws which segregate one race of people from another. Segregation itself is not immoral; we segregate the mentally sick, the carriers of infectious diseases, the ill-mannered. But race segregation, the almost religious expression of the infamous doctrine of race idolatry, brands with a stigma of inferiority the segregated people and is utterly to be condemned; not merely because of this, but primarily because it denies our common origin and our common redemption.

It must not be thought that in condemning thus, racial segregation, the Church thereby favours forced mixing of the races. No one can force you to mix with or demand that you accept into your home on terms of intimate friendship, those whom you do not much care for. Forced friendship is no friendship. Nevertheless the incontrovertible fact remains that here in Southern Rhodesia little or no contact between the two major races is made on anything other than the employer-employee level, and some serious effort at social understanding should be attempted if we are to hope to live in harmony.

Most Europeans in Southern Rhodesia know as much about the African way of life and its traditional social structure as they know about the Esquimaux. Not ten per cent of them can converse with an African in his language. Remember, that mongrel tongue 'Kitchen Kaffir' is not the native language of the African. He hears it for the first time when he goes to work in town or on a farm. Even less than five per cent of the white population knows anything at all about African customs or about the hundred and one delicate courtesies which dignify so much of the seemingly primitive life of the majority.

Nor are the Europeans alone in their ignorance. Africans are equally ill-informed about how the country is governed. They know little if anything at all about how money is found for public services, many of them imagining that Europeans pay no taxes because they pay no poll-tax. They have no understanding of the great influences at work in international politics. They do not realise that internal peace is essential if a country is to be able to attract the funds necessary for the development of its natural resources and for raising the living standards of its people. Surely some way can be found to bridge the gap between the two major races so that they may achieve social understanding? So far, very little has been done in the matter, though we still talk of 'partnership'.

Educational Opportunity

The other fundamental need of the African people is educational opportunity for their children. It is sheer deceit to talk of giving political equality to all races, if they are not given first of all, at least that educational opportunity which will enable them ultimately to qualify for the vote. An effort to bridge the educational gap between the two races must be made if there is to be any honesty in the much publicised policy of 'partnership' and any real attempt at distributive justice. The only feasible way to bridge that gap is by extending the educational opportunities of the African, not by lowering the standards of the European. At present, let us face the fact, the African is not treated as an equal in this regard at all. There is a general feeling that he is a peculiar kind of being, that he has no rights in the matter, and that it is presumptuous of him to expect the State to extend to his children the opportunities which it accords to others. In practice, there could scarcely be two more violently contrasting systems of educational opportunity than those made available by the State to the European and those which apply to the African child. One has practically everything provided for him freely; the other must struggle and pay for the little that he has at all. A more thoroughly unjust state of affairs it would be difficult to imagine in a country which is committed to a policy of 'partnership'.

Nor is this all: especially in regard to African education, the field of voluntary activity in which the Church traditionally excelled, has been grievously restricted over the years, and in recent times has been almost entirely closed by the gratuitous interference of the State, which apparently aims at exercising complete control over this, as over every other possible means of social influence. The Native Education Act 1959 confirming earlier legislation and imposing new penalties, assumes that only the State has authority to teach or to give others permission to teach, and is a notable example of such interference.

The essential evil of the Act consists in this, that once the State assumes a complete monopoly in the matter of education, the rights of the individual, the family, and the Church, are threatened; this all-important work of national development then runs the risk of becoming the instrument of Party Politics, and thereafter, each succeeding Party in power may impose on the youth of the nation its own ideas, while parents and Church are forbidden to interfere. The enormity of the crime thus committed is magnified by the situation as it exists in this country at present, when the moral and intellectual training of the emergent masses is by far the most important work to be done.

In particular, by exercising such radical control over African education, the State grievously obstructs a very important aspect of the missionary activity of the Church, and this is a most serious matter. Even though in special cases the Church is willing to build, equip, and pay the salaries required by the school, there is no guarantee that the State would then permit the school to function – this, in spite of the fact that our Catholic schools of all kinds have in general the reputation of being both efficient and well disciplined.

Education is not, nor never was, the exclusive concern of the State. It belongs properly to all three societies: the family, the State, and the Church, because it moulds man as a whole – man the individual, man the citizen of this world, man the heir of heaven. Yet, according to present legislation, the State presumptuously assumes the right to control everything, in defiance of the rights of parents and in flagrant violation of the rights and traditional function of the Church.

It is quite beside the point to argue that the Church is not thereby prevented from preaching its doctrines in its recognised places of worship. It is equally irrelevant to the principle at issue, to say that the Church can always be permitted to have 'Preaching Centres'. The Christian view of education is of something more comprehensive and profound than mere preaching can achieve.

This is made abundantly clear in the memorable encyclical *Divini Illius Magistri* of the late Pope Pius XI, when he says:

> The Church is independent of any sort of earthly power as well in the origin as in the exercise of her mission as educator; not merely in regard to her proper end and object, but also in regard to the means necessary and suitable to attain that end. Hence with regard to every other kind of human learning and instruction (besides faith and morals) which is the common patrimony of individuals and society, the Church has an independent right to make use of it, and above all to decide what may help or harm Christian education. All this must be so, because the Church as a perfect society has an independent right to the means conducive to its end, and because every form of instruction, no less than every human action, has a necessary connection with man's last end, and therefore cannot be withdrawn from the dictates of the divine law of which the Church is guardian, interpreter, and infallible mistress …
>
> Therefore with full right the Church promotes letters, science, art, in so far as necessary or helpful to Christian education, in addition to her work for the salvation of souls; founding and maintaining schools and institutions adapted to every branch of

learning and degree of culture … Nor does it interfere in the least with the regulations of the State, because the Church in her motherly prudence is not unwilling that her schools and institutions for the education of the laity be in keeping with the legitimate dispositions of civil authority; she is in every way ready to co-operate with this authority and to make provision for a mutual understanding, should difficulties arise.

It is worthwhile noting that the Supreme Pontiff says that the State may take a legitimate interest in schools and institutions for the education of the laity. He concedes to the civil authority no right whatsoever to interfere in the educational work of seminaries. Furthermore, though the Church is prepared to cooperate with the State in the work of education, she does not abrogate her fundamental independence and her right to open and conduct schools when she thinks it necessary. We have come to a pretty pass indeed, if the handing on of useful knowledge by anyone other than the State can be punished as a crime!

The Subsidiary Function

The well-known principle of 'The Subsidiary Function', according to which the State should not normally assume functions which some other smaller society can perfectly well undertake and fulfil, seems practically unknown in this country. The validity of the principle stems from the fact that the community is a greater concept than the State, and consequently the fostering of learning and the physical and mental care of the community are best organised by special agencies which encouraged and even if necessary subsidised by the State, are free of State control in their internal management. It is greatly to be regretted that the activity of such agencies (in origin usually the flowering of Christian charity in the Church) has been jeopardised by the influence even here, of the Welfare State. That they should be hampered in their activity or crushed out of existence altogether by unimaginative and secularist legislation, would be a real tragedy for Southern Rhodesia, as it would be for any country, because no matter how innocent and beneficient the Welfare State may appear to be, by exercising through a multiplicity of officials, control over even the most intimate concerns of man's daily life, it robs him of responsibility and in that measure strips him of his human dignity.

Division of Rights

Here too, in order to clarify the position still more, it will be useful to note that although the State has sovereign rights in its own sphere, the individual and the family are not only anterior to the State, but are in a very real sense far more important than it. The human person comes into the world through the family and has an eternal destiny; the State has not. Again, there need not necessarily be any conflict between Church and State; indeed there should not be, since God is the Author of both. Each has its own sphere of activity and its own proper end – that of the State being the highest natural good of mankind, and that of the Church, its supernatural and eternal good. Viewed from this aspect, Church and State are complementary, as are soul and body, and almost in that relationship. This does not involve any derogation in dignity from the State; on the contrary, just as the soul gives worth to the body, so too the Church enlightens and gives direction to the State, guards and strengthens its true vitality and consequently enhances its authority.

Regrettably however, this complementary character of Church and State is being less and less recognised nowadays in this country, and where grudgingly admitted, as in the sphere of African education, is being deprived of all real meaning. Under existing legislation, the Church in its mission as educator, has been reduced to the condition of an emaciated and etiolated prisoner of the State, which decides upon whom and when and where and in what degree it may be permitted to exercise its divine mandate to teach all nations. This constitutes the gravest threat to religion, because the more the State acquires a monopoly in education, the more the Christian quality of our civilisation will diminish and the more secularism will triumph. Once this happens it is only a short step to the position in which the Christian way of life will come to be regarded as an abnormal thing, a deviation from the general standard of social behaviour.

State Absolutism Denied

Until the State realises that it exists for the benefit of the community and to serve it; until it is convinced that the only justification for the curtailment of liberty is the extension of liberty; only when it recognises that the function of its paid officials is to frame and execute, not to decide, public policy, only then will there be any real order and only then can there be peace. It must never be forgotten that man is not the creature of the State but of God; that the dignity of man is equal in all men, and that governments themselves are limited by divine law which gives to every man inviolable rights, and provides the immutable basis on which all true law is founded. As a specific example of how far we are from having such standards, I note with dismay a report in a Rhodesian newspaper of today in which a Magistrate is quoted as saying that his judgment in a court case was delivered 'from a legal point of view and not from a moral standpoint' – as if law and morality had nothing in common!

Needs in Education

There can be no prospect of real peace or true progress in partnership in this country until the present disparity between the educational opportunity available to the European child and that available to the African child disappears. It is futile to expect mutual understanding when in so important a matter, such a radical distinction is made between the children of both races into whose hands the future of this country is to be committed.

Missionaries have been waiting, quite literally for years, for permission from the State to open the most elementary kind of village schools which the African people require and demand and are willing to erect at their own expense; and the applications, detailed and in writing, are still ungranted. Thousands of African children are every year thus deprived of any formal education whatsoever. Thousands more are forced to discontinue their schooling halfway through the elementary course, because no further classes are available for them. An increasingly great number of highly intelligent African children – for the same reason, dearth of schools – are unable to proceed to secondary education, although their parents make incredible sacrifices to provide the school fees – fees which are proportionately very much higher than those demanded of European children in State schools. But no European child need ever go without a school. Education is compulsory for him and is always provided and at little cost.

The State must see to it, and is in justice bound to see to it, if it has any idea of distributive justice at all, that at least equal consideration be given to the question of opportunity in education for the African majority. To argue that this shall be decided by the contribution which the African makes in taxation, is specious but immoral. People of all races are equally citizens of the State; legislation based on any other assumption is irrational and therefore morally unjustifiable; and the privileges of citizenship are surely not to be determined by the taxable capacity of the citizen. To deny educational opportunity to the African is not only a violation of distributive justice, but it gives substance to the arguments of those who foment disorder and claim that the responsible authorities subscribe to the wholly reprehensible doctrine of 'White Domination at any Cost'.

Before leaving this thorny problem of education, it will be useful to bear in mind that although we hear much about the increased sums of money now being allocated by the State to African education, these sums are as nothing compared with what has been contributed to this end by the various missionary bodies themselves. Since schools first began in this country, the State has been dependent on the charity of the missionaries of all denominations who have carried the burden of African education for years, have erected at no cost to the electorate practically all the school buildings, and in most cases have 'ploughed back' for further development, any salaries which they may have earned – all from motives untarnished by selfishness, all for the love and service of God and their neighbour. This is something which apparently is frequently ignored by those who, disturbed in their comfortable way of living by the African's growing awareness of his dignity as a human person, bitterly blame the Christian missionary for every social and political ill there is. Such people should remember before casting their stones of condemnation, that any lessening of the influence of missionaries in this country at the moment, places in jeopardy all hope of moderation.

Confidence in the Future

Wonderful things have already been accomplished in this young country and we have a proud record of peace, as proof of the general goodwill which has existed from the beginning between Rhodesians of all races. The future too, is full of promise and can be more glorious still, provided that we are prepared to build it on the immutable law of God and raise it up in justice and charity. Peace is the work of justice. It comes no other way. And basic justice involves equality of opportunity for all citizens, irrespective of race, colour or creed.

Times have changed. The gruff inflexible paternalism which the European has exercised over the African for so long must be modified and relaxed. It was useful while it lasted but it has had its day. The African, like an impatient teenager is aching to be off on his own. He must be taken into the confidence of the family. He must not be soured, but kindly and gently directed, so that his confidence be not lost but his affection retained. For too long has it been taken for granted that he was to remain indefinitely a 'minor'. He was not to be developed too rapidly. His advance was to be controlled, slowly – maybe too slowly. Perhaps all this did not take sufficiently into account his very considerable natural ability, his astonishing hunger for education, and the cumulative influences of travel, newspapers, radio, at play on him since the end of the war, and giving him for the first time some idea of how he stands in relation to this continent of Africa and to the world at large. Unfortunately, like many teenagers, he requires direction still and will need it for a long time to come. He has a better chance of getting real assistance from those whom he knows and who know him, than he has from others who would woo him with wild promises from afar. And as long as the direction given to him in the years ahead, is based on justice and enlightened by charity, the future of Rhodesia will be safe.

The Claims of the Church

The fearful apostasy from God which characterises so much of modern life, and the consequent ignorance of the nature of the Church, must indeed make its claims appear arrogant in the extreme. This is so because any divine society must necessarily seem arrogant to men who deny that divinity. A Church established by God cannot but claim to be superior to any mere creation of man's and though it be composed of sinners and not of angels, though like the Gospel net it contains good fish and bad fish, yet such is God's will to be near His people, that He closely identifies Himself with His Church and makes it His mouthpiece.

However embarrassing or intolerant this may appear to a secularist and myopic world in which 'Truth forsakes the single state to bear Half-Truths to Toleration', it is not in our power to change it or to be silent about it. A Bishop must, in virtue of his office, preach the living Christ, teaching, ruling, and sanctifying through His Church; not by a kind of remote power conferred two thousand years ago and strangely surviving still, but personally and at this moment, as He foretold when He promised to be with His Church always, even to the consummation of the world (Mt 28:20). No Bishop dare evade this truth, or with specious words or ambivalence shuffle off his glorious privilege of being Christ's witness. Fear of appearing intolerant must not make him ashamed of the Gospel (tolerance is for men, intolerance for error) because God's judgments await those who change the truth of God into a lie and worship and serve the creature rather than the Creator (Rom 1:25).

It is uncomfortable for some to be thus reminded that God has not retired from His world nor left it uncared for; that He has preserved through a multitude of betrayals and persecutions and martyrdoms, the Church which speaks with His authority and which will continue to speak till all earthly utterance is stilled. But we Catholics believe that this is so, that it is the most astonishing and comforting fact that there is, and we cannot be silent about it no matter what befalls. Whenever and wherever the malice or ignorance of men attempts to limit the essential liberty of the Church, the Bishops are in conscience bound strongly to protest and to assert her right to freedom. Other Bishops behind the Iron Curtain are in prison for precisely this. All have the same obligation.

Conclusion

Finally, no matter how reasonable the legislation or how anxious for harmony men may be, no one can hope to build for permanent peace unless he plans according to the Creator's laws. 'Unless the Lord build the house, they labour in vain who build it' (Ps 127:1). Just as in the natural order, architects and engineers must observe the natural laws of physics – laws which man has discovered but not made, which he has formulated but not imposed – so too in the moral order, God's laws for individual, family, State and Church, cannot be neglected with impunity. When the laws governing society are related to divine law, when they are based on justice and quickened by charity, the nation truly lives, because this is God's plan for it even in the natural order.

But we whom Our Divine Lord has redeemed and called His friends, we have higher motives still for practising the great virtues of justice and charity. His positive command to us is that we should do unto others as we would that they would do unto us (Lk 6:31) and His 'New Commandment', His final request to us on the night before His crucifixion, was that we should love one another, for by this could we claim to be truly His disciples (Jn 13:34).

The world passes and we with it, for even birth has in itself the germ of death. In a few years we shall all be compounded with the dust and probably forgotten. There will be no privilege then, no distinction of race or of colour, and there will be no segregation. And what will decide our eternity will be simply the charity which we have shown to our fellow man in this present life. Nothing else will count. Our Divine Lord Himself has assured us that this is so, and His words no man can gainsay:

And when the Son of Man shall come in his majesty, and all the angels with him then shall he sit upon the seat of his majesty: And all the nations shall be gathered together before him, and he shall

47

separate them one from another, as the shepherd separateth the sheep from the goats: And he shall set the sheep on his right hand but the goats on his left. Then shall the king say to them that shall be on his right hand: Come, ye blessed of my Father, possess you the kingdom prepared for you from the foundation of the world. For I was hungry and you gave me to eat; I was thirsty and you gave me to drink; I was a stranger and you took me in. Naked and you covered me: sick, and you visited me: I was in prison, and you came to me. Then shall the just answer him, saying: Lord, when did we see thee hungry, and fed thee; thirsty, and gave thee drink? And when did we see thee a stranger and took thee in? Or naked, and covered thee? Or when did we see thee sick or in prison, and came to thee? And the king answering, shall say to them: Amen I say to you, as long as you did it to one of these my least brethren, you did it to me (Mt 25:31ss).

✠ *Donal Raymond Lamont, O.Carm.*
Bishop of Umtali

'Drumfad',
P.O. Box 47,
Umtali, Southern Rhodesia.
Feast of SS. Peter and Paul, 1959.

*Introduction to
'Speech from the Dock'*

On Wednesday, 23 March 1977 Donal Lamont, the sixty-five year old Bishop of Umtali, was stripped of his Rhodesian citizenship and deported. This deportation marked the end of more than thirty years of ministry in Rhodesia and was the culmination of the regime's attempts to silence a consistently critical voice. Bishop Lamont had over the years become the symbol of the Church's conflict with the State on the rights of African Rhodesians to self-determination.

Bishop Lamont's deportation came at the end of an appeal against a ten-year prison sentence with labour, imposed on him by the Rhodesian courts in October 1976. He had pleaded guilty to four counts of failing to report the presence of guerrillas and of telling others to do likewise. The imposition of this sentence provoked a storm of international protest. Telegrams of support from religious and political leaders throughout the world flooded into Rhodesia; among them were messages from Pope Paul and Jimmy Carter.

While the international community wholeheartedly commended his identification with the aspirations of the black Rhodesian majority, Bishop Lamont was regarded by the Rhodesian government as a menace and by most white Rhodesians as a traitor. To understand the predicament of Christian missionaries in present-day Rhodesia, we must remember the nature of the society in which they exercise their ministry. Rhodesia is a country of over six million blacks and two hundred and fifty thousand whites. White Rhodesians have total political control of the country and are the beneficiaries of a grossly inegalitarian economic system. They occupy over half the land and have access to the most productive land in the country. In spite of United Nations sanctions living standards for white Rhodesians have risen considerably in the last twelve years and compare favourably with all western countries. In contrast, the vast majority of black Rhodesians live in poverty and are excluded from political life. Over the past ten years the differential between black and white average earnings has doubled. A senior welfare officer has recently estimated that some seventy-five per cent of urban Africans in Bulawayo where the breadwinner is in employment have incomes below subsistence levels, and this pattern is repeated throughout the country. All attempts to change this situation through constitutional means have failed.

Rhodesia is in practice a police state: strikes are effectively banned, the media are controlled, many political organisations are prohibited, whole communities are uprooted and forced to live as virtual prisoners in the so-called 'protected villages'. Laws have been enacted giving the Security Forces a blank cheque for any atrocities they wish to commit. Hundreds of people have been tried and executed in secret. Torture, intimidation and killings by the Security Forces are the order of the day.

Over the last few years the white minority has had to pay an ever-increasing price for the privileges it enjoys. The escalating civil war has affected virtually every Rhodesian home. Call-up into the armed forces has been progressively tightened. All white, coloured and asian males must, on leaving school, register with the armed forces and from that time, if they are under thirty, are not allowed to leave the country without special permission. After serving an initial eighteen months they are liable to be called up every few months. This total mobilisation of the white community puts immense strain on family life and, of course, on the Rhodesian economy.

The resulting low morale and confusion among whites has been intensified by the Rhodesia Front's apparent concession to the principle of majority rule. Many whites wonder exactly what they are fighting for. The loss of morale is reflected in emigration figures. During 1976 immigration statistics showed a net loss of some seven thousand people. This figure does not accurately reflect the true extent of emigration. The recruitment of between 1,200 and 1,600 mercenaries distorts this figure. Emigration would be massive but for the difficulty of selling assets and the stringent exchange control regulations. Indeed many people emigrate under the guise of taking a holiday because for a variety of reasons they do not want the government to know they are leaving the country. This hidden emigration does not, of course, appear in statistics.

If the war has seriously disrupted white Rhodesian society, its impact on African life has been disastrous. Hundreds of thousands of people have been forcibly driven from their homes and packed into 'protected villages' where in general conditions are appalling. Government propaganda portrays the 'protected villages' as being for the Africans' own protection, designed to be centres of development and a way of shortening the war against Communism by starving the guerrillas of their food supply. In fact most 'protected villages' are centres of hardship and misery – there is serious overcrowding, sanitary conditions are rudimentary and medical and welfare facilities are inadequate. The villagers are unable to tend their cattle and their lands properly and their crops, if they are not destroyed by the Security Forces, may be ruined by animals. A strict curfew is in operation in many areas which poses particular problems for rural Africans whose land is some distance from the 'protected village'. Curfew breakers are often shot without warning. Mr Ian Smith admitted that up to 24 February 1977, 632 Africans had been killed and 294 wounded 'while breaking the curfew or running with and assisting terrorists'.

Church and State in Rhodesia

Some cynics have accused the Church in Rhodesia of jumping on the bandwagon of African nationalism. However, the stand taken by the Church is not a recent one. Bishop Lamont's pastoral letter, *Purchased People*, issued in 1959, marked the beginning of the tension between Church and State in Rhodesia. The pastoral letter was by no means radical but it was the first time that a Bishop in Rhodesia had drawn such attention to the injustices of Rhodesian society and had identified himself with African aspirations:

> If nationalism as it manifests itself here among the African people means the desire of that people to participate fully in the life and in the development of their country; if it means a will to hold on to the things which they believe to have a traditional and cultural value and which are not contrary to the Moral Law; if it means a refusal to be stripped of their ancient character and turned out in mass production, de-characterised and presented to the world as ersatz Europeans; or if it means a sincere and simple wish to be regarded by all and to be treated by the State as equal citizens,

and not as second-class citizens, then obviously such aspirations are beyond reproach and the Church must support them.

The other Bishops refused to sign the pastoral letter and it was not until two years later that they issued their first joint pastoral letter, *Peace Through Justice*. In it they denounced racial discrimination and argued that 'there can be no stability in society while the few possess much and the majority have little or nothing.' They insisted that racial harmony 'is not simply one of social adjustment but of social justice. It is essentially a moral problem, a problem of right and wrong. When fundamental human rights are denied to any people, simply because of their race, a grievous wrong is perpetrated.'

Since that time at least thirteen joint statements have been made by the Rhodesian Catholic Bishops' Conference and also a number of statements by Bishop Lamont, which trace the increasing hostility in Church–State relations and the growing determination of the Church to speak out against injustice.

In 1965 Mr Ian Smith made his Unilateral Declaration of Independence and said in an address to the nation: 'We have struck a blow for the preservation of justice, civilisation and Christianity, and in the spirit of this belief we have this day assumed our sovereign independence.' Shortly afterwards the Bishops issued an outspoken and critical pastoral letter, *A Plea for Peace*.

The government censorship office in Salisbury censored the Shona and Ndebele translations of the letter and the Bishops subsequently refused to publish this censored version. One of the deleted passages read:

> Another thing which is quite clear to us is this: vast numbers of the people of Rhodesia are bitterly opposed to the Unilateral Declaration of Independence made recently. They are particularly angered that it should be stated publicly that this action was taken in the name of preserving Christian civilisation in this country. It is simply quite untrue to say that the masses are content with this recent decision or that they have consented by their silence. Their silence is the silence of fear, of disappointment, of hopelessness. It is dangerous silence; dangerous for the Church, for all of us.

> It comes as no surprise, therefore, that many are saying: 'So this is Christian civilisation! This is what Christianity is! The preservation of privilege for the few and well-to-do, and the neglect of the many who have nothing!' They also say: 'It seems as if we have been deceived by the exponents of Christianity, the missionaries. These have come here only to prepare the way for the racist state where we shall remain permanently the hewers of wood and drawers of water, and where a favoured handful can control and delay our development indefinitely.'

The Bishops were equally outspoken in their criticisms of the 1969 Constitution in their pastoral letter *A Call to Christians*, published in June that year. The 1969 Constitution was much more racist than the mildly liberal 1961 Constitution. In their letter the Bishops said:

> the proposals for the new Constitution are in many ways completely contrary to Christian teaching and we must therefore reject them for the benefit of our own people and on behalf of all men of good will publicly condemn them.

Indeed the Bishops have taken care to maintain throughout this conflict that their obligation to speak has been based on moral rather than political criteria: their primary concern has been for human rights. They have been criticised for their lack of political ideology and their failure to suggest concrete action to black Rhodesians faced with urgent political decisions.

Whilst these pastoral letters were signed by all the Bishops, their style and tone is that of Bishop Lamont. It is interesting to contrast the tone of earlier pastoral letters with Bishop Lamont's *Open Letter to the Rhodesian Government* issued on 11 August 1976. This Open Letter was written as Umtali was being shelled from Mozambique in retaliation for the Rhodesian army's massacre of hundreds of men, women and children in a refugee/training camp in Mozambique. It was probably this letter which finally provoked the Rhodesian regime into taking action to silence him, although the regime has publicly denied this. In it Bishop Lamont says:

Conscience compels me to state that your administration by its clearly racist and oppressive policies and by its stubborn refusal to change, is largely responsible for the injustices which have provoked the present disorder and it must in that measure be considered guilty of whatever misery or bloodshed may follow.

Far from your policies defending Christianity and Western Civilisation, as you claim, they mock the law of Christ and make Communism attractive to the African people … On whatever dubious grounds you may at one time have based your claim to rule, such argument no longer has any validity. You may rule with the consent of a small and selfish electorate, but you rule without the consent of the nation, which is the test of all legitimacy.

Many people, particularly inside Rhodesia, regard Bishop Lamont as a left-wing revolutionary, a sort of Rhodesian Camillo Torres. He is not. His theological formation is firmly rooted in mainstream Catholic-orthodox thought and is not derived from Latin American liberation theology or radical European political theology.

THE WAR

After a period of sporadic incursions beginning in late 1964, nationalist guerrillas launched a sustained offensive in north-east Rhodesia in December 1972. Since then, in the period up to March 1977, over 4,000 people have been killed – more than 2,727 guerrillas, more than 256 soldiers including a number of South African Police and some 1,473 civilians, including 79 whites. The figure for civilian dead includes some 632 who the government admit have been killed by the Security Forces for breaking the curfew or 'running with' the guerrillas. These are official government figures and therefore need to be treated with caution. They do, however, give some indication of the nature and the scale of the war.

Since 1972 the war has escalated not only in terms of numbers of people involved in the fighting, but also in terms of the areas in which the fighting is taking place. Since the collapse of the Portuguese Empire the major guerrilla offensive has been from across the Mozambique border. However, guerrillas are operating from each of the countries bordering Rhodesia, with the exception of South Africa. There are now very few rural areas in Rhodesia where there is no guerrilla presence and reliable sources indicate that guerrillas are establishing themselves in the urban townships. According to government estimates there are currently some 2,500 guerrillas operating inside the country. This figure does not include the countless numbers of Rhodesians who give material and other support to the guerrillas. The insurgents are able to melt in with the local population. They travel in small groups and rely on the local people for information, food and shelter.

The Rhodesian Security Forces are well aware that no guerrillas could operate inside the country without at least the tacit consent of the local people. They have therefore adopted policies of systematic harassment, intimidation and torture both to extract information about guerrilla movements and to deter potential supporters of the liberation struggle. One of the most controversial issues in the counter-insurgency campaign is the use of the Selous Scouts, a commando unit operating throughout the country. They often masquerade as guerrillas and exact retribution from those Africans who cooperate with them in this guise. By committing atrocities in the guise of guerrillas they aim to confuse and alienate the local people and to test their loyalty. The resulting dilemma was well expressed by one old villager who said:

> If we report the terrorists, they destroy our homes and fields and come and kill us. If we do not report them the soldiers come to torture us and to destroy our homes and fields. But even if we report the terrorists, the soldiers torture us all the same, for they think we are just trying to set them up.

The civil war in Rhodesia presents missionaries with difficult moral choices. Missionaries, although often white and albeit expatriate, live and work in mainly rural areas. They are thus an integral part of the local community. They are involved not only with the spiritual welfare of their parishioners but with the life of the community at all levels. Missionaries in rural areas make an essential contribution to health, education and community development. The problems and concerns of the community are therefore shared by missionaries.

When the Security Forces move into an area, uproot the local people and move them into 'protected villages', bomb their houses and destroy their crops, harass and torture people on suspicion of harbouring terrorists, shoot civilians on their way home from having a beer or tending their cattle, the missionaries cannot help but be involved. It is their own communities which are in danger. The people come to them for help and advice in the face of the Rhodesian government's policies. The missionaries experience with them the injustice of the system and share with them the desire for change. It is therefore not surprising that so many missionaries identify with the aspirations of their parishioners for a new and more just society.

Nor is it a situation in which the missionary can remain neutral. The regime defines the guerrillas as 'Communist terrorists' and demands total loyalty from the missionary in its efforts to wipe them out – even that he should act as informer on the movements of the insurgents. Not to inform the authorities when this occurs is a criminal offence. At the same time the missionary knows that if he notifies the authorities, the army is likely to saturate the area and exact terrible and indiscriminate retribution from the local people for assisting the guerrillas. What is the missionary to do?

Even those who do not feel that the guerrilla war is justified are convinced that the repressive policies of the regime have provoked the war. If it can be argued that the guerrillas have no legitimacy, it can be argued with greater force that neither does the present Rhodesian government. Is the execution of informants by the guerrillas any more illegal than the judicial murder of civilians by the illegal regime? The regime accuses the guerrillas of irresponsibility but has itself sanctioned irresponsibility on the part of the Security Forces by the enactment of laws such as the Indemnity and Compensation Act.

This still leaves the question of whether armed struggle is morally justifiable. Contrary to Western 'myth', the conscience of the guerrillas has been formed not by Marxist indoctrination but largely by Christian teaching in the mission schools. The Catholic

Bishops have proposed the conditions for armed revolt in their first joint pastoral letter:

> It must never be forgotten that only an insupportable tyranny or flagrant violation of the most obvious essential rights of the citizens, can give, after every other means of redress have failed, the right to revolt against the legitimate authority.

The decision whether or not to resort to violence as a means of overthrowing tyranny is a difficult one and can only be taken by those who are actually involved in the situation. It is clear that the vast majority of black Rhodesians have decided that the present Rhodesian regime is tyrannical and without legitimacy. They believe that all attempts to achieve their rights by peaceful means have failed. The guerrilla war is thus seen by them as an essential element in the overthrow of the regime.

THE LAMONT CASE

As the war intensified, increasing numbers of Africans mainly from rural areas made their way to the Justice and Peace Commission office in Salisbury with complaints of their treatment at the hands of the Security Forces. As the demands became more pressing, the Commission felt compelled to investigate the allegations and to take up the matter with the Rhodesian government.

The role of Bishop Lamont in the Commission, which was formed in 1972 and is an official body of the Roman Catholic hierarchy, was certainly a contributory factor to his deportation. The Rhodesian Commission has focused much of its attention on investigating allegations of brutality and murder of Africans by members of the Rhodesian Security Forces. Such investigations have inevitably attracted hostility from the Rhodesia Front government and its supporters. The officers of the regime – Security Forces, police, chiefs and any public servants – are protected from criticism by a series of 'emergency laws'. In publishing reports of carefully investigated cases of torture, intimidation and killings of Africans by Security Forces, in particular *The Man in the Middle* (May 1975) and *Civil War in Rhodesia* (October 1976), the Commission has taken up the gauntlet, strongly challenging the actions of the regime and its officers.

The government has accused the Commission of being a 'fifth column' and has used every means at its disposal to discredit its work. In September 1976 the Commission's president, Bishop Lamont, was charged. His trial symbolised the missionaries' dilemma and indeed almost any other missionary could have found himself in the dock faced with similar charges.

Aware of the significance of his trial, Bishop Lamont made a lengthy unsworn statement to the court. On the advice of his counsel, he did not make his statement on oath – not because he was afraid of cross-examination but for three very good reasons. Firstly, he wanted to avoid having nuns called as witnesses against their bishop. Secondly, he wanted the freedom to make a general statement about the situation in Rhodesia and not be confined to the technicalities of the charges levelled against him. Thirdly, he thought an oath unnecessary since he was pleading guilty.

The Appeal Court judgement in Bishop Lamont's case is a masterpiece of legal indiscretion. Justice MacDonald introduces extraneous material not led in evidence and uses his position to give vent to his personal feelings on the role of the Church in society, the aims and objectives of the guerrilla movements and the development of Rhodesia as a country. The Communist bogey looms large in the judgement. It assumed that black Rhodesians have no cause for dissatisfaction or for revolt against the Rhodesian government. It is his supremely paternalistic belief that white government has brought civilisation, stability and economic prosperity to Rhodesia. According to him the guerrillas fight against the government because they are pawns of the Communists. He condemns them as misguided, indoctrinated terrorists rather than freedom fighters who are attempting to overthrow a thoroughly corrupt and tyrannical regime. Justice MacDonald dismisses Bishop Lamont's indictment of the excesses of the Rhodesian Security Forces despite the overwhelming body of supportive evidence. He praises the achievements of the white regime, but glosses over the multiple and fundamental causes of the grievances which cause young African people to leave Rhodesia in droves to fight for the overthrow of the white minority government. The judgement is an apology for the white racist regime. He has no concept of the responsibilities of the Church in seeking social justice. He denies that the Church has an obligation in the sphere of temporal matters to oppose oppression, injustice and suffering and to refuse to comply with laws which have these effects.

CONCLUSION

It is hoped that this book will help to put into focus the stand taken by Bishop Lamont and many other missionaries in Rhodesia today. In Bishop Lamont's diocese alone, two priests, Fr Patrick Mutume and Fr Ignatius Mhonda, have been sentenced to four years' imprisonment (three years suspended) on similar charges and are waiting the decision of the Appeal Court. Both were assaulted in custody and Fr Mhonda sustained a perforated eardrum as a result of his treatment in detention. Both appeared at the local court handcuffed, barefooted and in prison garb. Fr Alexander Sakarombe was arrested and detained for eleven days. He has since been rearrested together with an Irish Carmelite priest, Fr Laurence Lynch.

It is hoped too that this book will provide a perspective for the tragic killings of missionaries which have taken place in Rhodesia recently. There are grave doubts as to who was responsible for their deaths and evidence is emerging which suggests that at least some of the murders were the work of the Selous Scouts. It is unlikely that the facts will ever be proven. However, if the massacres were perpetrated by guerrillas, it was a maverick band. It is certainly not the policy of the guerrilla movements. However, it would be naive to believe that guerrilla groups do not commit atrocities against civilians and such actions are to be deplored and condemned. At the same time, whilst in no way excusing such deeds, they must be seen side by side with what is tantamount to a deliberate policy of systematic brutality on the part of the Security Forces. Accounts of intimidation, torture and killings of civilians by the Rhodesian Security Forces are numerous and well documented in the reports from the Rhodesian Catholic Justice and Peace Commission.

Indeed the Rhodesian government itself has acknowledged the substance of the many allegations contained in the reports by refusing an independent enquiry and by refusing the Commission's challenge to prosecute them for making false allegations – a crime in Rhodesia. Furthermore, in 1975 the regime enacted the Indemnity and Compensation Act. This Act indemnifies from prosecution any public servant who commits *any act* 'in good faith' … 'for or in connection with the suppression of terrorism'. This Act was made retrospective to 1 December 1972. As the Commission said in a statement of protest about this Act, 'by thus exonerating the Security Forces in advance, this may amount to a mandate for illegalities'. This view was endorsed by the late Sir Robert Tredgold, the former Federal Chief Justice, who said: 'It is contrary to the rule of law and to our own system to give protection in advance to acts of the Executive or its officials that are illegal or of questionable legality.'

Tim Sheehy &
Eileen Sudworth
C. I. I. R.
20 April 1976

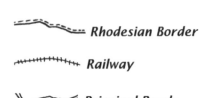

Rhodesian Border

Railway

Principal Roads

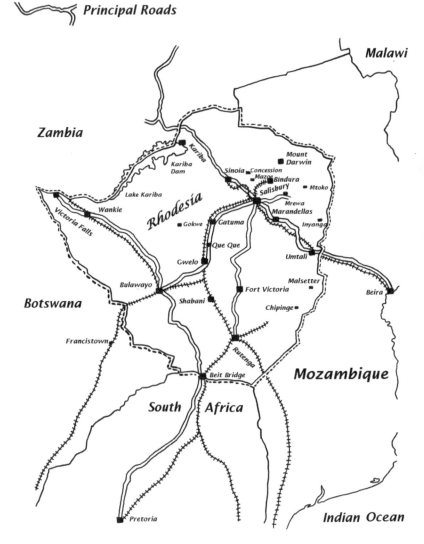

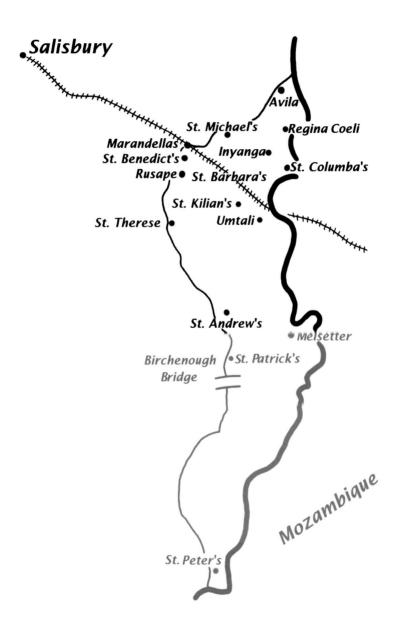

Salisbury

Avila

St. Michael's

Regina Coeli

Marandellas
St. Benedict's

Inyanga

Rusape

St. Columba's

St. Barbara's

St. Kilian's

St. Therese

Umtali

St. Andrew's

Melsetter

Birchenough
Bridge

St. Patrick's

Mozambique

St. Peter's

Speech from the Dock

My Personal History

I was born in 1911 in Northern Ireland into a middle class family of five boys and one girl. During my youth the Irish War of Independence was being waged all around us. The establishment of the Irish Free State meant a turning point for the lives of many of us who supported the nationalist cause.

I completed my secondary education at Terenure College in Dublin, where I had moderate academic success but satisfactory results in everything connected with games. I mention this to show that I was a very normal kind of youth. I had represented my Province of Ulster in schools hockey. I also played for the first XV in rugby and was *Victor Ludorum* at the College sports.

Having finished school I felt called to the priesthood and joined the Carmelite Order. After a year spent as a novice I took vows of religion for three years, and during this time studied at University College, Dublin, where I read an honours course in English Language, Philology and English Literature. I gained an Honours Degree in 1933. My superiors then sent me to the international College of the Carmelites in Rome where I spent the next five years studying Philosophy and Theology. This Philosophy course included Logic, Metaphysics, Psychology, Ethics, Cosmology and the History of Philosophy. The course in Theology involved the study of Dogmatic and Moral Theology, Canon Law, Church History, Holy Scripture, including some knowledge of Hebrew and Greek, Patristics, Ascetical and Pastoral Theology with the ancillary subjects, Christian Archaeology and Music. I had had some training in music and attended regularly as an external student the Pontifical Academy where I was particularly interested in Polyphony and Plainsong.

A most important feature of the years of study in Rome was that it brought me into contact with world opinion. I lived in an international community, my professors and fellow students coming from many different parts of the world.

Our life was primarily monastic and strictly disciplined. Our lectures were in Latin, though after a reasonably short time most of us became proficient in Italian, the official language of the community. For those interested in further study there was always the opportunity of learning other languages. We had to mix with the other students, whether we could speak their language or not, and through this initially difficult contact we soon learned a great deal of the social, political and religious conditions of many countries in the world. It was a most useful experience and prevented the development of any kind of narrow nationalism. We achieved a kind of world understanding and a sense of world concern. This was not all. The very international quality of Rome itself had an immense formative value in our lives.

The years 1933–1939, which I spent as a student in Rome, were crucial in the life of Central Europe. They were the years of Fascism and Nazism at their peak. The most indelible memory I have of that time is of the bitter tension that existed between the Fascist State and the Catholic Church. The Pope was vilified and obedience to the Church was denounced. We who walked, dressed as clerics, in the streets were apt to be shoved off the pavement by roaming gangs of Fascist youths. The walls were plastered with party propaganda at every turn. One could not only see but hear the official war cry everywhere: 'Viva Mussolini', 'Good old Mussolini'. The whole population, brainwashed by government-controlled press and radio, became a complacent herd. Men who should have known better put their principles in their pockets and became grovelling sycophants. From their very earliest schooldays children's minds were manipulated into State-worship and to the worship of 'Good old Mussolini'. They were called for Balilla drill on Sunday mornings precisely at the time when they should have been at Mass.

While all this was going on we knew of Catholics and other Christians who defied the law and hid their Jewish neighbours to prevent their being liquidated or imprisoned by a racist regime. During those years we suffered even hunger as the result of the grim economic sanctions. Money had to be found for the Abyssinian campaign and for the brief glorification of the 'sawdust Caesar', who celebrated his imitation triumph when it was over. During all this time I had as my Superior a saintly German Carmelite who kept us informed of the equal tragedy taking place in his own country. He warned us that as future priests it would be our work to promote God's justice on earth if we were to be authentic representatives of Christ. He insisted that the teaching of the Church was essentially personal; that its centre was the human person with all his rights, and that was the key to the understanding of all man's social and political rights.

Over and over again he warned us that the age of martyrdom would never leave the Church, and that some of us might even be called to enjoy that privilege. Some of those listening had just escaped death at the hands of the Communists in the Spanish Civil War. There were others in the class for whom the future held a much graver fate. Two of my companions were to die behind the Russian lines. Two others spent years in Dachau under Hitler. When he came to Rome we experienced the thrill of engaging in the conflict at close quarters. The Pope refused to see him and ordered the Vatican to be closed. In protest at his coming no one of our community went outside the doors of the college so that we should not even appear to welcome him. We would not risk being seen to be guilty by even the slightest association. We smiled with satisfaction when we heard of the powerless Palatine Guard with its antiquated musketry being drawn up outside the Vatican to prevent the entry of the armed might of the two dictators. 'Heil Hitler'. 'Good old Hitler'. 'Viva Mussolini'. 'Good old Mussolini' echoed all around us.

About that time the powerful arm of Fascism reached right into the college and deported out of the country after forty-eight hours' notice our Professor of Theology. Later on in Holland another Carmelite, the Rector of the Catholic University of Nijmegen, would be punished for his loyalty to principle. He had been appointed by the Dutch Bishops as their representative to press and radio, and when Hitler ordered him to use these means at his disposal to print and broadcast Nazi propaganda he chose to obey God rather than man and defied the might of the dictator. With that his fate was assured. He was dragged to Dachau and died there rather than betray his conscience and serve the State. He has been my hero.

All during the time of this tragedy of Europe, the Church, through its supreme authority, defended freedom of conscience and the natural rights of man against totalitarian Fascism, Nazism, Soviet Communism and the Mexican regime of 1917–1937. The teaching left an indelible impression on me and warned me for the rest of my life against the danger of State worship or the worship of political leaders. In 1937 I was ordained priest and completed my studies in 1938, when I received a Licentiate in Theology and left Rome to return to Ireland.

The Carmelite authorities in Rome wished me to return for doctoral studies, but in Ireland there was need of a teacher in my own college, and I was appointed there. I remained on the staff of the college until 1946. During that time I returned to University College, Dublin, and studied for a Higher Diploma in Education, which I obtained in 1939. In my special field of English Literature I worked for two years on a major thesis on one of the metaphysical poets and as a result was awarded an Honours Masters Degree in 1942.

Meanwhile, in my anxiety to be involved in more priestly work, I spent many of my weekends working at a hostel for 'down-and-out' men in the city of Dublin. I also coached rugby in the college, was involved in the production of a series of radio broadcast programmes of a religious nature for three years, and was also a founder member of Ireland's greatest choral society, which had as its director for many years Sir John Barbirolli. I was kept fully occupied.

In 1946 I volunteered to go to Southern Rhodesia, as it then was, to start mission work there under the then Bishop Chichester, and was appointed to lead a group of three priests who arrived in this country in November just thirty years ago. My first appointment was to Triashill Mission, Inyanga, and in and around Inyanga I remained as a missionary until 1950, when I became parish priest in Umtali. In 1953, having been joined in the interim by numbers of other Carmelite priests from Ireland, most of the province of Manicaland was, by agreement with Bishop Chichester, separated from his jurisdiction and put under my own control as Prefect Apostolic. This state of affairs continued until 1957, when Pope Pius XII constituted the area a Diocese and appointed me as its first Bishop.

It is a significant fact that when devising a motto for my episcopate I chose the Latin phrase *Ut placeam Deo*: 'That I may please God.' I so intended these words to be a programme of action for me that on the day of my consecration, during a luncheon in honour of the occasion, and in the presence of such distinguished political figures as the late Lord Malvern and the then prime minister, Mr Garfield Todd, I spoke of my motto and of my determination to live it through to the utmost, and I ended my speech by saying: 'As long as I am spared to rule this diocese I hope I shall please God, not men.'

THE DIOCESE DEVELOPS

I come to the development of the diocese. When I first came to Rhodesia in 1946, Bishop Chichester, whose jurisdiction included all of Manicaland, pointed out to me that the work of the Church in the Eastern districts had been very much neglected and that he expected the missionaries who came with me to make up for the time lost. The Jesuit Fathers had been unable to expand because so many of them were on active service during World War II. In the whole of Manicaland in 1946 there were only six priests and three lay brothers of my Church. Their average age at that time must have been well over sixty. There were three established Mission stations, about twenty-five primary schools for Africans in the tribal trust lands under the guidance of the Church, and a junior school for European girls in Umtali – nothing more.

It was my job, therefore, either personally or vicariously through the missionaries whom I might be able to recruit, to establish the Catholic Church from one end of Manicaland to the other, that is from Inyanga North to Mahenya country at the junction of the Sabi and the Lundi. This meant first of all making friendly contact with the people, obtaining the good will of the local chiefs and the official permission of the civil authority for the establishment of those works of charity and religion which brought to the African people the Church as a living entity, making present to them the healing, educating and liberating mission of Christ.

There was always the problem of recruiting missionary personnel, priests, brothers, nuns and lay workers, and of ensuring that among them there should be professionally qualified people, teachers, doctors, nurses, etc., who could satisfy the requirements of the State. Such dedicated people were not to be found in Rhodesia, so, as the ecclesiastical authority responsible, I had to seek abroad in countries as far afield as Germany, Holland, England, Ireland, Scotland, Canada, Australia and the United States for volunteers, prepared to leave their homes and dedicate their lives to the building up of the Christian faith in Rhodesia.

This was not all. Money had to be found almost entirely from outside Rhodesia. The local European Catholic population was never more than ten per cent of the total, and their financial contribution was scarcely enough to support each – as it was then – white parish. The African population, living in a subsistence economy, gave what it could, but found it hard to understand why it should be expected to maintain missionaries completely out of its penury.

To obtain finance for Church development, the Church in Manicaland depended on the generosity of the Holy See, on Catholic communities in Europe and in the United States, and on the efforts which I made personally in preaching and lecturing tours which brought me to many countries and involved very exhausting work. It is safe to say that in the past thirty years my missionaries and I have brought into Rhodesia for Church development not less than $6 million. It has all come from abroad, as have the people involved.

The institutions which have been set up have been an irreplaceable asset to Rhodesia, and I venture to say cannot be kept in existence by the State should the support, either in finance or human resources, be withdrawn. To give one example only, I hear it stated authoritatively that at this moment in Rhodesia eighty-five per cent of the population is being served medically by only eighty-five doctors. I wonder who would work to control disease, especially in the Tribal Trust Lands, if it were not for missionaries of all denominations who work so selflessly there and in such difficult conditions.

In short, Rhodesia itself provided neither the money nor the missionaries for the establishment or expansion of the Church in its own country. It was completely dependent on everything from abroad. Unhappily this situation remains unchanged, for all practical purposes, as far as the European population is concerned. African vocations, both to the priesthood and to the sisterhoods, are steadily on the increase, and give great promise of becoming self-sufficient before the end of the century.

In the course of the last thirty years under my direction my fellow missionaries have established in the Diocese of Umtali the following institutions for the benefit of Rhodesia:

1. Between sixty and seventy primary schools, most of which have, in recent years, been ceded without any recompense to local Councils.
2. Eleven Central Mission Stations, each with its own dispensary, school, and its own group of orphans.
3. Six FI schools, that is African academic schools going up to Form four.
4. Three FII schools – African secondary technical schools.
5. One teachers' training college in Chiduku Reserve.
6. One Nursing Assistants' Training School at Nyamaropa Reserve.
7. Regina Coeli Hospital with one hundred and ten beds in Nyamaropa.
8. A tuberculosis hospital in Umtali with one hundred beds established at the request of the local authorities because they could not cope with their then existing facilities with the number of tubercular patients. We have been running that place for the last twenty years.
9. Moreover, I have established eight rural hospitals at Mission stations with an average of forty-four beds. Four of these small hospitals receive no government aid whatsoever.

Besides these institutions the Diocese of Umtali, during my episcopate, established other institutions of benefit to the country such as Marymount College, a secondary school for girls which, unfortunately, is soon to close because of the deteriorating political situation; and Carmel College, an interracial school for boys which has already closed down for the same reason.

During the same time the Diocese built a Minor Seminary near Melsetter for aspirants to the priesthood and in another place a Novitiate for African Sisters. The building of places of worship has kept pace with the natural extension of the Catholic religion, and again, chiefly owing to money brought into Rhodesia from benefactors overseas, we have been able to build between twenty-five and thirty smaller churches in the Diocese, as well as the Cathedral in Umtali.

I mention this to show that my missionaries and I have not been idle during our years in Rhodesia. Whether Rhodesia approves of this activity or not, at least no one can deny that all this development has provided employment and in other ways has done no harm whatsoever to the economy of the country. Certainly we cannot be accused of sponging on Rhodesia, or of growing wealthy as a result of our labours. Not one single missionary retains a cent of any of the emoluments received from any source. All is ploughed back into the work of the Church and for the benefit of this country.

Since we are especially concerned in this court with a Mission hospital and with medicines and nurses, I would like very briefly to indicate the services provided by the Church throughout the Diocese, for example, last year, 1975. These figures have been provided through the good offices of the organisation called The Association of Rhodesian Church Hospitals, an inter-denominational body which deals with the hospitals of all denominations.

In 1975, my Diocese and its ten Mission hospitals, stretching from Inyanga North to Chisumbanje, had 559 beds. It treated in that year 13,281 in-patients and 50,386 out-patients, while 2,192 births are recorded. The cost to the State was exactly $62,124,57. The cost to the Diocese, to me, which my missionaries and I obtained from overseas, was $76,970,95. This is small compared with what is done in other Dioceses.

I mention this to show that even if the modest contribution to public health which my Diocese makes to Rhodesia were withdrawn by the return to their home countries of our nursing sisters, the loss to Rhodesia would be very serious indeed.

No less serious in another field of activity of immense value to Rhodesia would be the closing down of all Church schools of whatever kind. I am proud of what, in the name of the Church, I have been able to provide in the realm of education for children of all races during my thirty years in Rhodesia, just as I am proud in the same cause of having been able to promote the Church's ministry of healing and aid to the sick and infirm. It is this knowledge that enables me to bear with equanimity the remarks published in the *Umtali Post* some months ago: 'There is a certain prelate living not far from here who has done more harm to Rhodesia than all the terrorists put together.' My old Professors of Philosophy, knowing the facts, would have passed their own sober Latin judgment on such an accusation, and would have said: *Disputatur inter Auctores*; 'That is a disputed question.'

Briefly, my contention is this: The work the Church does in Umtali Diocese is too valuable to jeopardise. Its continuance depends on the ability of the Bishop to recruit personnel from overseas and to find the money to keep the various institutions going. Government subsidies are minimal. Should relations between Church and State in this country deteriorate, should Rhodesia continue to reflect to the outside world a racist character, inimical to the Gospel teaching of seeing Christ in one's fellow man, no matter how underdeveloped or physically repulsive or bodily ill, then it would be impossible to attract missionaries of any Christian creed to come to Rhodesia and the protestations of the Government about preserving Christianity and Western civilisation will be proved to be merely words. Words signifying nothing.

Worst of all, should missionaries be by law constrained to violate conscience and to be seen to collaborate with an administration which does not mete out even-handed justice to all in every field of human activity, then Christianity itself would be brought in to disrepute and the way laid open for atheistic Communism.

PASTORAL TEACHING

I come to my pastoral teaching. When I was consecrated Bishop in 1957, my earlier experience of racist ideology in Europe, my training in social ethics and, by that time, my nine years of living in Rhodesia, working mostly among the African people, made me see more clearly the disabilities they suffered. In spite of the advances which they had made through their own initiative, the devoted service of all the Christian Churches, and the cooperation of an increasingly liberal civil administration, they were still marginal to society, still offered only crumbs from the privileged white man's table, still with no real and effective share in economic, political, cultural or social life. Even in the life of the Church the African seemed to be regarded patronisingly and as a second-class member. I recall my own shock when I discovered that in our city churches African Catholics were not normally admitted into the body of the church but had to worship from the sacristy, segregated from the rest of what we ought to have recognised as the one community of faith, of worship and of common Christian concern.

This fact, more than anything else, drove me to a realisation of the disparity that existed between our preaching and our practice. It made clear to me the dullness and superficial quality of our living; our unquestioning acceptance of a situation based on unchristian principles, on a racist ethic; our insensitivity to the conditions of the local indigenous people. Not only – as I recently stated in my Open Letter to the Rhodesian Government – were they marginal to society, but they were likely to remain so. Not that the then civil administration was consciously racist: it simply took for granted as 'the accepted thing', without attempting to analyse the consequences, that in Southern Rhodesia there were different moral standards applicable to the 'superior' and the 'inferior' peoples – standards which enabled the 'advanced' classes to have an easy conscience while making the 'inferior' classes an object of exploitation.

In 1958, a year after my consecration as Bishop, I preached for the first time in the Catholic Cathedral in Salisbury to a multiracial congregation, including the Vatican representative to Southern Africa, representatives of the Government and members of the Diplomatic Corps, and clearly expressed my ideas on the need for the abolition of racism if we were really to be true to Christ's command to do unto others as we would be done by ourselves, and if we were ever going to be able to lay the foundations of a stable society in Southern Rhodesia.

In the months that followed I set to work on the theme, and finally produced a fairly extensive Pastoral Letter entitled *Purchased People*, addressed to my own diocesans and published on 29 June 1959. The document had little effect in Rhodesia, but was immediately noticed outside the country. I understand it has been translated into fifteen languages. Copies were ordered by the United Nations, and extracts appeared in translation in many countries. The Italian journal of sociological studies *Aggiornamenti Sociali* published the document *in toto*.

I had just begun my episcopate and was, as it were, the new boy in the Bishop's Conference. My Pastoral Letter clearly shows how seriously I considered my office. I quote from it:

> Preach, a bishop must, not permitting himself to be silenced by merely human fears or temporal considerations; not watering down his message for the sake of spurious peace, or loss of friendship with any worldly authority, or possibility of being deliberately misinterpreted by wicked men ... There are some who would confine all church activity to the sacristy, demanding of the Church the subservience of silence in all public affairs. Yet ... it is precisely such people who most bitterly and vociferously condemn the Church for failing to influence our modern life.

'States', I said, 'may persistently disregard or repudiate the rights of the spiritual power, rejecting its tutelage and claiming in their blindness absolute sovereignty, but whether they like it or not, the Church must insist on her imprescriptible right to intervene in temporal matters insofar as these affect the spiritual order of salvation, for example, the denouncing or avoiding of sin, the preservation of the order established by God, or the maintenance of her own liberty'.

One can immediately recognise in all this the influence of my experience of the totalitarian states' oppression of the Church in Central and Eastern Europe.

Continuing to explain the current problem of race relations, and attempting to show how it was at its roots a religious problem to be solved only when men recognise their common brotherhood in God, I stated:

> Once religion goes from public life, society loses its vitality and social decay sets in; law itself becomes a lawless thing; legal positivism takes the place of divine ordinance; public men forget

that they are responsible to God for their official actions and confusion becomes inevitable.

Our Divine Lord's doctrine of justice and charity can alone provide the basis for mutual understanding and peace (in Rhodesia) … That doctrine has in other ages proved successful in reconciling the varied social conditions of men, has civilised barbarous races, has made clear how master and servant can live in the peace of the one great Christian family.

I continued: 'Such is the tragedy of the world's forgetfulness of God that men look down on, and treat with contempt, and persecute, and deny ordinary justice to their fellow men and continue to call themselves Christians.'

Blaming much of the disorder on the neglect of Natural Law, I said: 'Wherever the genius of law seeks out its origins, there it will find Natural Law', and added:

Wherever, as here in Central Africa, it is neglected, grave injustices are inflicted and prolonged on whole groups of people, family life is disrupted, the liberty of the individual is needlessly constrained, uninstructed masses are confused about what is their duty and what is their due, and legislators themselves, with no very clear idea of the essential nature of man or of his destiny, and with no unalterable principles to guide them enact measures so ill-considered and immature that they make a mockery of justice itself.

Next in this Pastoral Letter I dealt briefly with the crucial problem of African nationalism which was then revealing itself in all its complexity throughout Rhodesia. I said: 'The desire of a national group to be free from subjection to a foreign ruler is a most legitimate one, provided it can be achieved without any violation of justice.'

Pleading for a change of outlook on the part of extremists on both African and European sides, I said that a vocal minority of Europeans was responsible for much of the ill-feeling which exists. 'This minority', I said, 'basing its cause on the plea that control of the country must always remain in the hands of civilised persons, perverts that excellent sentiment into meaning that one race of people, their own, shall dominate for all time and at any cost', and I added:

> The treasured belief that they are a courageous, confident, virile, fair-minded and adventurous people must surely be dismissed as an illusion, if the Europeans of this country are not prepared or are incapable of moderating their outlook, to meet the challenge of a changing world in which the barriers of space and time have so rapidly been broken down that men of different nations and of different racial origins are brought more quickly and closely together than ever before.

I wrote that nearly twenty years ago. It seems still appropriate today.

I have devoted a good deal of time to describing this document, because I wish to indicate the character of my criticism of the national scene. The same style of philosophical argument pervades all the statements of the Catholic Bishops of Rhodesia in the years that followed, because I played some considerable part in framing them.

Unfortunately the people of this country either did not take the trouble to study what the other Bishops and I had to say, lest perhaps their conscience be disturbed, or maybe because the sober philosophical argument was beyond their comprehension.

The result of all this was that I acquired a reputation of being simply a troublemaker, a political agitator who was, as the Irish are alleged to be, just against the Government for the heck of it. I was written off, as one clerical visitor to Rhodesia put it to an appreciative public last year, as 'a lovable lunatic, who really should not be listened to or allowed to remain in the country at all'.

Such an opinion was formalised some years later by the Chichester Club, a society of Catholic business and professional men in Salisbury who, in fact, made an official request to Pope Paul to have me removed from the office of Bishop of Umtali.

My Pastoral Letter of 1959 was followed by a similar instruction to all the Catholics of Rhodesia two years later and signed by all the Bishops of this country. The theme was clearly expressed in the title: *Peace through Justice*. It was an effort to ensure that the Church should be seen to advocate a cessation to the disturbances that took place throughout the country at the time when a new Constitution for the country was being framed.

From 1962 to 1965 I was almost totally concerned with that historic event which was the Second Vatican Council held at Rome during those years, and attended by all the Catholic Bishops of the world. Over one hundred years had passed since there bad been such a gathering. The aim of the Council was the reform of the Church in every aspect of its activity where reform was necessary, and a renewal of its own understanding of its mission in the world.

Although I was completely unknown in such a distinguished gathering, in the first session I received almost one thousand votes and was elected a member of the important Secretariat for the Promotion of Christian Unity, a group of twenty-four Cardinals and Bishops whose objective was to make contact with the heads of other Christian denominations in the hope that through studying our differences and achieving mutual understanding we might possibly, in time to come, achieve corporate unity.

Once again the experience of four years working in an international atmosphere, meeting intelligent and disciplined men from every corner of the globe, influenced my under-standing of world affairs and made me realise that there was emerging in history a planetary unity of mankind and a notion of international community. The contrast with the parochial, morally primitive and racist existence of Rhodesia provided a revelation and a shock from which I have never recovered.

In the Second Session of the Council during 1963 I delivered my first speech in Latin to the Bishops assembled in St Peter's Basilica in Rome. Looking back on it now, it is interesting to note that it was a denunciation of racism as it had been applied to the first people of God, the Jews.

As a member of the Unity Secretariat, I was involved every day with the most intelligent minds of the Church in framing documents which were afterwards approved as bearing the most authoritative character for Catholics all over the world. We were blessed too with the aid of all other Churches and with lay experts from many nations. My particular Secretariat was especially concerned with the framing of the historic Declaration on Religious Liberty, a declaration on Anti-Semitism, and an extremely important Decree on Ecumenism.

Here again the seminal ideas of religious liberty and racism, with their correlative problems of the relationship between Church and State and the rights of racial groups and religious and political minorities, matured in my mind and much influenced my thinking in relation to Rhodesia.

In 1964 I achieved some international notoriety for an important address to the Council delivered in Latin to the 2,300 Bishops in which I criticised proposed legislation about the Church's missionary activity, and by my intervention I managed to have the proposals rejected and a new document substituted. In the following, final year of the Council I was chosen to address the gathering in the name of all the Church's missionary Orders when the definitive document on mission endeavour was voted and approved.

I mention this particularly because the document seemed to have the official approval of the Holy See and was presented to the assembled Bishops as having that character. In spite of that, I recognised that as a loyal son of the Church I had not only the freedom to object to it, but even the duty to do so. I understood that it would be an act of disloyalty not to say, and to say fearlessly, what I considered to be wrong with the document.

I mention this to illustrate the fact that in criticising the State of Rhodesia I am not behaving as an enemy, but rather as a responsible citizen, and it is in this attitude that I persist to this day.

My learned counsel have encouraged me to give all these details of my activity, possibly to refute the opinion held by many of my critics in this country that I am simply an irresponsible troublemaker with no understanding whatsoever of the grave issues affecting this country, and possibly one who would have no hesitation in promoting violence or encouraging Communism. At best I am dismissed by many simply as a talkative 'do-gooder' who has no intention of remaining permanently in Rhodesia and who would leave the country and fly to safety elsewhere should danger ever arise.

In regard to this latter accusation which, indeed, has been made many times, I might say that I have never been dispossessed of my passport. The authorities have paid me the compliment of presuming that I would do nothing so dishonourable as running away, even when faced with this trial and its serious consequences.

For the other supposition that I am simply a 'do-gooder' with no logical reason for my rejection of racism, may I here make explicit my belief that unless a man has cultivated in himself a contemplative mind, unless his life is characterised by inwardness, by an appreciation of his own identity, by an understanding that he is not mass-produced, but purpose-made, that his possession of intellect and will prove to him that he has been called into existence by Someone – not just by Some Thing, by some blind cosmic force, unless a man realises all this profoundly in his own heart and recognises that such is the condition, the privilege of existence of every other human being, no matter what his race or colour or condition or creed, unless he realises precisely this, he can have no solid foundation for his denunciation of racism and must be prepared to be described as a mere 'do-gooder'.

My rejection of the evil of racism is founded, I believe, on such a contemplative conclusion and is supported by the Gospel of Christ as clearly expressed in St Matthew's Gospel. Christ wishes to be served and to be seen in the most abject and neglected of his fellow men. This should be taught and practised by all who profess to follow him.

I think of an Anglican priest missionary, known throughout the length and breadth of Rhodesia, Fr Arthur Shearly Cripps, who, with the vision of a very special grace, saw Christ in this way in his fellow man, in his black African servant, and who wrote:

> Oh, happy eyes are mine
> That pierce the black disguise
> And see Our Lord!
> Oh, woe of woes!
> That I should see, that I should know
> Whom 'tis they use that use Him so!

The years following the Vatican Council were crucial as far as my attitude to the problems of Rhodesia were concerned. I was now able to recognise, as never before, how the rights of human persons were being systematically violated in many countries and communities. Some of these rights, though thankfully not all of them, were violated in Rhodesia, yet no one recognised them, or if so, dared to protest against them, though Rhodesia claimed to have declared its political independence in the name of God and for the preservation of Christianity and Western Civilisation.

Recognition of this widespread moral malaise inspired the Catholic Church to convene a Synod of its Bishops in Rome in 1971 to examine the whole problem and search for solutions based on a firm and radical conviction that it is God's will that justice be done on earth, that therefore the Church cannot remain indifferent to the deplorable state of affairs which existed throughout the world to the widespread neglect of justice, both in the profession of law and in the practice of politics.

I had the privilege of representing the Bishops of Rhodesia at that Synod, and I carried out my duty of illustrating to the assembled prelates the racist character of our society, both in political, social, economic and cultural life. It was at the meeting that I coined the phrase which has since passed into common use to describe our political structure. I said: 'Rhodesia is a political absurdity. It is a State without a nation.'

The official document published at the end of the Synod and entitled *Justice in the World* clearly stated the obligation imposed by conscience and by the Christian faith on all who professed that faith to take positive action to promote justice in the world and to work through peaceful means for the dismantling of those unjust structures which denied other human beings integral human development. This directive is summed up in the following magisterial sentence from the document: 'Action on behalf of justice and participation in the transformation of the world fully appear to us, the Bishops, as a constitutive dimension of the preaching of the Gospel, or, in other words, of the Church's mission for the redemption of the human race and its liberation from every oppressive situation.'

After such a clear indication of where my duty lay, how could I, or any other Bishop, for that matter, remain indifferent to the gross injustice which existed all around me and which especially had to be borne by the vast majority of the Rhodesian population?

Pope Paul himself made explicit what should be done. It would not be enough, he said, just to publish statements pointing out and denouncing injustice wherever it might be found. Positive and prophetic action ought to be taken, the lead ought to be given by the Church if it is to maintain any shadow of credibility in its mission. These are his words:

> It is not enough to recall principles, state intentions, point to crying injustices and utter prophetic denunciations. These words will lack real weight unless they are accompanied for each individual by a livelier awareness of personal responsibility and by effective action.

This ought to explain much of my activity here in Rhodesia in my work for the promotion of a sane order and the eradication of injustices in any shape or form. It was a work inspired by Christian teaching and based on the belief that peace can only be achieved where justice is sought, protected and practised.

In all my criticism there was nothing whatsoever of a spirit of anarchy. I had experienced in my young manhood the tragedies of State absolutism, of blind following of political figures. I was convinced that the old moral and paternalistic concept of the State should be replaced by a juridical and constitutional one in which the true subject of politics is the human person, the citizen. I believed that it was morally wrong and pregnant with danger for the future of Rhodesia to banish the majority population, the African people, to the fringe of society, to deny them the right of self-determination and independence. I held as fundamental for the pursuit of lasting peace that power, responsibility and decision-making should be shared by all who could reasonably take part in it, and that these activities should not be the monopoly of one group or race segment of the people. I understood that democracy, to fulfil its true functions, requires an aristocracy of mind and character, and that neither one element nor the other, nor indeed both were the exclusive possession of the ruling white minority in Rhodesia. With St Thomas Aquinas I knew well that not all citizens have either the will or the capacity to concern themselves with politics, but that in practice any good form of government ought to incorporate the democratic principle.

Above all I detested and denounced at every possible opportunity the use of violence, whether the institutional violence created and made respectable by parliamentary legislation, or the brutal, physical violence which is more easily recognised, but no less detestable.

As far back as my Pastoral Letter of 1959 I had stated that any organised attempt to overthrow a legally constituted government can only be justified by the presence of the following conditions:

1. If there be on the part of the government grave and prolonged violation of the rights of the subject;
2. If all constitutional methods of obtaining redress have been seriously tried and have failed;
3. If there be a reasonable prospect of success and of setting up an objectively better government; because, as I said, unless there be, the common good demands that civil war be averted.

I would like to point out here that at no time in my life have I ever taken part in Party Politics. Even now after thirty years in Rhodesia, I know hardly any of the prominent political leaders. I stand apart from them and prefer it that way.

The changing of unjust and oppressive social structures, and hence planned and organised action in the political field, is mainly the task of the laity, because the political field is their proper field of action. The priest normally should not involve himself in ideological and partisan disputes, since this would jeopardise his function as a mediator and would possibly tarnish the purity of his message and indeed his freedom as a representative of the Church.

In 1970 I was elected President of the Rhodesia Catholic Bishops' Conference, and held that office for two years. It was during that time that I strenuously opposed the recognition of the Land Tenure Act, which would have made it impossible for the Church to be faithful to its mandate to treat all human beings as equal members of the one family of God through creation and redemption. At a meeting of all the Bishops and the heads of all the religious Orders working in this country, I proposed that we should close all our institutions, all our schools, hospitals, orphanages, homes for the aged – everything – rather than be false to the principle which we preached as the fundamental tenet of our faith, namely that we call God 'Our Father', that we must do to others as we would like to be done by ourselves, that we must try to see Christ in our fellow man – the hungry, the thirsty, the naked, the stranger, the prisoner. Above all, I argued, we must say with the same resolution as the first Christians: 'We must obey God rather than men.'

The government has been prudent enough to let our decision and its consequences go unchallenged. The contribution made by all the Christian Churches and ecclesiastical communities to the life of the nation has been so widespread and beneficial that were they to be forced to close down their institutions rather than be false to principle, the loss to Rhodesia would be enormous.

Certainly it seems that the government appeared by this to recognise that the Christian Church in Rhodesia could not continue to exist if, because of the colour of a person's skin, or his racial origin, it could be forced to refuse its mission of healing or of educating to any human being who came to our hospitals or schools and requested the service of charity which the Church professes to offer in the name of its founder. By taking no action, when the Church did not observe the law as laid down in the Land Tenure Act, the State seemed to indicate that it gave due and proper recognition to the primacy of conscience.

In the past five or six years, as everyone knows, restrictive legislation has been greatly increased and today has reached unbelievable proportions. The growth in African nationalist consciousness and political activity, both within and outside Rhodesia's borders, has largely been responsible for it. Particularly the monolithic fracture of the Portuguese colonial empire has been instrumental in bringing into existence African nationalist parties whose aim is the overthrow of the present government of Rhodesia and the setting up of another administration based on black majority rule.

The determination of both sides to the struggle not to give in has brought Rhodesia to a state of war and has given reason for the daily increase in oppressive legislation. The machinery of coercion is multiplied and legalised without any apparent end to it in sight. Wherever such a condition of affairs obtains, it is symptomatic of serious social disorder. Wherever the civil state is well ordered and firmly established on the consent of the people, the machinery of coercion should not obtrude itself on the notice of the citizens.

Unhappily, this is not so in Rhodesia, and as a result the Catholic Commission for Justice and Peace has had increasingly to concern itself with the proliferation of acts of violence brought to its attention by the general public, almost entirely by the African population, in its effort to obtain redress through a legitimate Church authority.

I have had the honour of being President of the Rhodesia Justice and Peace Commission for the past two years. The majority of its members are young Europeans, professional men, who, with their African fellows, give unlimited time and expert attention to the searching out of acts of injustice and the obtaining of redress or compensation. It is a joy for me to report that although the Commission acts under the aegis of the Catholic Bishops' Conference, its members belong to different Christian denominations and sometimes to none. The work of the Commission has at various times been greatly supported by the heads of other Churches, particularly when it has had to make representations to Government requesting a public inquiry into some of the more serious matters brought to its attention by complainants who had no other help available.

Sad to say, the response of the State to these appeals made by responsible people for the investigation of injustices has not been what might have been expected from an administration which not only claims to be democratic, but which actually proclaims that it is the defender of Christianity and Western Civilisation. In spite of all the appeals and personal approaches made to the Government, no independent inquiry into allegations of brutality has yet been carried out. Instead, abuse of the most bitter and defamatory type has been heaped on the Commission and its members from all parts of the country, by Government supporters in Parliament and out of it, by a cowardly and sycophantic Press, and above all by the State-controlled and manipulated television and broadcasting systems.

It is history, well recorded, both in the Press and in Hansard at the time, how the Justice and Peace Commission's charges, compiled with meticulous and professional skill and published in the pamphlet *The Man in the Middle*, were rejected without examination, and how people like me, who were associated in the preparation of the document, were reviled, both in the House of Assembly and in the Senate.

And so, instead of accepting the challenge to investigate and thus manifest a proper concern that justice should be done and be seen to be done, the security of the House of Assembly and of the Senate was used to attack the Commission and defame its members.

However, out of such attacks much good eventually came. The African people, whose grievances we had attempted to present to the authorities in a responsible manner, and for whom we sought justice, now recognised that there were in the country some people, surprisingly to them, even Europeans, who were concerned on their behalf, and as a result the racial tensions, which were daily increasing in the densely populated townships, were relaxed, and the suffering people felt that someone at least was speaking on their behalf. The Justice and Peace Commission acted as a relief valve for the pent-up emotions of the black people, made marginal in their own country, and it thus provided a service of extremely great value to Rhodesia.

Not only that. The Commission's work quite categorically offset the propaganda of those who tried to enlist the African population of Rhodesia to Communism. The Christian Church, as represented by the efforts of the Commission, was seen to be the support of the underprivileged, the advocate of the voiceless, the tireless defender of the rights of the human person, the friend of the disenfranchised masses. That was perfectly clear to great numbers of the young African intelligentsia who otherwise, in their unhappy condition, might easily have been swayed by the Communist cry that the Christian Church will not stir a finger to help the underdog, but simply preaches pious platitudes to him, counsels him to be even more long-suffering, not to challenge the privileged few who manipulate him for their own selfish gain, and that whatever the hardships of this life, it would be all made right in the next; there would be pie in the sky when you die.

Having personally received much of the abuse from Cabinet Ministers and members of the Senate – from their seat of safety –

because of my being President of the Justice and Peace Commission, I was on one notable occasion last year delighted to be able to use, on behalf of the Church, one of the more scurrilous attacks made on us by the then Minister of Justice, Law and Order. It is appropriate to my argument that I should record the incident.

I was invited to an important conference in Bonn in November of last year, sponsored by the Justice and Peace Commission of West Germany. The purpose of the conference was to find out how the Christian West could best assist the newly independent African nations so as to wean them away from the advances of Communism. At one point during the formal discussions at the conference table, one of the sixteen African ambassadors complained that the Christian West had been silent for many years, and had connived, by its silence, in benefiting by the exploitation of the masses in the colonies. I jumped at this opportunity to reply, and produced from my briefcase the front page of *The Rhodesia Herald*, which carried the headline: 'Church acts as Fifth Column', an accusation made some time earlier in the House of Assembly by the Minister for Justice, Law and Order.

In the widespread denunciation of the Justice and Peace Commission, the media of communication in Rhodesia used all the means at their disposal to bring the Commission, and me, its President, into disrepute so as to nullify all our efforts. Nothing was too despicable to be attempted. In the Senate, not only did a Senator Chief propose that I should be removed, but a hitherto highly respected Senator Chairman of the Senate Legal Committee defamed me in the Chamber by asserting that I exercised a dictatorial influence in the Commission and appointed and dismissed its Chairman as I thought fit. Such an accusation made in the Senate by a man who bore an honourable name I found intolerable, and through the medium of the national Press I challenged him to substantiate or refute his defamatory remark. To this day he has refused to accept the challenge. It seems that defamation of my character from the safe sanctuary of the Senate is justifiable, according to Rhodesian standards.

I cannot too greatly emphasise the need for the Church to be seen here and now as a courageous voice in the denunciation of acts of injustice, particularly those felt by the African people, and as a committed and active agent in the peaceful dismantling of unjust social structures wherever they exist. Such clear-cut and public denunciation and action is especially necessary when we are told that Communists threaten the whole of Southern Africa, and that all along the Eastern border, that is all along my Diocese, the forces of Marxism are already at work to invade and take over Rhodesia. I must say at once that personally I doubt every bit of government propaganda that I hear on the RBC or RTV, just as I read with the greatest sense of scepticism much that is printed in our Rhodesian newspapers. I do not believe that Rhodesian Africans want Communism, or Russia, or China, or Cuba. I believe that they want to be with the West, and with the English-speaking world.

One highly gifted African of great academic distinction told me, when I asked him if his people felt any natural inclination towards Communism: 'My lord, Communism is completely alien to us. Can you imagine our giving our cattle, let alone our children, to the State? We are capitalists at heart. Unfortunately we have no capital.'

One way or the other, however, it is vital for the preservation of the Christian Church in this country that it be clearly seen by the underprivileged masses and by those who endeavour to attract them to Communism to be prepared to practise what it preaches, to be unpopular when need be, to stand up and suffer for the underprivileged, to be known to be opposed to all unjust agencies, no matter how powerful, and not even by fear of persecution to be terrified into the silence of complicity.

As far as I am concerned in my Diocese at this time, no Communist agent, I pray, will ever be able to accuse me or my missionaries of being indifferent to the appeal of the sick, the hungry or the naked. No Communist agent will ever be able to say that by our silence we gave consent to discrimination based on race or religion or political belief. Whatever befalls, I and those wonderful missionaries I am privileged to have with me will always try to do God's will, not men's.

In saying all this, I realise it will be claimed by the State that its very *raison d'être* is the preservation of Christianity and of

Western civilisation. To this I reply that surely that civilisation which we now call Western, and which was once significantly called Christian, is based on effort made to achieve a social order directed towards the good of the person, on an acceptance of the fact that everyone is a person endowed with intelligence and free will, and that the human person is and must be the source, subject and goal of all its social institutions.

The philosophical principle here enunciated finds little acceptance in the thinking of those who rule Rhodesia. Neither would they, in practice, agree to the assertion that all men and nations enjoy the right to development regarded as a dynamic interpretation of all those fundamental human rights on which the aspirations of individuals and nations are based, which includes the right to equal opportunities in the cultural, civic, social and economic spheres, and to an equitable distribution of the natural resources. Such doctrine is utterly at variance with what obtains in practice, and is sanctified by legislation in this so-called bastion of Western civilisation.

As for our being a free Christian society at all, I doubt it very much. The very racist ethic which is the fount of all our discriminatory legislation, which informs the minds of the electorate and determines the customs of the privileged ruling class is utterly alien to the mind of Christ. As I wrote in my Pastoral Message in 1959:

> What is really at the heart of the trouble is that God has been banished politely from public life, His eternal law has been quietly set aside, hesitant lip-service is paid to Him only , and thoughtless men attempt to order society without taking the Maker's rules into account.

In Rhodesia, for instance, at this moment it seems that only a State-censored form of Christianity is permitted to be broadcast from RBC or RTV. Every single religious script has to be submitted, and if necessary censored by some State official before it can be delivered to the general public. This is fact, not hearsay.

One Anglican Bishop told me of the preposterous pre-sumption of one official of the RBC who corrected his text – the Bishop's text – before it could be broadcast. One of the priests in my own Diocese had his text completely rejected. That I could understand. The good man was either so innocent or so imprudent as to think that he might be permitted to speak on our national broadcasting station on such a delicate subject as the saintly Lord Chancellor of England, Sir Thomas More, who gladly laid his head on the executioner's block to show that his first duty was to conscience and the Church, that he had first to serve God, and only then, if it were in accordance with God's will, to serve his King.

And this is not the only way in which it is evident that a new form or interpretation of Christianity exists in our midst and enjoys the blessing of the State.

Morality has, in many respects, been banned from public life by order of the Ministers of State and some of their subjects. This is true. I recall the order of him who until recently was Minister of Defence, an order which I challenged in the national Press and which has not been answered. The Minister told the security forces, in effect, not to hesitate to kill and destroy anyone and any place where there might be terrorists, and said that if innocent people were killed or maimed in the process, it was just too bad. It was their misfortune, not his fault. I reminded him and other members of the Government, in a letter to the Press, that political authority must always be exercised within the limits of morality, and of course, for that, drew down upon myself the wrath of all Rhodesian white racists, with their telephone calls in the middle of the night to disturb my sleep, these brave people, their threats in the street, their unspeakably filthy letters and their drawings of abuse. Such is the penalty for presuming to suggest that morality has any place in public life.

You think this is exaggerated? May I read for you, as reported in *The Rhodesia Herald* of 30 July 1976, the directive given by the Secretary for Law and Order to recruit patrol officers during their passing-out parade at the Morris Depot in Salisbury. He told them 'not to be too squeamish in departing from the niceties of established procedures which are appropriate for more normal times'. What is this but an indication by a State authority that excessive punitive measures may be exercised without fear against the general public? Is this not another indication that political authority and morality, in the mind of the State, have no natural correlation?

I very well realise that when the security of any State is threatened, extreme measures may have to be taken for the common good. But in a so-called Christian State, how does it accord with the declared principle of preserving Christian civilisation that the government has now, I understand, in a high state of preparedness, a plan for the taking over of Christian Missions of all denominations everywhere in Rhodesia?

What, for instance, is one to say of a government which claims to be Christian and which allows its officers to burst, fully armed, into a church while Mass, divine worship, is being celebrated, and order the priest to hurry up and leave the altar, chomping their rifles to intimidate him into obeying them? This happened to one of my priests at one of my Missions in my Diocese a few weeks ago, and, strange to say, I first got the news of it on the day when I read in *The Rhodesia Herald* of 25 August 1976, of a similar case which took place in Uganda, when a Catholic priest was dragged from the altar in his church by another kind of soldiery.

Is this what one expects from the Government of Rhodesia? And when the unfortunate priest was finally locked up in a cell, and I was allowed to see him, I was shocked to the core that he, or any human being, should be housed in such appalling conditions. This was not in Uganda, or in some country of Eastern Europe. It was not in a Communist country, or in some remote South American republic, this was here in Rhodesia. It was not perpetrated by some sadist in some remote corner of Rhodesia, where no responsible authority could see it and later on protest that it was done without his approval. This was here, just beyond those walls, not twenty yards away from where we are assembled.

Let me tell you what I saw. After the lawyer whom I had employed had been refused permission to see the unfortunate priest alone, after bail had been offered and refused because no charge had been laid, through the kindness of some humane officials of the police service, I was permitted to see my brother priest. A great steel door with two bars was opened, and inside, to my horror, I saw the priest standing barefoot on a cold cement floor. His shoes and socks had been removed. His belt, his watch, his rosary had all been taken from him. In one corner, near the door, four or five narrow slats of wood battened together close to the floor made what passed for a bed. The unfortunate man had to sleep on that as if on rails. There were three blankets, but no pillow and no mattress whatsoever. In a far corner of the room a square cement block about two or two-and-a-half feet high, was built solidly into the wall. There was a hole in the centre and a push button at the side. This was the toilet. To use it the prisoner had to climb up and somehow try to squat. There were two small windows very high up close to the ceiling. There was no table, no chair, no stool, nothing whatsoever to sit on. Food, consisting of porridge and beans, was brought to the prisoner at six o'clock in the morning, and he had nothing more to eat until six o' clock in the evening.

Thanks to the humanity of the officer-in-charge, after some days I was permitted to send him a New Testament and a Breviary, the priest's prayerbook. But try as I could I was unable to find out when this unfortunate man might be brought to trial or how his condition might further be improved. Then, suddenly, eleven days later he was called out of his cell, given his shoes and socks and other belongings and told that he might go; that he was free.

It is safe to presume that this priest is not the only one who has had to suffer like this without any charge whatsoever being laid against him. Is this the sort of treatment one expects from civilised beings? Is this the way Christian governments with Western civilised traditions deal with their citizens who have been guilty of no crime? Is it not right that I should speak and denounce such injustice for all the world to hear, such Pharisaism, such hypocrisy?

The whole world is alerted and alarmed, and no expense is spared to seek out and recover a sophisticated instrument of war, either sunk in the ocean or hijacked in another country. But the same world is indifferent to human beings locked up and forgotten and sunk in gaols and in internment camps all over the world.

The general public knows nothing about all this, I am sure. The electorate would not believe it were it to be made known. They would not credit that the men they elected to Parliament would ever allow such things to happen.

I wrote about this general condition of affairs in an English newspaper on 3 April of this year.

> For the most part the ordinary European does not realise that anything like this appalling system exists. He has been brain-washed by the officially-controlled media and by a subservient Press. He has heard of such things happening during the last war in Central Europe, but he will simply not believe that this happens right under his nose in Rhodesia. That a previous prime minister, Garfield Todd, is still under house arrest worries him not at all, neither does the daily tally of murdered Africans, shot dead merely for breaking the curfew. He is not in the least troubled at the fact that the Government censors every single radio talk given by ministers of religion, and chooses 'safe' men to be given time on the air. That no member of the parliamentary opposition is ever heard on radio or television he regards as only proper. It never occurs to him that there is anything unusual in all this. Were he to hear African nationalists speak of the need for another Nuremberg, he probably would not see that either.

In writing this way about such things, I believe I do a service of great value to the people of Rhodesia and to free men the world over. I believe that if this system of government be permitted to continue without any change whatsoever, without any attempt at providing equality under the law and equal opportunity for all men, then the danger of another Nuremberg could be very real indeed.

Neither time nor numbers are on the side of those who rule us today. The moral state of the country gives little hope for the future either. We have one of the highest divorce rates in the world. Our maternity homes have been turned into geriatric units. The civil administration seems to have lost all capacity for self-examination, for self-discipline, for self-regulation, and to my mind it is heading for chaos. And still the selfish electorate, callous and insensitive to the condition of the masses, thinks it can carry on regardless.

Selfishness or avarice in men or in nations is a sure sign of moral underdevelopment. If this is true, and I believe it is, then those who rule us must be regarded by thinking men the world over as moral primitives. Yet to those who do not see beneath the surface, Rhodesia appears a haven of order and cleanliness and discipline. Yes, indeed. It is the same order, discipline and cleanliness that one finds in prison compounds and cemeteries. The good life, the power and the wealth which people in Rhodesia claim as the culmination of their so-called civilising presence in Africa, of their professional and technical achievement, divorced as it is from basic morality, must surely be regarded as nothing more than, if I may quote Toynbee in his *Study of History*: 'The opening chapters of complete decline.'

I have said that in speaking openly of these things and criticising them, no matter how unpopular these truths may be, I am doing a service to Rhodesia and its people. Anyone who loves Rhodesia and its people, anyone who wants peace here, must surely recognise that the laws which have built up and continue to maintain such national disorder must quickly be revoked by the rulers: the unjust social structures must, without delay, be dismantled. In short, institutional violence must be abolished if racial war, with the most horrible consequences, is to be avoided.

Were there to be an African Government in this country – and indeed this seems inevitable, and very soon – and if the present laws which have been enacted and applied to create and preserve privilege – if these were retained and applied in reverse against the European, what a protest there would be! For instance, only a small number of European children would be allowed to attend school, and an even smaller percentage would be permitted to pass the State examinations. Employment and access to apprentice-ships would be reserved to black people only. All officers – and I believe this will change – in the Army and police would belong to the governing race. Prison sentences for Europeans could be served in cells similar to the one I have described, and with the same civilised amenities. Thousands of whites could be driven from their homes and farms without compensation and housed in the open veld behind wire fences with lights blazing all night, with limited sanitation and under curfew, as is now done with certainly at least 100,000 Africans in the so-called 'protected villages'.

But perhaps an African Government might be more consider-ate. Europeans might possibly be treated better than Africans were. They could even be given alternative accommodation. It might be possible to arrange for them to have at least a roof over their heads during the rainy season as many Africans had not. In Salisbury, for instance, houses in Highfields might be given in exchange for those in Highlands. With laws in force now, but applied in reverse, white people, children among them, could be arrested or restricted without trial, and any brutalities practised by the Security Forces could be withdrawn from the jurisdiction of the courts, as has been done by the application of the Indemnity and Compensation Act. Trials could be held *in camera* and sentence of death by hanging carried out without it being necessary to inform anyone, including the closest relatives, that the executions had taken place.

Should anyone feel that he could no longer live in such a country, the Departure from Rhodesia Act of 1972 could be invoked to prevent his leaving. Moreover, should he manifest in any way contempt for an officer of the State, he could be severely punished, and if under the age of eighteen, could be given a whipping, provided the whipping did not exceed eight strokes.

These are only a few of the disabilities which the African majority now suffers in Rhodesia and has had to tolerate for years 'to maintain standards', to preserve Christianity and Western civilisation. I believe that there are two notions of Christianity abroad in this country, that promoted by the official Christian missionary bodies, who have done so much for Rhodesia, and that peculiar form based on a racist blasphemy and sponsored by the Government.

Rhodesians are prepared, by their peripheral activities, to rewrite the *Guinness Book of Records* in every single endurance test, as long as they are not required to do to their neighbour what they would like done to themselves in this so-called Christian country.

The Avila Situation

Your worship and gentlemen, in the course of this next part of my unsworn statement there will be many references to the priest who has been the Superior at Avila Mission, and who has since left the country. I would like permission, instead of using his full name, and for his own security, to be permitted to refer to him as 'Father X'.

I want to tell you exactly what happened in regard to the first offence with which I am charged by the State. What I have to say is taken from my diary which I have kept with considerable detail for some years past.

On Wednesday, 21 April 1976, I was at Regina Coeli Mission in Nyamaropa Reserve on an ordinary visit. As the Mission is situated within a very short distance of the Mozambique border, and since it comprises not only a secondary school but also a large hospital and a training centre for African nurse-assistants, I was particularly anxious that things should be running smoothly and that all was well. The fact that the Mission had been cut off for some weeks by swollen rivers during the rainy season, and the further fact that it had no telephone connection with the outside world, had always given me reason for special concern. Besides the two priests at the Mission there were five Franciscan Sisters, some from Scotland and some from Ireland. I was very happy to realise during my visit that everything was proceeding normally and that the community was quite happy, although two of the Sisters were on that particular day in Melsetter.

I drove from Regina Coeli Mission to Avila in Inyanga North on 21 April, and shortly after arrival was informed that a letter had been handed into the Mission requesting medicines. I was shown the note and, as far as I can remember, it asked for anti-malarial tablets and medicines for diarrhoea. My recollection of the incident is that I was told that the letter had been delivered by a villager, a man, on behalf of what are in the summons called 'terrorists'. I was asked what ought to be done about it, and I replied that we ought to give medical aid to anyone who asked, and that the nurses should not argue about the matter. I have a distinct recollection of saying that as far as medical help was concerned, no missionary should inquire about the religion or politics of those who asked for help. I remember also saying that if the Security Forces came looking for medicines, they too were to be given whatever they needed and whatever the Mission could afford to give.

I realised clearly what my decision involved. It was a decision which I had arrived at long before, knowing that what had already happened in other parts of the country when terrorists came to Mission stations would, in all probability, happen in my Diocese. First of all, having thought the matter out, I realised that any request for food or medical help made a particular claim on the Church's ministry of charity, and that, were it to be refused, the Church might easily be accused of preaching one thing and doing another. I remembered Christ's words in which he reprimanded those who lacked charity and failed to see Him in the suffering poor. His words, which are known to you all, are these: 'I was hungry and you gave me not to eat, thirsty and you gave me not to drink, naked and you did not clothe me ...', etc.

It was of paramount importance to me that the Church should not suffer in its reputation by failing in charity. In particular I realised that in nearby Mozambique the Church had suffered greatly because of its century-old association with a colonial regime, and that a Marxist ideology was now actively being promoted among the people of that country. I had heard too that this ideology was shared by those who came armed into Rhodesia determined to achieve equality under the law and equal opportunity for all the citizens of Rhodesia. It seemed vitally important to me that these people should not, on their contact with the Church in Rhodesia, be made to believe that it collaborated with the regime which they considered oppressive. Rather it was necessary for the Church, as represented by our Missions, to manifest a courageous and generous Christian concern, even for the wayward.

This was the first thing which decided my thinking in regard to the attitude to be adopted by the missionaries should they be approached by terrorists.

The second decisive motive was the safety of the personnel involved. What would happen, then, were they, few in number, without any means of defence whatever, without even a telephone closer than a two-hour journey – I did not know at the time there was a telephone at the police station – what would these helpless people do were they to refuse the things demanded of them? Certainly, from all the government propaganda that we had listened to, one could only conclude that their lives would be in imminent danger. Informers were given little mercy, we were told. We had been provided with gruesome Government agency reports of how unfortunate people, forced to inform, had been either brutally murdered or savagely mutilated by having their lips and ears cut off.

Here was my problem. If our missionaries deny the medicines, there is nothing to prevent armed men from invading the Mission at any hour of the day or night and forcibly taking what they wanted. As a matter of fact, some time later another group of armed men, Europeans this time, members of the Security Force, came to the Mission clinic, came into the premises, asked for what they wanted, were given it, and even demanded Penbriton, the most expensive drug which the Mission had, and went off. Nobody reported such an incident.

Suppose then the Mission authorities were not to inform, they were guilty of a most serious crime to which was attached the gravest punishment. Rather than have anyone of my missionaries involved in such an issue, I had resolved long before, and now at Avila Mission I made my resolution clear to all the Mission staff, that I alone would be guilty of any crime involved through giving food or medical help to forbidden persons, and that I would also be responsible for the further crime of not reporting their presence. For this I stand here today. I alone am guilty. All other members of the Mission staff who acted in defiance of the law did so under obedience from me.

The person who had come looking for medicines had gone off and it was understood that a parcel containing what was requested, or as much as was available and what we could afford to give, was to be left until called for. Meanwhile the Superior of the Mission, a European priest, and the two European nursing Sisters left that very afternoon to attend a function at another convent of their Order in Marandellas. I remained on at the Mission that afternoon, and while I was out for a walk after the others had gone to Marandellas some European and African soldiers arrived at the Mission and told the African priest stationed there that a group of terrorists had robbed a store and a bus somewhere north of the Mission. I recollect nothing more of that day, but the next morning I set off for Umtali.

That afternoon, having arrived at Umtali, I was visited by the Mission doctor from Regina Coeli hospital, which is very near the border. He came with his wife and baby. The man in question had come a few months before to work at Regina Coeli hospital on a three-year contract. He seemed perfectly happy at first, but after working to get Rhodesian experience in the General Hospital in Umtali, he realised, from the number of war casualties being treated there, that the situation along the border was much more serious than was generally believed. On that day he came to inform me that he could no longer remain in the country, and he wished to terminate his contract. He said that the situation was much too dangerous, and, however much he regretted it, he thought that his obligation to his family came first. With this I agreed. It was proposed then that he might exchange places with another doctor, a nun of the same Order as those working in Regina Coeli, and that she might perhaps come from her hospital in the Transkei and go there to take his place.

Two days later I set off for another Mission, in Chiduku Reserve in the Rusape area, but when I arrived at the priest's house at Rusape I received an urgent message to go to Triashill Mission in the Inyanga area to meet the priest and two European Sisters from Avila Mission. When I arrived there I heard to my great dismay that Father X had left the Mission early in the morning, bringing with him the two Sisters and all their belongings because of threats from terrorists who had come to Avila the night before.

The story, as I heard it from him, was that on the previous night, while at supper, he and Sister Vianney were summoned out into the darkness by two men who had guns at the ready. When they met they saw some other armed men lurking in the shadows some distance away. According to the priest, he and the Sister were lectured on the glories of Communism and the evils of capitalism as represented by the Kennedys, the Rockefellers and the Catholic Church. The visitors ordered the priest to reduce the school fees and the charges made at the Mission clinic. He replied that the clinic was unaided, receiving no support from the State, and that the Sisters were unpaid and the medicines had to be bought by the Mission. The terrorists told him that the

Church could well afford to provide medicines freely. They then threatened that the Mission would be destroyed and other vengeance taken if their other requests for watches, radios, cameras, etc., were not granted.

After a long interview, the men went off, the priest having told them that he could not possibly meet their demands.

Naturally both he and the other members of the Mission staff were greatly frightened by the visit, and they decided that it would be unsafe for them to remain there any longer. They packed up and left early next morning, drove to Inyanga, informed the civil authorities, and without further delay arrived at Triashill Mission, a hundred miles away from Avila, where I met them and heard their story.

The priest was very distraught and wondered if he had acted correctly in leaving the Mission and informing the authorities. I consoled him by saying that if what he told me were true, and that his night visitors were Communists who had said that they wanted to destroy the Church and its Missions, then he had acted correctly. There was a long discussion at the Mission that evening, and other missionaries joined us to decide what ought to be done, especially about Regina Coeli Mission, which was so completely isolated and so close to the Mozambique border.

It was the opinion of the majority of those discussing the matter that someone ought to go at once to Regina Coeli and find out what was happening there. I heard that the Mother Superior and one of her Sisters from Regina Coeli were at Melsetter that evening, so I phoned through and asked them to come very early in the morning, meet me at the Montclair Hotel in Inyanga where I would explain everything, and then return to their Mission in Nyamaropa. I also phoned the African priest at Mount Melleray Mission and asked him to go up as quickly as possible over the mountain to Regina Coeli to be of aid to the three European Sisters who were at the Mission.

The next day was Sunday. I celebrated Mass and preached against Communism. I met the two Franciscan Sisters at the Montclair Hotel, they having come all the way from Melsetter. I told them what had happened at Avila Mission two days earlier, and of the fears for their safety at Regina Coeli. Leading the way,

I drove in my own car, with the Sisters following in theirs, up past Troutbeck Hotel and down the escarpment to Regina Coeli Mission.

All was quiet there. The African priest had arrived, and after a short time I called together all the Sisters and the priests for a conference. I repeated what Father X had told me concerning the visitors at Avila and told the Sisters that the same might happen to them and that therefore they must consider themselves absolutely free to leave the Mission if they so wished. I told them that I could not possibly expect them to remain in such an isolated place without any protection and without even the comfort of a telephone.

Their reply was marvellous and edifying. Without any hesitation they said that they wanted to stay, that they had a duty to the patients, to the student nurses and to the Church. I informed them that the doctor and his wife would not be returning as he considered the situation too dangerous. I asked them if there was anything that I could do to make their safety more secure. They replied that they would like to have another priest at the Mission, one who could drive the car if they could possibly have the Land Rover that had been taken from Avila Mission. We had a very pleasant evening. All was well.

The next morning, 26 April, I drove back to Inyanga and on to Mount Melleray Mission, and from that point travelled with Fr Mutume to Avila. There were many European soldiers at the priest's house. I heard from the Mission personnel that after Father X reported the terrorists at Inyanga, helicopters flew in over the Mission area and army trucks full of soldiers arrived. Shooting started in the village nearby and helicopters swooped low over the fields. One African woman, Mrs Maida Nyamapfeni, who was working in the field, ran in fright for a grass shelter nearby, and was badly wounded in the air attack. She was shot in the face, side and in both legs, but was afterwards picked up by the helicopter and flown to Bindura Hospital.

On the same day, Sunday, Mr Vinyu, on his way to Mass at the Mission, was interrogated and beaten by the Security Forces. The villagers came and reported all this at the Mission, and said that it was all Father X's fault, and that it would not have happened had he not informed. All the Mission staff were very gravely upset, so I called them, the two Sisters, the teachers, nurses, Red Cross students and kitchen staff, and in a classroom I tried to calm them, telling them that if the Sisters' safety could be guaranteed, I would try to get them to come back to the Mission. I told them that whatever Father X had done, the Security Forces themselves knew, as far back as the previous Wednesday, that terrorists had robbed a store.

I drove back that day all the way to Umtali and made arrangements to send another priest to Regina Coeli Mission as I had promised. That night the Regional Superior of the Avila Sisters, i.e. the one who is in charge of all the Sisters who are in Rhodesia, phoned from Salisbury and expressed the hope to me that whatever about Father X, 'our own two Sisters might be able to return to their Mission at Avila'. Next morning I phoned her again, asking permission to send to Avila, accompanied by two priests, one of her Sisters stationed at Mount Melleray, and to see if it would be safe for the two Sisters to go back. My diary says about this request: 'Safe from the anger of both villagers and terrorists'.

About the same time, one of my African priests came to see me, and I told him of his brother's interrogation and beating, and then, because he is a native of the Avila district, I asked him to go at once to that Mission and try to explain to the local people Father X's problem and departure from the Mission, and to endeavour to restore confidence in the missionaries. That same day also the doctor of Regina Coeli and his wife called to finalise their plans to terminate their contract of service at Regina Coeli Mission.

The news of the Avila episode travelled quickly to all parts of the country, and the very next day, 28 April, the Rhodesia Superior of the Marist Brothers, who have a large secondary school at Mount Melleray Mission, phoned me to inquire if it was safe for his community of Brothers to remain on at the Mission. The day after that I was requested by the community of Sisters of Marymount College, Umtali, to meet them for a formal discussion about the closing of their College at the end of the year. It seemed that all the institutions of the Diocese were already feeling themselves threatened.

On Friday, 30 April, I received a phone call from a represent-ative of South African newspapers asking me if it was true that I intended to withdraw all my missionaries from what he called the operational area. I replied that it was not true, and asked him – and these are the words of my diary: 'to kill the story for the safety of the Mission's Sisters'.

Shortly afterwards I had a visit from my two African priests who had come back from Avila. They asked me to do everything I could to send a European priest back there to take Father X's place, and, as they put it, to restore faith in the white missionary. I drove at once from Umtali to Avila myself, because I had to officiate at a wedding at one of the villages. I think it is useful to explain that the Government does not recognise every ordained priest as a marriage officer, and I was the only one available to get to Avila in time.

After the wedding ceremony I drove down the road that leads from Avila to Regina Coeli Mission fairly close to the Mozambique border. I found there the Sisters of Regina Coeli very concerned, because the student nurses had organised a protest on hearing of the sudden departure of their doctor. For their nursing course to be recognised by the State it is necessary for them to be under the direction of a qualified medical doctor. Sister explained to them that in a short time one of my own priests, who is a highly qualified doctor, and who was at the time lecturing in the Royal College of Surgeons in Dublin, would be back in the country and would be available at Regina Coeli to make the nurses' course valid.

On the same day I drove to Umtali, where I found waiting for me the African Regional Superior of another Order of nuns who work at St Peter's Mission in my Diocese near Chisumbanje. This nun too, having heard of the Avila incident, was deeply concerned about the safety of the Sisters of her Order in Chisumbanje, and had come all the way from Pretoria to see for herself how things stood. I volunteered to drive her to Chisumbanje the next morning. We set off the following morning, joined the convoy and went with it as far as Hot Springs. From there we proceeded to Chisumbanje, where we found everything quiet and the Sisters happy to stay on, in spite of what they had heard about Avila.

Next morning I had a phone call from the Regional Superior of the Avila Sisters telling me that her Superior General had cabled her from England saying that Father X had called on her and told her about what happened at Avila, and as a result of that she ordered that the two Avila Sisters should be sent back to Britain at once for their own safety. I told the Regional Superior to cable the Mother General in England and ask her to reconsider her decision and to inform her that I would telephone her myself as soon as I got out of the bush and away from the party line.

I returned to Umtali next day, and was delighted to hear that the two Sisters from Avila, in their anxiety to restore their good name by serving the people, had taken the risk of going back to their Mission for a quick visit. The following day I tried to phone the Superior General in England, but failed. However, subsequently, on 6 May, I did get through to her by phone and explained that it would be very bad for the reputation of the Church in Rhodesia if the Sisters were to leave the country. I even asked her to wait until I could go to Rome myself and get another opinion about the Church's reputation which would ensue were our missionaries to leave. I got in touch with the Archbishop of Salisbury, explained the situation to him and asked him to support my request that the Sisters remain on in Rhodesia.

Two days later, while in Salisbury, I was told by the Regional Superior of the Sisters that they had sent a further appeal to their Head House in England requesting permission for the Sisters to remain on in the country.

It is remarkable how, just at this time, representatives of the various religious Orders in the country suddenly expressed their concern about the future. For example, I had acted on behalf of the Rector of St George's College and the Headmistresses both of Nagle House, Marandellas, and of Marymount College, Umtali, to discuss with the other Bishops what ought to be done should further deterioration in the political situation lead to the closing down of their schools. On this very day too the Superior of another Order of nuns came from Rome to visit her Sister in Rhodesia and to find out if they were safe.

On 10 May I received another disappointment, when, from the Superior of the nuns in New York, I received a letter telling me of her Order's final decision to close down Marymount College, Umtali, at the end of the year.

On 13 May I had a meeting of my Bishop's Council, and it was agreed that I personally should go to Avila Mission and stay there alone for about a week to keep the European presence there and to allow the African priest who had been in charge to go home for a break. On that same day the Provincial Education Officer telephoned to inquire if it was true that all our teachers had left Avila Mission. I assured him that there was no truth at all in this, but I suggested that the continued presence of Security Forces on the Mission would make it a target for terrorists and would endanger the safety of the school children when they returned after the school holidays. That explains my reference to requiring the Security Forces not to remain there. The Provincial Educational Officer got in touch with the Ministry of Education and the matter was dealt with there.

On 14 May I went to Avila and took charge there for about a week. On 17 May two of the Sisters came from Mount Melleray and worked for two days at the Mission hospital. I heard from them that finally their Mother General had decided not to withdraw the Sisters permanently from Rhodesia. On 23 May the Regional Superior phoned to say that the two Sisters were ready to return to Avila. On 27 May I drove from Umtali to the Mission. While there I interviewed the African woman who had been wounded during the helicopter raid on 25 April. She was still receiving treatment at the Mission for her wounds. I discussed with the Mission personnel how we could best provide for the safety of the Sisters when they returned permanently.

On 1 June an incident took place which, in the light of events, proved important. A young European girl had disappeared from her home in Umtali into Mozambique and caused great concern to her parents, who were my parishioners. Her father came to my house that evening with the senior officer of the CID, and we discussed how I perhaps might act as intermediary in getting the child back to Rhodesia. In the course of the long conversation, the CID officer told me that the Church had failed in Avila by not maintaining a European presence there. The priest who had informed on the terrorists should not have run away, he said, but should have stayed on. He added: 'That is just what the Communists want – Europeans to clear out so that they can take over.'

I explained that I had gone back to the Mission myself to show the flag, as it were, and that the European Sisters were themselves anxious to return permanently so that the *status quo ante* should be restored. I told him of all my efforts with the Mother Superior General in England, and reminded him that if he liked to check up on me, my telephone calls would have been recorded as proof of what I had done.

Next day I was informed of the two Avila Sisters, who were already on their way back and had arrived at Mount Melleray Mission. I drove there next morning with supplies and brought the two Sisters back to the Mission which they had left with Father X on 24 April. We received a wonderful welcome from all of the villagers, but especially from the hospital staff.

To show the character of Sister Vianney and her willingness to serve in spite of danger, I would like to tell you that on the very next morning, 5 June, she received a sick call asking her to go out to a distant village to assist a woman who had already been a full day in labour. The only motor car available at the Mission was my little Volkswagen, which was quite useless for the purpose. Straight away Sister solved the problem by getting a driver for the Mission tractor and trailer and set off with it into the bundu. Hours later she returned on the tractor with the baby safely delivered and the mother well.

I go on following my diary to 20 June, when in Umtali I met the Superior General of the nuns who work at Regina Coeli hospital. She had come all the way from Ireland to visit the convents of her Order in Ethiopia, Kenya, Zambia and South Africa, but her great concern was for the safety of those at Regina Coeli. Fortunately she had gone there, spent some days with the nuns, and was returning to Ireland confident that they could remain there in safety.

On 26 June the Regional Superior of the Avila Sisters wished to visit the Mission and see for herself how the nuns were settling in before leaving for England to report to the Superior General. I brought her there where she remained until the following day. I then drove her back to another convent of her Sisters near Headlands. During the time of my visit to the Mission I heard that terrorists were in the vicinity and I did not report their presence for the reasons which I will soon explain to the court.

The Why

Before I endeavour to explain to the court my reasons for acting as I did, permit me to outline some of the principles which influenced my decision. I accept, first of all, that obedience to legal authority is a moral duty. However, if the State demands obedience against the antecedent duty of fulfilling one's existential ends, then obedience becomes evil.

Again I must ask the court to bear in mind that the Church, and churchmen such as I, are conscious of the strong distinction between morality and law. They regard human rights and their correlative duties as a manifestation in human nature of God's eternal law, and in consequence they hold that they are anterior to society, to any arbitrary contract, majority principle, public opinion or poll. Into this category, and I mention those only which are pertinent to the present issue, fall such rights as the right to life, to bodily integrity and well-being, the right to a good reputation, to an honest representation, the right to act in accordance with the right norms of one's conscience, the right to worship God, to practise one's religion, both in public and in private, and to enjoy religious liberty. Man has the imprescriptible right also to be correctly informed about public events, and, as if to crown it all, he has the right to have all his rights – I have, as I say, only mentioned a few of them – safeguarded by law. Finally, he has a right to a protection that is impartial, effective and inspired by true justice.

Man perceives and acknowledges the imperative of the divine law through the mediation of conscience, properly informed. The protection and promotion in an effective manner of such freedoms ranks among the essential duties of Government.

Another matter of great importance in my case is that, as a Bishop of the Church, I have a particular obligation to build up and to preserve what Christian teaching calls the Kingdom of God on earth. The whole reason for my office is that I should dedicate myself completely to the work of advancing the

Christian religion. Should this task of penetrating and perfecting the temporal sphere of things with the spirit of the Gospel of Jesus Christ conflict with my obligation of obedience to the civil authority, I know at once where my duty lies. No matter what the consequences may be for myself personally, should it even involve my life, I must always put what I regard as the good of the Church before my own personal convenience, even before what the State commands. In other words, I must obey God rather than men.

This does not mean that between Church and State there need necessarily be any conflict. The political community exists for the common good, and so it follows that the Church regards as worthy of praise and consideration the work of all those who, as a service to others, dedicate themselves to the welfare of the State and undertake the burdens of the task.

But, and this is vital in my consideration, political authority, whether in the community as such or in institutions represented by the State, must always be exercised within the limits of morality and on behalf of a dynamically conceived common good, according to a juridical order enjoying legal status. When such is the case, citizens are conscience-bound to obey. This fact, which I here acknowledge clearly, reveals the responsibility, dignity and importance of those who govern.

Two phrases just used call for comment: 'enjoying legal status' and 'conscience-bound'. Although the community of nations disputes the claim, the Government of Rhodesia believes that it enjoys legal status. I am here in court at this moment for this reason. I have no alternative.

That is not quite correct. I could have refused to attend the court voluntarily, and might instead have been brought here by force. Alternatively, having my passport still in my possession, I might have fled the country, putting myself beyond the jurisdiction of this court.

However, I am still here, first of all because I believe that I have been, by divine providence, appointed to promote God's work in the Diocese of Umtali, and here is where my duty lies, hence here I must remain. Secondly, even in the court I welcome the opportunity of explaining my behaviour and of giving concrete witness to the concern of the Church for social justice. Finally I am here because, however unpleasant my situation, both to me and to my people, I recognise that there has to be some legal authority. The alternative is anarchy.

I am not an anarchist. Through all the thirty years I have lived in Rhodesia and worked for the welfare of all its people, I have counselled the use of constitutional means for obtaining redress of grievances, grievances affecting the vast majority of the population. Such grievances, based on a racist ethic, denied them equality under the law, equal admittance to the economic, cultural, social and political life of the country, and a fair share in the nation's wealth, and left power, responsibility and decision making in the hands of a race segment of the people.

Moreover, I would like to insist on this, my criticisms of the civil administration have not been confined to the present Government. Long before the Rhodesia Front Party was even heard of, I was exercising my duty as a citizen by openly and lawfully pointing out certain evils in the State in an effort to obtain redress of grievances, and ultimately that peace which it is greatly the work of churchmen to promote.

Never once have I advocated the use of violence. Instead I have consistently acted in the belief that the two classic non-violent means of protest were the only means justifiable, that is, the mobilisation of public opinion and an appeal to a superior forum of justice.

These methods have been tried and have failed. Instead of hearing the joint appeals of the Christian leaders in this country, the Government has refused to do anything really significant to change the unjust social structures which call down on us the condemnation of the free world. Even at this crucial moment of our history, the really vital proposals of the Quénet Report have been rejected. And the electorate, anaesthetised by State-controlled radio and television, remains unmoved.

Neither did an appeal to a superior forum of justice make any difference. The authoritative report on *Racial Discrimination and Repression in Southern Rhodesia*, a legal study prepared by the International Commission of Jurists and published in March of this year, 1976, might as well never have been written as far as those who rule Rhodesia are concerned.

It was the same most recently with my Open Letter to the Government.

This being so, and since all other legitimate means of redress of serious violations of human rights have been tried without success, surely it is not only permissible but even an obligation that forms of passive resistance should be exercised in defence of the human condition against the intransigent oppression of the State?

Both politically and morally, passive resistance I look upon, as indeed the Church looks upon it, as the only proper means of protecting the liberties of citizens, when, as I believe in this case, the Government abuses its powers.

It is clear from what I have already said that I cannot and never did in conscience approve of the racist ideology, which I see at the basis of life in Rhodesia today. Equally it should be clear that I have never, in the course of all my years here, seemed by my silence to connive with the unjust situation. I could not. The teaching of the Church utterly condemns racial discrimination as contrary to the natural dignity of the human person and to the brotherhood of men. There has never been any doubt in my mind about the matter. Christianity and any teaching of racial discrimination are mutually exclusive.

Addressing the United Nations on apartheid in 1974, Pope Paul stated:

Men rightly consider unjustifiable and reject as inadmissible the tendency to maintain or introduce legislation or behaviour systematically inspired by racialist prejudice ... As long as the rights of all the peoples, among them the right to self-determination and independence, are not duly recognised and honoured, there cannot be true and lasting peace, even though the abusive power of arms may for a time prevail over the reactions of those opposed. For as long as, within individual natural communities, those in power do not nobly respect the rights and legitimate freedoms of the citizens, tranquility and order, even though they can be maintained by force, remain nothing but a deceptive and insecure sham no longer worthy of a society of civilised men.

These words of Pope Paul are directed to men of all faiths and of none, but in the Rhodesian situation they appear to have a pointed validity, and I have accepted them as a directive for pastoral action. To professing Christians, however, the Pontiff gave more specific reasons for denouncing racial injustices when he added, 'The message which we offer – and it is at the same time advice, counsel and injunction for Christian consciences – to every group or state or nation, is what we have learned from Him, whom we represent (meaning Christ): You are all brothers.'

I pay particular attention to this argument in order to show that I could not possibly, as an ordinary human being concerned with social justice, much less as a Christian, and never under any circumstances as a Bishop, encourage or support by my silence any regime which grossly and blatantly promotes legislation and behaviour systematically inspired by racialist prejudice, and as a consequence so utterly opposed to the teaching of Christ. To permit myself, or those working under my jurisdiction, to appear to collaborate with such an unjust and unchristian system for the sake of avoiding the penalties of the law, even death or imprisonment, would destroy not only our credibility as Christians, but would cause irreparable damage to the Christian message among all thinking people, especially among the African population of this country at this time.

Were this to happen, Christian missionaries might as well withdraw from the country, because the people would reject them as deceivers: men and women who preached one thing but practised another. The chances of Christianity, even in its Government-sponsored, controlled and emasculated form, being tolerated here in time to come, would, by such connivance, appear minimal.

And this, I hope, illustrates one aspect of the dilemma which not only I have to face, but all my missionaries, and, indeed, everyone who takes his Christian faith seriously in this country today. To support racial discrimination, either directly by practising it oneself, or by aiding those institutions based on it, and at the same time to claim to be a Christian, is to bring Christianity into disrepute and – this is important in the context of Southern Africa at this time – to leave the way open for Communism.

From 21 April until the end of June, I had travelled from one end of the Diocese to the other with the Superiors of the different orders of nuns who had come all the way from Europe to see for themselves whether it would be safe for their Sisters to continue working here. You will remember too how strenuously I worked to persuade them that the Sisters should be permitted to remain; how I also told the Superior of the Marist Brothers that his subjects too should stay and continue their work for the Diocese. At the same time I received from the Mother Superior of another Order, the Marymount Sisters, official intimation that they would have to close the College in Umtali at the end of the year. The Junior School at the Dominican Convent in Umtali was also due to close for good at the end of this year, and now I was faced with the very real problem of having to close down all our other Church institutions in the African areas, if, by reporting the presence of terrorists, these institutions would have to close and the missionaries leave Rhodesia.

A senior officer of the CID exhorted me to keep all the Missions going and not give terrorists the impression that they were in control of the country.

Another important aspect of the problem lies in this, that the dilemma I was placed in would not be confined to me, or to my Diocese, or to any one Christian denomination. It would soon become commonplace, as the infiltrations of terrorists increased and the intransigent attitude of the Government made the local people more ready to receive them as liberators.

I have already pointed out some of the benefits which accrue to Rhodesia by the presence of missionaries. In particular I showed what a small unit such as the Diocese of Umtali, with its educational and health services, has done to develop the country and benefit all sections of the community. Were we and all other Christian missionaries to be forced to close down all these institutions by being compelled to violate conscience and obey the laws of men rather than those of God, Rhodesia would very greatly suffer.

One may well ask, is this what the Government wants? Is this what the legislation we are dealing with envisages? I might well ask myself also which is better, to keep my Missions in existence and my missionaries in the field for the general good of Rhodesia, a good which can be equated with the good of the Christian Church, or must I, in blind obedience, obey a particular ordinance of men and so bring the whole work of Christianity to an end?

What does the Government want? Obedience to its laws about reporting the presence of its enemies, which it probably knows about anyway, or the continuing presence of the Christian Churches and the consequent benefit to Rhodesia now and in the years to come?

I certainly know where my duty lies. It lies in preserving the good name and consequently the continued presence of the Church in Rhodesia, no matter what the laws of men demand. I cannot be false to conscience. The law cannot compel me.

In my belief that passive resistance is permissible when other means of protest have failed, I would like to remind the court that in the case we are dealing with there was no kind of exceptional contribution made by me or by any of my missionaries enabling the enemies of the State to continue their campaign of rebellion. There was no question of our providing the weapons of war or the financial means of obtaining such military equipment. In this respect we are pacifist. Simple medical aid was all that was permitted and given, and that in virtue of the Christian imperative of charity. Could anything be more consonant with a non-violent approach to the problem, more in conformity with the practice of passive resistance?

On the very problem presented to missionaries when they are confronted with requests from the enemies of the State for medical aid, or even food and clothing – anything, in fact, apart from the arms of war – may I attempt to describe in some detail the very situation at Avila Mission when a letter asking for medical help was handed in to the Mission hospital on behalf of terrorists.

The Church staff consisted of two African Sisters, two European Sisters – both State Registered Nurses – and two priests, one a European and the other an African. They live in a very isolated part of the country, as the map shows. They are at least ten miles away from the nearest telephone, and that has only been introduced fairly recently, I believe, into a new police camp. The road leading to the Mission is hazardous at all times of the year. Their nearest European neighbours are at another Mission, twelve miles south of them. There cannot be, in normal times, more than fifteen Europeans in the whole area, which is contiguous with Mozambique, and in most difficult terrain.

What is anyone, missionary or lay person, African or European, to do when approached for medical help in such circumstances? To deny such help in peacetime, or to inquire into the religious or political beliefs of the needy person before giving aid, is quite contrary to the Christian conscience, as it is to the high principles of the profession of medicine.

In these conditions, particularly the conditions of a guerrilla war, when the guerrillas, heavily armed, come to lonely outposts where there is neither the protection of weapons and ammunition or even the comfort and relative protection of a telephone, what can anyone do but obey demands made under threats, expressed or implied, of violent retaliation?

Government propaganda has, as I said, given gruesome details of the mutilation alleged to have been carried out by terrorists on those who have dared to inform on them. We have been told that such informers have had their lips and ears hacked off, and even worse.

What is the unfortunate missionary, defenceless and isolated, expected to do under the circumstances? Inform and be mutilated or murdered sooner or later, when the Security Forces have been and gone and the missionary is quite alone again?

What does the State expect? Heroic resistance, superhuman courage, martyrdom, to maintain a system which compounds social injustices and supports the privileged conditions of the few, a system condemned by the civilised world? What does the State demand of this young nun who has given up home and family and who has dedicated herself for life under the vows of poverty, chastity and obedience to the service of the underprivileged, the hungry, the thirsty, the naked, the stranger, the prisoner – in whom Christ himself says He is to be found, in whom He is to be seen and served?

Does the State believe that it can so compel the conscience as to make such a person as Sister Vianney, or, indeed, any other

Christian, deny her faith and renounce her duty and be disloyal to the Church she belongs to? Does the Government of Rhodesia insist, for the preservation of its own narrow needs, that we must serve men rather than God?

Is not this precisely a violation of the basic human right to freedom of conscience, freedom to worship God according to the right norm of conscience, freedom to practise religion both in public and in private?

I keep in mind that the service of the sick and the needy, in the name of God, is every bit an act of religion as is public or private worship.

Nor is this all. Has not the person in the circumstances described, threatened on the one hand by the penalties of the law and on the other by the extreme and immediate danger of death or mutilation – has not such a person the fundamental right to life? To compel anyone, like this young nun, to endanger herself, or to sacrifice her life for the maintenance of an unjust social system, is surely more than any civilised, legal authority can demand. Does the order to report in such circumstances not, in principle at least, mean a violation of the citizen's right to life itself? Is this not another human right lightly violated?

Does this court believe that the State can compel anyone to give his life, or risk it recklessly, for the observance of its laws? I do not think so; though, indeed, in these days, anything can happen. This, however, I can say: I, as a Bishop of a Diocese, cannot, by any authority which I possess, and would not, were it within my power, compel any subject of mine to risk life or mutilation under any circumstances whatsoever, least of all in the circumstances we are dealing with, when to obey the law of this land would bring discredit to the Church. In fact, during the days of the Avila incident, I went myself to the Mission rather than insist that another should put himself in danger.

And this brings me to another aspect of the right to life and its relevance to the present issue. By informing, not only does the informer prejudice his own safety, but he deliberately endangers the lives of others. The moment the Security Forces hear of the presence of terrorists, they at once embark on their mission of extermination. All that is required of them is, as the law (Indemnity and Compensation Act 1976) itself declares, that they should act in good faith. The terrorists themselves, of course, are the first victims to be sought out and mercilessly annihilated.

What of the informer? Is he or she not responsible for the deaths of such persons? What of the missionary, who knows more intimately than anyone else the daily sufferings of the African people, their near despair, as they see the State make little effort to treat them as full citizens in their own country? Is the missionary-informer not responsible for the death of any young man or woman who, in defence of his own fundamental rights, takes up arms for what he believes is a just cause?

But what about the other people who become the victims of the informer's cooperation? I refer, of course, to the villagers in the area where the terrorists are known to have been. Rhodesia knows what their fate is likely to be. Certainly the missionaries and the African people know. Once the informer speaks, the unfortunate villagers can themselves expect to come under attack from the Security Forces, as indeed happened at Avila the day after the presence of the terrorists was revealed.

First come the helicopters, sweeping low and firing at anything black and bifurcated moving suspiciously in the village or the bush nearby. Then come the troops, armed to the teeth with all their modern weaponry. Then others with trained and fierce dogs, and the comfort of the law to encourage everybody. In their determination to seek out and destroy their enemies, they know that they can carry on regardless, there are no holds barred.

The former Minister of Defence has given them a clear directive granting them unlimited freedom of action. Speaking in the House of Assembly on 2 July 1976, the Minister declared: 'If villagers harbour terrorists, and terrorists are found running about in the villages, naturally they will be bombed and destroyed in any manner which the commander on the spot considers desirable in the suitable prosecution of a successful campaign.' He added: 'My first concern is to eradicate the terrorists, and civilians mixed up with them have only themselves to blame.'

Shocked by such remarks, I wrote a letter published in *The Rhodesia Herald* on 10 July 1976, where I said:

It is necessary to remind the Government, and the Minister of Defence in particular, that political authority must always be exercised within the limits of morality. The successful prosecution of a war cannot justify the indiscriminate killing of people. Such a wicked and cowardly preparedness to bomb whole villages and perhaps kill innocent people, children particularly, who would have had no responsible contacts with terrorists, is wholly reprehensible and unpardonable in a Minister of the Government.

I was, of course, at once attacked in the Press and misrepresented. But what I insist on here is another of the effects of informing. When the local people in their villages become the immediate target for the indiscriminate attacks of the Security Forces, if the Christian missionary is the informer, the whole local community understandably blame him. And they blame not only him but the whole organisation to which he belongs. Not only his Church gets the blame, but Christianity itself is condemned as a fraud, as the agent of oppression, and is accused of teaching the brotherhood of all men in creation and in redemption, and of contradicting it in practice – even becoming the willing accomplice in the bombing and destroying of villages and in the killing of innocent women and children.

This is fact. The village next to Avila was attacked. I myself recorded the details of the terrifying event from a young African woman who was machine-gunned from a helicopter. Her hospital charts from Bindura, Inyanga and Avila hospitals are in the keeping of the Justice and Peace Commission of which I am President.

Apart from my inability and unwillingness to command my missionaries to report and so imperil their own lives, the lives of the local people are endangered, and in consequence harm is done to the good name of the Christian Church. I believe that, as the Church's responsible authority, I have the prior and more compelling obligation of doing all in my power to protect the lives of my people than to protect the lives of the Security Forces.

It is an accepted principle in the Christian Church that the Bishop must act as the shepherd of the flock, the pastor of his people. It is his duty, as a spiritual Father, so to protect all who look to him for leadership that, if it should be necessary, he should not hesitate to shield them from danger. He should be prepared to give his life for his people, especially if their actions, performed in the service of the Church, should put them in danger.

With that ideal before me, I told my missionaries that I would hold myself entirely responsible for their actions, both in giving medicines to the terrorists and in not reporting their presence. In doing so, I am convinced, not only that I was acting correctly as their Bishop, but that I was actually fulfilling a further obligation, namely of taking more care of the defenceless missionaries than of the armed forces, who, I presumed, were well able and well equipped to defend themselves. In short, I believe my greater duty, from every point of view, lay more in protecting the lives of innocent and defenceless people than in protecting soldiers.

There is even more to it. Those of us who live close to the African people in these difficult days and who enjoy their confidence know how difficult it is to identify strangers who come into the villages, and indeed how unreliable their messages can sometimes be, and even for what purpose they issue commands.

It is widely believed, and I think the State will readily admit it, that African members of the Security Forces have been infiltrated among the terrorists and masquerade in their guise.

The danger of reporting terrorists who deliberately make their presence known is that the terrorists might be laying a trap for the Security Forces. If this succeeds, the African missionary may be accused of being a party to the trap.

I come now to an aspect of the problem which concerns anyone who, like myself, belongs to the clerical profession. It is a generally accepted principle, in Western society at least, that the State recognises and respects the confidence which the laity of all denominations place in their clergy. As a Catholic Bishop may I make it at once quite clear that I am not here speaking of that peculiar quality of confidence which, in our Church, is given to a priest under the seal of the Confessional. That is a special matter altogether and need not be discussed here. It does not concern us.

What I am concerned with, however, is the widely acknow-ledged immunity which the custom of Western nations allows to the confidences which a citizen places in a minister of religion. I believe that the basis for this immunity lies in the recognition by the State of its subsidiary function in human affairs, and its acknowledgement of the supremacy of the moral order, in which the sacred relationship between man and his God is given primacy.

The Christian clergyman, in terms of his very function, must appear to men as offering to them the mercy and reconciliation of his God. No one, even the greatest criminal, the most debased, the most hardened sinner, may ever be refused his counsel or his word of mercy. He must be prepared to understand the frailty of human nature, man's tendency to evil, the almost overpowering compulsion of temptation.

What a loss to society if such a source of good were to be set aside. After all, it is the *ought*, the power of conscience, the sense of religion, not physical necessity, which determines man's actions and which can reform society itself by inculcating obedience to the Creator's laws. By such willing obedience men may even be brought to achieve, in their daily lives, something of that order and peace which is manifest through physical necessity in the rest of creation.

Take the case in question, the Avila incident. Were anyone, even a terrorist, to approach me for food or clothing or medicine, I would certainly not refuse him, if it were at all possible for me to give him ordinary help. Neither would I place his life in danger by informing on him. If such a one were to come to me for counsel, I would deal with him in the same manner and would consider myself bound in conscience to remind him of God's command 'Thou shalt not kill', and try to persuade him to use nonviolent means of seeking redress of his grievances. All of which sounds very well, and presumes the man to be well-disposed and docile. Were he otherwise, were he to threaten me with death or mutilation or anything similar, I suppose I would be as cowardly as any other ordinary person in the same circumstances.

But there is another possible variation in the case. Suppose, for instance, I am conducting a religious service, and I notice, or have brought to my attention by others, an enemy of the State among the congregation of worshippers. Am I supposed to report his presence to the Security Forces, and so make his act of worship the occasion of capture or death? Is obedience to the State to be regarded as a greater good to be sought and obtained than an individual's act of acknowledging the worship he owes to his God? Am I, the minister of religion, to play the turncoat and become the servant of the State rather than the servant of God? In other words, am I bound to obey men rather than God?

I cannot see that as a Christian, and certainly as a Bishop, I will be performing a service to my God or to His Church, or even to civil society itself, if I be compelled by law to make my ministry in this manner a servant of the State, no longer a ministry of mercy or reconciliation, but rather an instrument of vengeance. Rather, I choose what I conceive to be the greater good, and with a clear and informed conscience accept what penalty the law may provide for my disobedience. I do not despise the law. I simply obey a higher law. I must obey God rather than men. I cannot do both simultaneously in these circumstances.

It seems, therefore, that in demanding that I obey its laws and inform about the presence of its enemies, the State of Rhodesia, as at present constituted, and with its present unwillingness to modify its policies, places an intolerable burden, not only on me as a Catholic Bishop, but, in fact, on every other Christian worthy of the name. It is asking what is morally impossible. It is coercing conscience. *Ad impossile nemo tenetur*. No one is bound to perform the impossible.

In stating this ancient legal truth, one is reminded of another problem. Let me put it this way: Can the State, under the threat of death or of any other serious punishment, such as would be a long period of imprisonment, compel a citizen to perform an act which is not absolutely, but only relatively necessary to the common weal? This is the situation, I believe, in many instances where people are expected to report the presence of terrorists. In fact in many cases the Security Forces are already aware that terrorists are around. They obtain this information as a result of their own activities, and they also get it from the hundreds of paid informers, people who are prepared to play the traitor, very often simply to revenge themselves on their own personal enemies.

Take the Avila incident, for example. The very day I arrived at the Mission and was informed of the note handed in on behalf of the terrorists asking for medicines – on that very afternoon Security Forces visited the Mission and informed the priest there that terrorists were in the neighbourhood and had the previous day robbed a store and a bus. Is not any additional reporting by a missionary or anyone else in such a case a work of supererogation? Is one to be severely punished for not performing such a duty? In any well-ordered political community where authority is solidly based on the consent of the governed, such unnecessary legislation should not obtrude itself on our notice.

Closely connected with this argument is the fact that the Security Forces are not really in control of the situation anywhere in the operational area of Rhodesia. I say this in spite of all the State propaganda to the contrary.

Missionaries of all denominations are in a far better position to know what is, in fact, taking place than the Government is. They are widely placed all over the country; they live close to the people; they know them intimately and enjoy their confidence. They are with their people all the time, and not like the members of the Security Forces, here one day and gone the next. Scarcely a thing happens in the Tribal Trust Lands that does not come quickly to the notice of the missionaries. Theirs is a closely knit organisation, and the news of the happenings in one area quickly travels to another.

It is simple fact that the general public in Rhodesia, certainly the European population, knows only a fraction of the activities of the nationalists everywhere throughout the country. All the Security Forces are able to do is to move into an area where terrorists are reported to have appeared, carry out punitive raids, stay on for a little while and then move on to another disturbed area to do the same.

Moreover, the strength of the African people's opposition to the present Government is daily on the increase. Time and numbers are on their side, and they know it. No matter what the State propaganda may declare, the African people already sense that the Security Forces are no longer in control of events.

The practice of informing is, as far as the successful prosecution of the war goes, quite useless. The Security Forces generally manage to kill only innocent villagers in retaliation for the presence of the guerrillas. Moreover, by such action they not only further antagonise the African people, but they promote the cause of those whom they seek to eliminate.

I have pleaded guilty to the charges preferred against me, and welcome this opportunity of explaining to the court the reasons for my actions. I believe that I had no alternative but to act as I did. The good reputation of the Church had, in my opinion, to be preserved at all costs. The lives of local villagers, innocent and unarmed, had also to be protected as had – and in this case as their Bishop I had a very compelling responsibility – the lives of my missionary personnel. The cumulative effect of these arguments convinced me at the time, and is even more coercive now, that I have no alternative but to break the law. In doing so, I believe that I was not in any way acting as an anarchist. I believe that, since neither I nor any of my missionaries made any positive contribution to the promoting of violence through providing arms or ammunition, my actions can reasonably be regarded as legitimate acts of passive resistance – nothing more.

It is most important that a solution to this problem be found as soon as possible. The incident which took place at Avila is not an isolated one, as is well known to the authorities. It is repeated frequently in different forms. The common good is bound to suffer if, throughout the country, the problem is left unsolved, and if members of the medical profession, churchmen and others in allied occupations, do not know how they are to reconcile the commands of conscience with those of the civil authority.

While I was still struggling to keep all our missionary activity alive and to preserve the medical and educational services they provide for the country, the general situation continued to deteriorate. Outside pressures on Rhodesia increased, yet within the country itself the authorities continued in their determination to resist meaningful change of the unhappy social structures. The hopes once placed in the Quénet Report on Racial Discrimination were dashed and seen to have been illusory. Meanwhile, from every corner of the country, through the information that missionaries possessed, came increasing evidence of further infiltration by members of the nationalist movement, and a growing realisation that the masses of the African people were welcoming them and affording them every support.

On the morning of 11 August, Umtali came under mortar and rocket attack from Mozambique. On that very morning too I received news of the arrest and detention without charge of one of my African priests. Even at that late hour I decided that I would make a further appeal to the Government by sending to the prime minister and to each member of his Cabinet an open letter pleading for an immediate change in what I called 'its present tragic course of action'. I indicated quite clearly the increasing difficulty that Church leaders were having in reconciling their Christian principles with the demands made on them by racist legislation. The very problem of medical or other non-military aid to the enemies of the State was discreetly indicated in my letter to let the authorities know that it was an urgent and widespread one. A mission doctor was at that time still awaiting trial for a somewhat similar offence.

In my Open Letter I put it this way to the members of the Cabinet:

> Over the years, and as a matter of principle, the Catholic Church has had to refuse to practise racial segregation in its schools and hospitals, or to limit to the percentage laid down by your administration the service of Christian charity which is commanded of it by the Gospel. Today an equally important decision will have to be taken whenever or wherever the charity of the Church is sought by those who are in conscience opposed to your regime. Have not those who honestly believe that they fight for the basic human rights of the people a justifiable claim on the Church for the spiritual administration of the clergy? How can one counsel loyalty and obedience to your ordinances when to do so is tantamount to giving approval to the manifold injustices you inflict? To keep silence about one reign of oppression in order the better to combat what you alone consider to be another, is wholly unacceptable.

And then I ended by saying:

> If intensification of racial hatred, widespread urban guerilla activity, increased destruction of property and fearful loss of life

are to be avoided, if the whole subcontinent of Africa is not to be engulfed in a cruel war, you must without delay change your present course of action.

Notice I did not attempt – because it is not within my competency – to give any specific solutions. That is for men of state, not for me. All I begged for – and I think this is the right of any citizen, as it is his duty to point out defects if he sees that anything is wrong – was that the Government should, without delay, change its present course of action. My final words were: 'It is up to you to give the lead. The fate of Rhodesia and its people is in your hands.'

And what did Government do about my appeal? Some will say that it filed these charges against me. The State has officially denied this. At least one Minister commented not too politely on my Open Letter in the House of Assembly. But even now nothing really worthwhile has been done, and people like me, who work for the welfare of Rhodesia, are regarded as its enemies.

What a frightful comment on our society. As I said in the beginning of this statement, I am concerned in this problem at its local and at its international level with the human person; with the need for the recognition in law and in fact of his unique identity, with his fundamental dignity, with his imprescriptible rights as a purpose-made creature of the Almighty with his rights and duties as a member of society.

This has been the leitmotiv of this whole unsworn statement of mine. Think of it in this way: The whole civilised world is appalled and reacts with horror, humiliation and hurt when a mentally deranged person attacks and tries to mutilate a great work of artistic genius, such as the Pietà of Michelangelo, and yet he can remain unmoved and unconcerned when God's own handiwork, that is the human person himself, is attacked in his very essence, in his basic rights and is mutilated and treated as non-man by his fellows who claim to be sane and civilised. Is this not the tragedy and horror of the racist state?

However, I am glad to be here today to bear witness to the practical concern of the Church that God's will, manifested in social justice, be done in Rhodesia. I am grateful to you, your worship and gentlemen, and to your associates, for your quite exceptional patience. I thank for their testimony to the truth all those who have given evidence.

Throughout the weeks that have passed since I was first indicted, I have been greatly comforted by the words which the first Bishop of Rome, Peter the Fisherman, addressed to those who might, in the centuries to come, have to appear before magistrates to answer for their adherence to the faith which they were given. He said:

> No one can hurt you if you are determined to do only what is right. If you do have to suffer for being good, you will count it a blessing. There is no need to be afraid or to worry about them. Simply reverence the Lord Christ in your hearts, and always have your answer ready for people who ask you the reason for the hope that you all have. But give it with courtesy and respect and with a clear conscience, so that those who slander you when you are living a good life in Christ may be proved wrong in the accusations that they bring. And if it is the will of God that you should suffer, it is better to suffer for doing right than for doing wrong.

I. The Judgement

What follows is the main part of the judgement of the High Court of Rhodesia by Chief Justice MacDonald. The technicalities of Bishop Lamont's appeal have been omitted.

The appellant's statement contained many expressions of opinion of a political nature which are inextricably interwoven with the purely factual and legal aspects of this case. These political views are introduced in mitigation of his offences, and it is not possible for this Court to avoid dealing with them in assessing the weight of the plea in mitigation.

The appellant in his statement acknowledges that as a priest he must not concern himself with politics. He says:

> The priest normally should not involve himself in ideological and partisan disputes, since this would jeopardise his function as a mediator and would possibly tarnish the purity of his message and indeed his freedom as a representative of the Church.

He acknowledges that there must be some legal authority and that obedience to legal authority is a moral duty. In conformity with his view that a priest should not involve himself in politics, the appellant says that it is not within his 'competence to give specific solutions' and adds 'that is for men of state, not for me'.

For obvious reasons the Church may not make itself responsible for the political structures of a country. If it were to do so, it would immediately assume a political role and, to use a favourite word of the appellant, would lose 'credibility' as a church. But just as a church may not accept the responsibility for creating political structures, so too, for precisely the same reason, it cannot accept the responsibility of destroying them. Indeed, the arguments against a destructive role in politics are even more compelling than the argument against a creative role.

Wholly inexcusably and quite inconsistently, the appellant throughout his statement indicates in the clearest terms that he is prepared to accept the role of a political activist in 'dismantling unjust social structures …'. The following passages reveal the appellant's political activities:

> The official document published at the end of the Synod and entitled *Justice in the World* clearly stated the obligation imposed by conscience and by the Christian faith on all who professed that faith to take positive action to promote justice in the world and to work through peaceful means *for the dismantling of those unjust structures which denied other human beings integral human development.*

> This ought to explain much of my activity here in Rhodesia *in my work for the promotion of a sane order and the eradication of injustices in any shape or form.*

> I cannot too greatly emphasise the need for the Church to be seen here and now as a courageous voice in the denunciation of injustice, particularly those felt by the African people, and *as a committed and active agent in the peaceful dismantling of unjust social structures wherever they exist.*

> *I believe that if this system of government be permitted to continue without any change whatsoever*, without any attempt at providing equality under the law and equal opportunity for all men, then the danger of another Nuremberg could be very real indeed.

> … anyone who wants peace here, must surely recognise that *the laws* which have built up and continue to maintain such national disorder *must quickly be revoked by the rulers; the unjust social structures must, without delay, be dismantled.* In short, institutional violence must be abolished if racial war, with the most horrible consequences, is to be avoided.

> Instead of hearing the joint appeal of the Christian leaders of this country, the Government refused to do anything really significant *to change the unjust social structure*, which calls down on us the condemnation of the free world.

> This being so and since all other legitimate means of redress of serious violations of human rights have been tried without success, *surely it is not only permissible but even an obligation that forms of passive resistance should be exercised in defence of the human condition against the intransigent oppression of the State.*

As a young Carmelite, by the lake in Terenure College.

Donal Lamont as a young bishop, 1957.

Carmelites who took part in the Second Vatican Council.

Back Row, L–R: Bartholomé Xiberta (Theclogian, Spain), Redemptus Gauci (Bishop, Peru), Raimundo Lui (Bishop, Brazil), Nevin Hayes (Bishop, Peru).

Front Row, L–R: Gabriel Bueno Couto (Bishop, Brazil), Avertanus Albers (Bishop, Indonesia), Kilian Healy (Prior General), Telesforo Cioli (Bishop, Italy), Donal Lamont (Bishop, Rhodesia).

On the way into a council session, 1963.
L–R: Redemptus Gauci, Kilian Healy and Donal Lamont.

Donal Lamont leads this group of bishops exiting a
session of the Second Vatican Council.

Four honorary doctorates from Notre Dame University in 1987. L–R: Stephen Kim, Jimmy Carter, Paolo Evaristo Arns and Donal Lamont.

Donal Lamont on a Kenyan postage stamp in 1978.

Donal Lamont in one of several meetings with Pope Paul VI.

Donal Lamont, expelled from Rhodesia, arriving at Dublin Airport in 1977. Archbishop Dermot Ryan is with him.

As a retired bishop, by the lake in Terenure College.

> *Both politically and morally, passive resistance* I look upon, as indeed the Church looks upon it, *as the only proper means of protecting the liberties of citizens*, when, as I believe in this case, the Government abuses its powers.

What the appellant is saying in the clearest terms is that he is prepared to work actively to 'dismantle social structures'. Moreover, he is prepared to take active steps to bring about these changes without first satisfying one of the criteria which the appellant says must be fulfilled before revolutionary activity is permissible, namely that 'there be a reasonable prospect of success and of the setting up of an objectively better government'. Since the appellant has expressed the view that the terrorists will win, and since the evidence is overwhelming that the terrorists are members of a Communist organisation, how is he able to satisfy himself that his support for the terrorists would result in 'an objectively better government'?

In the course of his statement the appellant on more than one occasion makes the generalisation that Africans in Rhodesia have been oppressed by European rule.

Missionaries work almost exclusively in the African field, more often than not in remote areas of the country. Some serve for a short period only in Rhodesia and then move on to another country or return to their country of origin. Others devote a lifetime in the secular and religious service of the Africans in this country. It is understandable, in these circumstances, that missionaries tend to identify themselves with African causes and aspirations and to see the problems of the country through the eyes of the African with whom they work closely at all times, in much the same way as Europeans, living in a wholly European environment, tend to see the problems through European eyes. Neither, in the result, achieves a wholly balanced view and the realisation that both sections of the community are completely interdependent and complementary to each other.

In assessing the moral guilt of the appellant it is important not to lose sight of these tendencies. Unhappily, some missionaries appear to have a preconceived idea that their mission in life, in part at least, will be to save and deliver the African from what he or she has been led to believe is the exploitation by and rapacity of the European. The truth is that each section of the community is heavily in debt to the other: the European to the African for providing, in the formative years of Rhodesia, the sinew and muscle of all that has been achieved in so short a time, the African to the European for establishing law and order, without which nothing, least of all missionary work, could prosper and for introducing much-needed skills and expertise. It serves no good purpose and leads only to acrimony to attempt to make a comparative assessment of the contribution made by each section of the community. Such an attempt will always prove to be a sterile exercise because the truth is simply that the changes which have been brought about, transforming Rhodesia from a primitive country, racked by tribal division and conflict and plagued by barbaric practices of witchcraft, to a country with a highly sophisticated twentieth century economy with a higher average standard of living for both African and European than almost any other African country, could not have been achieved by either section of the community without the other.

The problems which now exist are not the bitter fruit of a colonial experiment which has failed, but, on the contrary, stem directly from the success of that experiment in creating the peaceful climate in which there has been a burgeoning, not only of commerce and industry, but also of the potential of all its inhabitants. Within the lifetime of a single person, this country has witnessed a very substantial number of the African section of the community moving swiftly from a wholly rural and primitive existence to participate in a modern Western society and from a pagan and barbaric society to a substantially Christian society. So swift has been this transformation that the institutions created by the Europeans when Rhodesia was established have not fully adapted themselves to it and it is understandable that the emerging African is impatient with the speed with which desirable changes have come about. No fair-minded person, however, would stigmatise what has been achieved in the short history of this country as constituting 'oppression'. Indeed, these beneficent changes could not possibly have resulted from oppression. Beyond question the progress has been the result of cooperation between the races and, should it come to an end, progress will cease and there will be a sharp retrogression in every aspect of life for all the inhabitants of this country.

The charge of oppression levelled against the European of this country by the appellant is as a generalisation false and provides a spurious justification for the terrorist atrocities committed against the civilian population. If any generalisation is to be made it is that the progress made by Africans under European rule has been remarkable and much greater than the progress made over the same period of time in any other African country.

No country in the history of the world can claim to have established a system of government or institutions which at any given time have been perfect and Rhodesia is no exception to the general rule. What is certain is that nothing has happened in the very short and successful history of Rhodesia remotely to justify the bestial acts of terrorism committed against civilians and, what is no less certain is that on a balanced and comprehensive assessment of all that has been achieved, it is a monstrous travesty of the truth to describe the history or this country under European rule as one of oppression.

The only oppression in the recent history of Rhodesia occurred during the short period of the Matabele domination from 1840–1893, the year in which the Matabele were defeated by the Pioneers. That defeat ended the despotic reign of Lobengula, who had kept the whole of this country in thrall by the barbaric and savage use of witchcraft and the unbridled use of military power. For a detailed account of the excesses committed during this period and the life of the ordinary African before the conquest of Matabeleland, such works as the *Diaries of the Jesuit Missionaries at Bulawayo from 1879–1881* should be consulted. The diaries conclude with the following assessment of the Matabele at that time:

> Living entirely by pillage and by war, they seem to refuse any progress at all and are, in this respect, the most backward and the most barbarous of all the natives of Southern Africa.

That that stricture is not true today is a tribute to the cooperation between African and European, a cooperation which has outlawed internecine tribal war and pillage and which, to a very great extent, has eliminated the more barbaric practices of witchcraft.

Oppression by invaders of an indigenous people has, in a large number of countries, been characterised by the decimation of the indigenous inhabitants. It is quite unnecessary to mention the countries in which this has happened. They readily identify themselves and, paradoxically, are among Rhodesia's most strident critics. In Rhodesia the reverse has happened and with the establishment of law and order and the creation of a burgeoning economy, there has been a population explosion. A fair-minded person will not readily accept that this could happen as a result of oppression.

Two main arguments were advanced by the appellant for not obeying the law. The first was that it would not be possible to keep open the various institutions under his jurisdiction if they were seen to be collaborating with the Government. The second was that the law that terrorists should be reported was unjust, that the terrorists are justified in taking up arms against the Government, because it is oppressive and that it would be wrong for 'any Christian worthy of the name' as well as any tribesman 'playing the traitor' to report them.

Subsidiary arguments are advanced in support of these two main arguments and, in addition, the appellant has raised a number of arguments unrelated to them.

The appellant also used the occasion to launch an attack on the Security Forces. This would seem to be part of his general attack on the Government. Conscious of the fact that it would be inexcusable to collaborate with the terrorists by refusing to report them if they were guilty of the atrocities against the African and European civilian population attributed to them and that it would be even more inexcusable for a Roman Catholic prelate to do so if the terrorists belonged to a Communist organisation, the appellant, in his statement, mentions that he has 'heard' and has been 'told' by the Government propaganda agencies and by the RBC and the RTV of these atrocities and the fact that they have been committed by Communist terrorists, but casts doubt on these sources by saying:

I must say at once that personally I doubt every bit of Government propaganda that I hear on the RBC or RTV, just as I read with the greatest sense of scepticism much that is printed in our Rhodesian newspapers.

In the result, the appellant manages to convey the impression that, while the Security Forces are evil and should not be supported, the terrorists are justified in taking up arms.

But in marked contrast to his attitude to the Security Forces, the appellant adroitly avoids expressing any view on whether or not the terrorists are guilty of atrocities against the civilian population and whether or not they are Communist. While claiming an unrivalled knowledge of what is happening in the operational area and using this knowledge as a basis for his attack on the Security Forces, he omits to say what his own information concerning the terrorists is or to say what this information leads him to believe.

In common with all reasonably well-informed persons living in this country the appellant knows only too well what the terrorists are doing but, to confess this and reveal the nature of their actions, would reveal his stand for what it is; support for Communist terrorists who do not shrink from committing the most bestial acts against defenceless civilians not in any way actively involved in the struggle between the terrorists and the Security Forces. The appellant, in company with the World Council of Churches, adopts the tactic of condemning all acts of violence, but at the same time studiously refrains from identifying the perpetrators of the crimes involved whenever the evidence points unerringly in the direction of the terrorists. By refusing to identify the perpetrators of such acts when they are committed by terrorists, the appellant manages to convey the idea that since the acts must, of necessity, have been committed by one side or the other the Security Forces could possibly be responsible for them. His dishonest conduct in this regard is particularly reprehensible in a person occupying such a high clerical office.

In the result the appellant nowhere in his very long statement acknowledges that terrorists belong to a Marxist/Leninist organisation. From the innumerable terrorist cases which have come before this Court as well as from other sources, the following facts are notorious:

1. Many terrorists have received their training in Russia, China and Eastern European countries under Russian domination.
2. Many who have not been trained in countries outside Africa have been trained by Communist instructors in Tanzania and other African countries orientated towards Communism.
3. In the result, the tactics used by the terrorists are similar to those used by Communists in subverting law and order in other parts of the world.
4. The terrorists operate from Mozambique which makes no secret of the fact that it has embraced Marxist/Leninist principles.
5. It is improbable that terrorists would be acceptable to the Mozambique Government if they embraced a wholly different political philosophy.
6. It is inconceivable that Mozambique would allow, much less welcome, the establishment of a system of government in this country different from and opposed to its own, and Mozambique is in the position of being able to dictate to the terrorists at the present time.
7. The terrorists' debt to their Communist sponsors is such that it would be unreasonable to expect that in the unlikely event of their achieving victory they would forsake the Communists and transfer their allegiance to the countries of the Western World. In the light of the fact that Russia is steadily expanding its influence in Africa, while at the same time and to a corresponding extent the countries of the Western World withdraw, it is too much to expect that such a transfer of allegiance would come about.
8. Statements have been made by the terrorist leaders that a solution to the problems of Rhodesia can only be brought about by violence. The idea that revolutionary change can only be brought about by violence is a corner stone of the Communist philosophy and is expressed in the following words by Marx in his Communist manifesto:

    The Communists disdain to conceal their views and aims. They openly declare that their ends can be attained only by the forcible overthrow of all existing social conditions.

9. Before a Special Court convened to consider the detention of the Rev. Ndabaningi Sithole, documentary evidence led the State to establish that the terrorists were a Communist organisation. The documents consisted of the official pamphlets published by the terrorist organisation and their authenticity was not challenged by Mr Maisels, Q.C., who appeared for the Rev. Ndabaningi Sithole. The documents were obviously authentic and were available for inspection by the press and members of

the public. They showed beyond any doubt at all that the terrorist organisation operating from Mozambique has adopted the Marxist/Leninist principles. A copy of the judgement is annexed to this judgement.

Communism is not only atheistic, it is actively anti-Christian and since the appellant acknowledges to quote his own words that 'The whole reason for my office is that I should dedicate myself completely to the work of advancing the Christian Religion', he must necessarily take up the position that in collaborating with the terrorists by refusing to report their presence to the Security Forces, he is collaborating with a Communist organisation. He attempts to establish, as far as it is in his limited power to do so, that the terrorists are a respectable organisation, fighting with every justification against an oppressive government. That this is the image he seeks to create for them is shown very clearly by the following passages in his statement dealing with the terrorists:

> I had heard too that this ideology (the appellant is referring to the Marxist ideology) was shared by those who came armed into Rhodesia determined to achieve equality under the law and equal opportunity for all the citizens of Rhodesia. It seemed vitally important to me that these people should not, on their contact with the Church in Rhodesia, be made to believe that it collaborated with the regime which they considered oppressive. Rather it was necessary for the Church, as represented by our Missions, to manifest a courageous and generous Christian concern, even for the wayward.
>
> This was the first thing which decided my thinking in regard to the attitude to be adopted by the missionaries should they be approached by terrorists.

And the appellant poses the question:

> Is the missionary-informer not responsible for the death of any young man or woman who, in defence of his own fundamental rights, takes up arms for what he believes is a just cause?

It will be noticed that the appellant, in the first passage cited above, uses the words 'I had heard too' and not 'I knew that this

135

Marxist ideology was shared' by them. Had the appellant confessed he knew they were Marxist/Leninist terrorists, could he then have said, as he did, that they 'came armed into Rhodesia determined to achieve equality under the law and equal opportunity for all the citizens of Rhodesia'? Could this possibly be the appellant's assessment of what Communists do?

The appellant speaks of propaganda but is there a more subtle propaganda device than to state a fact as being no more than a rumour and to then offset the rumour by stating categorically that the terrorists are dedicated to 'achieving equality under the law and equal opportunity for all the citizens of Rhodesia'?

Dealing with the visit of terrorists to the Avila Mission on the night of 25 April, the appellant gives the following account of his conversation with Father X after the latter had left the Mission, and his reaction to Father X's departure from the mission:

> When I arrived there I heard *to my great dismay* that Father X had left the mission early in the morning, bringing with him the two Sisters and all their belongings because of threats from terrorists who had come to Avila the night before.
>
> *The story, as I heard it from him*, was that on the previous night, while at supper, he and Sister Vianney were summoned out into the darkness by two men who had guns at the ready. When they met they saw some other armed men lurking in the shadows some distance away. *According to the priest*, he and the sister were lectured on the glories of Communism and the evils of capitalism as represented by the Kennedys, the Rockefellers and the Catholic Church. The visitors ordered the priest to reduce the school fees and the charges made at the Mission clinic. He replied that the clinic was unaided, receiving no support from the State, and that the sisters were unpaid and the medicines had to be bought by the Mission. The terrorists told him that the Church could well afford to provide medicines freely. They then threatened that the Mission would be destroyed and other vengeance taken if their other requests for watches, radios, cameras, etc., were not granted.
>
> After a long interview, the men went off, the priest having told them that he could not possibly meet their demands.
>
> Naturally both he and the other members of the Mission staff were greatly frightened by the visit, and they decided that it would be unsafe for them to remain there any longer. They

136

packed up and left early next morning, drove to Inyanga, informed the civil authorities, and without further delay arrived at Triashill Mission, a hundred miles away from Avila, where I met them and heard their story.

The priest was very distraught and wondered if he had acted correctly in leaving the Mission and informing the authorities. I consoled him by saying that *if what he told me were true,* and that his night visitors were Communists who had said that they wanted to destroy the Church and its Missions, *then* he had acted correctly. [My italics.]

In the course of this conversation, the appellant received from Father X the most cogent evidence that terrorists are in fact Communists and if he doubted Father X's uncorroborated evidence, it was always possible for him to obtain Sister Vianney's version of what was said and done by the terrorists. Notwithstanding the overwhelming evidence available to him on this occasion, it is of the greatest significance that the appellant uses the words in italics in the above passage. These words are intended to convey that until the appellant has heard the terrorists' version of what was said and done by them, he is not prepared to accept the version received from his own priest as being the truth. He says: 'The story, as I heard it from him …' and '… if what he told me were true' … 'then he acted correctly.' It could reasonably be expected that having regard to the trust which should necessarily exist between a bishop and one of his priests, he would have said: 'I consoled him by saying that since his night visitors were Communists who had said they wanted to destroy the Church and its Missions, he had acted correctly.'

In the light of overwhelming evidence that the terrorists are Communists, it is amazing that the appellant, with his means of knowledge, should evade this fact; it is even more astounding that he should be at pains to avoid making a frank acknowledgement that the *modus operandi* of the terrorists is to attack African and European civilians, murdering and mutilating them, and to avoid contact with the Security Forces by every possible means, including threats that any person reporting their presence will be murdered. So notorious are the atrocities committed by the terrorists that knowledge of what they have done and are doing is shared by everyone living in this country and is certainly not confined to persons with access to the records of cases coming before the courts. The terrorists are selective in the atrocities they commit against African civilians – murder and mutilation is reserved for those Africans who oppose or are suspected of opposing them, that is the so-called 'sellouts'. European civilians, both male and female, with the exception of the Europeans working in the institutions under the appellant's jurisdiction, are murdered indiscriminately whenever the opportunity occurs. We deal elsewhere in this judgement with the reasons why the exception is made in the case of Europeans working under the appellant's jurisdiction.

The first of the appellant's main arguments, that it would not be possible to keep the various institutions under his jurisdiction open if the terrorists had reason to believe the personnel of these institutions were hostile to them and were reporting their presence to the Security Forces, is an argument of substance, and a strong mitigating factor. The recent massacre at Musami has shown conclusively that the terrorists do not stop short of murdering Roman Catholic missionaries.

It is understandable that the appellant is most reluctant to see institutions under his jurisdiction close down. Once personnel were dispersed, it would be extremely difficult, and might even prove impossible in some instances, to re-open. The appellant has devoted thirty years of his life to building up these institutions and their closure would be a bitter blow to him. The fact that the appellant has expressed views which are quite untenable and intemperate and that in some respects he has been dishonest, must not be allowed to obscure the dilemma in which the appellant is unquestionably placed by the situation which has developed.

It is necessary in assessing the strength of this mitigating factor to bear in mind that missionaries are not prepared, because of their religious convictions, to take up arms in defence of either the missions or their own lives. It follows that the various institutions are defenceless and it is acknowledged that it would not be possible for the Security Forces to provide every missionary institution in the operational area with a permanent guard. The only way in the circumstances in which the appellant, to use his own words, can 'guarantee the safety of his Sisters' and other personnel is to satisfy the terrorists that these institutions are well disposed towards them and, conversely, are hostile to the Government, and that they can be relied upon not to report their presence in the area. The appellant, we are satisfied, has succeeded in convincing the terrorists of this and it is for that reason that no institution under his control has been attacked, notwithstanding that they are all in the operational area and that some are very close to the border. While this reason for the appellant's desire to collaborate with the terrorists, by not reporting their presence, clearly emerges, it is not a reason which this Court accepts as valid and, for the reasons given elsewhere in this judgement, it cannot possibly serve the long-term interests of the Roman Catholic Church. Nevertheless, in assessing the appropriate sentence, full weight must be given to it. The appellant also says:

> I told my missionaries that I would hold myself entirely responsible for their actions, both in giving medicines to the terrorists and in not reporting their presence. In doing so, I am convinced, not only that I was acting correctly as their Bishop, but that I was actually fulfilling a further obligation, namely of taking more care of the defenceless missionaries than of the armed forces, who, I presumed, were well able and well equipped to defend themselves. In short, I believe my greater duty, from every point of view, lay in protecting the lives of innocent and defenceless people than in protecting soldiers.

This reason, if it stood alone, would be a very strong mitigating factor, because, for the reasons which I have given earlier in this judgement, there is no doubt at all that missionaries are placed in a most invidious position. It is very clear, however, that the appellant has been motivated to a large extent by sympathy for the terrorists and hostility towards the Government. He says, for example:

> In fact in many cases the Security Forces are already aware that terrorists are around. They obtain this information as a result of

their own activities, and they also get it from the hundreds of paid informers, *people who are prepared to play the traitor,* very often simply to revenge themselves on their own personal enemies.

The words 'prepared to play the traitor' reveal the extent of the appellant's sympathy for the terrorists. They reveal that the appellant believes that members of the public, who are not in the invidious position of a minister of religion, should also refuse to report. The view is clearly expressed that no person, Christian or pagan, should assist the Government by reporting terrorists. Tribesmen also face difficulties and problems in reporting as this Court has had occasion to point out in a series of judgements, but these difficulties are of an entirely different kind and the view contained in the above statement shows the extravagant lengths to which the appellant is prepared to go in justifying his attitude.

The appellant makes a point that it is not always possible for a person to serve both God and the State and that an informed Christian conscience not infrequently dictates that a person 'please God, not men'. What the appellant has done in the commission of these offences is undoubtedly extremely displeasing to many men in Rhodesia. On the other hand, his conduct must necessarily be extremely pleasing to the men who make up the terrorist gangs, and such as to endear him to them. This is necessarily so since it is an attitude which ensures that, so long as the appellant is in charge, neither he nor anyone acting on his advice will report the presence of terrorists in his diocese. This means that terrorists may come and go from any of the institutions under his control without fear of a report being made to the Security Forces by any member of the institution. This must be well known to the terrorists by now since express directions have been given by the appellant to all persons under his jurisdiction not to report and, as the appellant rightly says, there is the closest contact between the various institutions and the African people of the areas which they cover. In his address he indicates clearly that the safety of the staff and the various institutions under his control is dependent on the terrorists being made fully aware that these institutions are not 'collaborating' with the men who constitute the Government.

The appellant devotes much of his statement to showing how it comes about there is a coincidence between his belief that what he has done and is doing is pleasing to God and the fact that his actions must unquestionably be pleasing and a continuing source of comfort to the men who make up the terrorist gangs in his area. To show that this coincidence in no way invalidates his belief that what he is doing 'pleases God', the appellant sets out to make a case that the real villains are not the men who constitute the terrorist gangs, but the Europeans, in particular the Europeans who constitute the Government, and the members of the Security Forces of all races. In his enthusiasm to establish this premise he falls into the understandable but inexcusable error in a man of such erudition and in such a calling, of grossly exaggerating the faults of the men he condemns and grossly understating the faults of those with whom he collaborates. The appellant, in the course of his statement said:

> Were we and all other Christian missionaries to be forced to close down all these institutions by being compelled to violate conscience and obey the laws of men rather than those of God, Rhodesia would very greatly suffer.

The reason for closing down would, in fact, as the appellant admits elsewhere in his statement, result directly from the hostility of the Communist terrorists and only indirectly from compliance by the institutions under the appellant's jurisdiction with the law that persons should report a terrorist presence. But the appellant, in the above passage, by a process of circuitous reasoning, attempts to establish that the blame for any such closure would be attributable not to the activities of the Communist terrorists but to compulsion brought to bear on those institutions by the Government 'to violate conscience and obey the laws of men rather than those of God ...' In short, collaboration with the terrorists and refusal to collaborate with Government, by this process of circuitous reasoning, becomes 'the divine law through the mediation of conscience, properly informed'. By collaborating with the Communist terrorists, the appellant, in the result, sees himself as 'obeying God and not men'. It is only possible to comment that the appellant is possessed of a singularly malleable conscience, capable of being shaped in a most unusual way to accord with his preconceived ideas. The appellant continues:

> One may well ask, is this what the Government wants? Is this what the legislation we are dealing with envisages? I might well ask myself also which is better, to keep my Missions in existence and my missionaries in the field for the general good of Rhodesia, a good which can be equated with the good of the Christian Church, or must I, in blind obedience, obey a particular ordinance of men and so bring the whole work of Christianity to an end?

This statement postulates that the good of the Church is to be measured in the short term, that if the missions and other institutions are forced to close down, the whole work of Christianity is brought to an end. The truth, as we see it, is that what would bring 'the whole work of Christianity to an end' permanently is not the temporary closure of any of the appellant's institutions made necessary by the need to fight and overcome Communist terrorism, but the victory of Communism in this country. It is not understood how a person with the appellant's background and high office in the Roman Catholic Church can overlook the long-term interests of Christianity and adopt the short-term expediency of collaboration with Communist terrorism, a collaboration which, if it led to a Communist victory, could only spell the end of everything the appellant maintains he stands for. There would not, with a Communist victory, be 'a continuing presence of the Christian Church and a consequent benefit to Rhodesia now and in the years to come', as the appellant says in his statement. It is charitable to believe that the appellant is not being deliberately dishonest when he implies very clearly that collaboration with the terrorists and opposition to the present Government is 'the imperative of the divine law through the mediation of conscience, properly informed', but rather that his hostility to the Government has become obsessive and has led to a situation in which he has become blinded by his bias to any other point of view.

The appellant's high regard for the Communist terrorists and

142

his corresponding contempt for the Security Forces fighting against them is manifest in the following passages:

> Closely connected with this argument is the fact that the Security Forces are not really in control of the situation anywhere in the operational area of Rhodesia. I say this in spite of all the State propaganda to the contrary.
>
> All the Security Forces are able to do is to move into an area where terrorists are reported to have appeared, carry out punitive raids, stay on for a little while and then move on to another disturbed area to do the same.
>
> Moreover, the strength of the African people's opposition to the present Government is daily on the increase. Time and numbers are on their side, and they know it. No matter what the State propaganda may declare, the African people already sense that the Security Forces are no longer in control of events.
>
> The practice of informing is, as far as the successful prosecution of the war goes, quite useless. The Security Forces generally only manage to kill innocent villagers in retaliation for the presence of guerrillas. Moreover, by such action they not only further antagonise the African people, but they promote the cause of those whom they seek to eliminate.

The above passages from the appellant's statement are all part of the appellant's theme that the terrorists are going to win and there is a note of exultation in the passages. Had a Communist propagandist set out to give comfort and encouragement to the terrorists, it would not have been possible for him to have done better than the appellant has in these passages. His words reveal not the balanced and moderate viewpoint of a prelate, but the diatribe of a political activist, anxious to promote by any means the victory of Communist terrorism. The appellant dare not admit that the terrorists are both bestial and Communist and dare not even admit that this is a possibility because once he does, the whole of his violent and intemperate opposition to the Security Forces and his collaboration on the other hand with the terrorists, would become suspect to say the least. In his statement the appellant says: 'I am not an anarchist' and at another point: 'I believe that I was not acting as an anarchist', and also 'In all my criticism there was nothing whatsoever of a spirit of anarchy.'

Why should it be necessary for a bishop to emphasise more than once in the course of his statement that he is not an anarchist? In the ordinary way, his calling and position would be sufficient to make such a suggestion absurd. The appellant is, however, aware that collaboration with the terrorists and opposition to the Government of the kind evinced in his statement, is conduct which is calculated to encourage persons who respect his opinion as a prelate to indulge in revolutionary action. It is no use for a bishop who employs inflammatory language to protest that he is against violence. If he is truly against violence, let him refrain from using language which leads logically and inevitably to it. A young African, with little knowledge of the achievements which have been brought about by the very successful cooperation between the races in Rhodesia over a very short period of time and of the changes which have steadily taken place, would, on hearing the words of the appellant laying stress in extravagant language on the allegedly evil and oppressive conduct of the European and Government, be left in no doubt that he should resort to violence in order to overthrow the Government.

The appellant in his statement raises a number of excuses for his conduct unrelated to his two main arguments mentioned earlier in this judgement. He says:

> The Christian clergyman, in terms of his very function, must appear to men as offering to them the mercy and reconciliation of his God. No one, even the greatest criminal, the most debased, the most hardened sinner, may ever be refused his counsel or his words of mercy.

This is another excuse which simply does not bear examination. The terrorists did not on any of the occasions on which the appellant failed to report, come to him for 'his counsel or his words of mercy'. Since they are fighting in a Communist organisation, it is most improbable that they are practising Christians. He says:

> But there is another possible variation in the case. Suppose, for instance, I am conducting a religious service, and I notice, or have

brought to my attention by others an enemy of the State amongst the congregation of worshippers. Am I supposed to report his presence to the Security Forces, and so make his act of worship the occasion of capture or death? Is obedience to the State to be regarded as the greater good to be sought and obtained than an individual's act of acknowledging the worship he owes to his God? Am I, the minister of religion, to play the turncoat and become the servant of the State rather than the servant of God? In other words, am I bound to obey men rather than God?

Once again, these were not the circumstances in which the appellant failed to report the presence of terrorists. Had they been, it is quite possible the Attorney-General would not have instituted a prosecution. He says:

> The danger of reporting terrorists who deliberately make their presence known is that the terrorists might be laying a trap for the Security Forces. If this succeeds, the African missionary may be accused of being a party to the trap.

Any excuse, no matter how far-fetched, is used in justification of his failure to obey the law. When such an improbable argument as that above is used, the inference to be drawn is that there is an absence of sincerity in advancing it.

In justification of his conduct the appellant cites a number of directives received from the Holy See of his Church. We have read these directives and we are satisfied that they do not direct priests to become involved in political activity and cannot be reasonably interpreted as doing so. In particular we are satisfied that these directives do not direct that priests should become actively engaged in dismantling political structures or systems. To attack the structure or system of a government would bring the Church and State into conflict. Such a conflict would only be justified where the State, as in Communist countries, attempts to suppress the Church itself. It is unlikely, we think, that it can be the policy of the Roman Catholic Church to permit a priest to indulge in political activities of the kind mentioned by the appellant in his statement. Nor are we impressed by the attempt he makes to elevate purely secular and political issues to the spiritual plane.

Political activity by a priest can only lead to dissension and controversy within the Church he serves and the appellant's revelation in his statement that an official request was made to Pope Paul by some members of the laity of his Church to remove him from his office comes as no surprise.

While we agree that the factors which the trial court took into account in arriving at sentence were properly taken into account, we are of the opinion that insufficient weight was given to the dilemma which missionaries experience in their struggle and determination to keep their Missions and other institutions open in the operational areas. In a series of judgements this Court has emphasised that persons who are in an invidious position when the duty arises of making a report are not to be punished as severely as those who are not. We are satisfied that because of the failure of the trial court to give sufficient weight to this aspect of the case the sentence imposed was manifestly excessive.

As stated earlier in this judgement the safety of missionaries in the operational areas depends, regrettably, to a large extent on their ability to satisfy the terrorist organisation that they are not hostile to it. It is very clear indeed that the terrorists, because they are Communists, have no respect at all for the sanctity of a Church or of the priests and nuns who serve it.

But for the seriously aggravating factors in the appellant's conduct referred to in this judgement, the dilemma which exists and the invidious position of the priests and nuns in the light of that dilemma would make a substantial prison sentence inappropriate. Because of those aggravating factors, however, a substantial prison sentence is called for.

Having studied the appellant's statement with care we are conscious of the fact that the appellant believes that any sentence imposed on him will be unjust and that by going to prison he will suffer martyrdom.

In his statement, the appellant deals with the subject of martyrdom. Referring to the views of the Superior under whom he studied in Rome, he says: 'Over and over again he warned us that the age of martyrdom would never leave the Church and that some of us might even be called to enjoy that privilege', and he ends his statement by quoting the words of St Peter:

No one can hurt you if you are determined to do only what is right. If you do have to suffer for being good, you will count it a blessing. There is no need to be afraid or to worry about them. Simply reverence the Lord Christ in your hearts, and always have your answer ready for people who ask you the reason for the hope that you all have. But give it with courtesy and respect and with a clear conscience, so that those who slander you when you are living a good life in Christ may be proved wrong in the accusations that they bring. And if it is the will of God that you should suffer, it is better to suffer for doing right than for doing wrong.

The appellant, unhappily, appears to be under the impression that his judgement of what is right or wrong is infallible, and that those who challenge his judgement are wrong, even 'moral primitives', and that should he be punished it will be given to him 'to enjoy the privilege' of martyrdom and the satisfaction of suffering 'for doing what is right' rather 'than for doing what is wrong'. We entertain no doubt that the appellant would enjoy the notoriety of serving a prison sentence.

From the purely subjective point of view, therefore, a prison sentence will serve no purpose but such a sentence is necessary to mark the seriousness of the offence and to deter others from behaving in the same way.

In substitution of the sentence imposed by the trial court and giving full weight to the submissions of counsel, we would impose the following sentence:

Four years' imprisonment with labour, three years of which will be suspended for five years on condition that the appellant is not convicted during that period of any offence under the Law and Order (Maintenance) Act [Cap. 65] and sentenced to imprisonment without the option of a fine.

II. An Independent Report

The report on Bishop Lamont's trial which follows is by Seamus Henchy,
Judge of the Supreme Court of Ireland, who attended the trial on behalf
of the International Commission of Jurists.

APPEARANCES

The accused was represented by Mr Lionel Weinstock, S.C., of the
South African Bar, Mr A. Gubbay, S.C., of the Rhodesian Bar, and
Mr C. Jordan (instructed by Mr M. Muller of Messrs Scanlen and
Holderness).

Mr J. A. R. Giles and Mr I. Donovan appeared for the prosecution.

THE COURT

The court of trial was the court of a regional magistrate, Mr W. R.
Henning, who sat with two assessors.

The offences charged carried a sentence of death or life
imprisonment under s.51(1)(c) of the Law and Order (Maintenance) Act, 1970, but, because the trial was before a regional
magistrate, his sentencing powers were limited by s.63(1)(c) of
that Act to a fine not exceeding 2,000 Rhodesian dollars or
imprisonment for a period not exceeding fifteen years.

THE PLEA

Before the accused pleaded to the charges, his counsel submitted
that Counts 1 and 2 amounted to an impermissible splitting of a
single offence. He submitted that Count 1 should be quashed on
the ground that it was simply the completed offence charged in
Count 2 with the added ingredient of incitement, and that on the

authorities an accused could be charged with inciting another to commit an offence which he had jointly committed with that other.

Having heard legal argument, the magistrate refused the application to quash Count 1.

The accused then pleaded guilty to all four Counts.

THE FACTS

The essential facts in relation to the four Counts were agreed to be those set out in a written statement of agreed facts handed in to the Court with the consent of counsel for the prosecution and of counsel for the defence.

THE EVIDENCE

The only evidence called by the prosecution was that of Detective Officer Williams of the Rhodesian Special Branch, who dealt mainly with geographical and locational matters, including the nature and disposition of Security Forces in the relevant area at the time of the charges.

The only witnesses called for the defence were the Anglican Bishop of Mashonaland (which includes Salisbury), Rt Rev Paul Burrough, and the Anglican Bishop of Matabeleland, Rt Rev Mark Wood. Both of those witnesses gave their evidence after the accused had made his address to the Court, but without having heard that address. Their evidence stressed the dilemma of Church authorities when mission workers are visited by terrorists. They both said they found it impossible to give a 'straight reply' as to what they would do in the accused's position when a mission had been visited by terrorists seeking medical supplies. Bishop Burrough said that if the terrorists did not threaten violence he would not report them; otherwise he would. He would not give a general direction to mission personnel not to report terrorists who came to them. Both bishops expressed the view that whether they would instruct or incite Mission personnel not to report the presence of terrorists would depend on the circumstances of the particular case; it was a moral decision to be made in each case in the light of the particular circumstances of the case.

THE ACCUSED'S ADDRESS TO THE COURT

Bishop Lamont stated that he would not give sworn testimony, for the sole reason that by doing so he would leave himself open to cross-examination which would elicit from him answers which might incriminate particular priests and nuns in his diocese. Instead, he elected to give an unsworn statement from the dock. This unsworn statement was made from a lengthy written document in five parts, each part of which was handed in to the Court in turn. Some alterations and interpolations were made in the written version as it was being delivered.

COUNSEL'S CLOSING ADDRESS

Mr Weinstock, in addressing the Court on behalf of the accused, was naturally circumscribed, not only by the plea of guilty, but also by the manner in which the accused in his unsworn statement had justified his conduct. He urged that the accused was not a man of violence who had opted for the course of assisting terrorists. Rather, he was a man who opposed violence and who, when confronted with the dilemma of deciding whether Sister Vianney or he should report the presence of terrorists in the Inyanga mission, made a conscientious decision not to report, in the interests of the safety of those working in the Mission. He suggested to the magistrate that, in exercise of the powers vested in him by s. 337 of the Criminal Procedure and Evidence Act 1970, he should suspend the operation of any sentence imposed or, alternatively, postpone the passing of sentence for a period not less than the three years allowed by that section, subject to such conditions as he might think proper to impose.

On the 23 September 1976 the magistrate postponed his judgement on sentence until the 1 October 1976.

THE SENTENCE

On the 1 October 1976 the magistrate imposed a sentence of ten years' imprisonment with hard labour. By then I had left Rhodesia, so I did not hear the reasons put forward by the magistrate for the measurement of punishment in those terms. A transcript of the judgement has not yet come to hand. I understand, however, that the sentence imposed was stated to be deterrent as well as punitive, and was so imposed on the ground that the accused had misused his position of authority by giving, and inciting the giving of, aid to terrorists, because he had not expressed any regret for doing so, and because in his statement in court he had attacked the Government of Rhodesia and not the terrorists. Apparently, the only matters reckoned in his favour were his age and the fact that he had pleaded guilty.

OBSERVATIONS

The trial, as I saw it, was conducted in a fair and courteous manner. Criticism, if it is to be made, must be directed against the nature of the offences charged and against the severity of the sentence.

The dilemma in which Bishop Lamont found himself is but another addition to the tragic catalogue of cases of persons caught up in the struggle between the Rhodesian Security Forces and the terrorists. The evils resulting from the measures adopted by the Rhodesian authorities for dealing with that armed conflict have been highlighted in the ICJ Report on *Racial Discrimination and Repression in Southern Rhodesia*. The law bears so harshly and arbitrarily on a person who unwillingly finds himself assisting terrorists that any missionary or other person in one of the 'operational areas' of Rhodesia might easily be charged, convicted and sentenced as Bishop Lamont has been.

It would, of course, be tragic if Bishop Lamont, who is now sixty-six years old and who has given the past thirty years of his life in the service of the people of Umtali, black and white equally, were to become one of the first prisoners of conscience in the new State of Zimbabwe which is about to replace Rhodesia. At present he is on bail pending appeal, and it seems likely that his appeal will not be heard until well into 1977. By then the legal background of the case may be overshadowed by political developments, for those now labelled terrorists or supporters of terrorists may have come to share political power. It is to be hoped that a political settlement will carry with it an amnesty for those imprisoned under the present emergency legislation. Even if there is no general amnesty, there is a strong case to be made for giving special consideration to Bishop Lamont's case. If his sentence is allowed to stand, the missionary work of the Christian churches, which is so important in Rhodesia, will be imperilled, for all missionaries in the 'operational areas' will be at risk. More particularly, the life-work of a great humanitarian will have been cruelly and prematurely cut short. It is to be hoped that the International Commission of Jurists will use its good offices to ensure that those charged with bringing the State of Zimbabwe into existence will undo the sentence on Bishop Lamont – if it has not already been set aside on appeal. His statement to the court that tried him proclaims him to be a man of principle, courage, compassion and talent. It would be wholly regrettable if his life's contribution to the people of Rhodesia, in particular the black people of Rhodesia, were to be snuffed out by his harsh sentence.

Donal Lamont
– The Man and His Work

*To the Carmelites of the Irish Province,
with fraternal affection and gratitude.*

INTRODUCTION

The Carmelite Order, throughout the complex and turbulent twentieth century, produced a number of people of great human, intellectual and spiritual stature: Blessed Titus Brandsma, journalist, professor and Rector of the University of Nijmegen, executed in the Dachau concentration camp; Blessed Hilarion Januszewski, martyr for love in the same concentration camp; Bartolomé Xiberta, theologian, whose process of beatification is in train; Dom Gabriel Bueno Couto, Brazilian, Carmelite bishop, great pastor and model of holiness, and many more theologians, pastors and saints of one kind or another, who blazed a trail for the Carmelite Family and provided witness for the world. One of the figures that has stood out is Bishop Donal Raymond Lamont, the first bishop of Umtali (Mutare today) in Zimbabwe, who set himself against the racial discrimination that was part of the life of what was then called Southern Rhodesia, and who received a nomination for the Nobel Peace Prize. He took part in the Second Vatican Council and his intervention was decisive in establishing the orientation of what would turn out to be the decree, *Ad Gentes*.

In 1959 Bishop Lamont wrote a famous pastoral letter entitled, *Purchased People*, which was a landmark in the modern history of the African continent, since it represented the adoption of a very clear stand by a member of the Catholic hierarchy against racial discrimination and against the methods that were used to restrict the liberty of African people, who, little by little, and with considerable difficulty, were moving to ever greater in-dependence from the colonising powers.

This study of the life and work of Bishop Donal Lamont, along with the study by Carmen Márquez Beunza of the theological problem that lay behind his important pastoral letter, was published as an introduction to the Spanish translation of *Purchased People*, and the *Speech from the Dock*, spoken at his trial in 1976,[1] in the prestigious collection that bears the title, *Textos para un Milenio* ('Texts for a Millennium').[2] I am totally convinced that in these writings by Bishop Lamont we will find reasons for genuine pride in relation to our past, inspiration for the present – in its own way a complex and difficult time, similar to the times that Lamont would have known – and hope for the future. Now we offer the text in English, thanks to the translation by Fr Míceál O'Neill, an Irish Carmelite, currently the Prior of St Albert's International Centre in Rome, where Donal Lamont lived for a number of years, as we will see later on.

Early days and Formation

Bishop Donal Lamont was an Irish Carmelite. He was born into a large family in Ballycastle, County Antrim, in 1911. His parents sent him to Terenure College[3] in Dublin for his secondary education, at the end of which he entered the Carmelite Order. He made his novitiate in Kinsale, in Cork in 1929. There, like all Carmelite novices, he learned the traditions of the Order, with its spirituality and rich world of symbols. Following his Simple Profession he went to University College Dublin for his studies.

Having completed his civil degree in Ireland, in 1933 the young Lamont was sent to Rome to study theology at the international house of the Order, St Albert's International College, which at that time, and despite a considerable number of difficulties, had a very respectable set of teachers, among whom Bartolomé Xiberta, Alberto Grammatico and John of the Cross Brenninger (who left a deep imprint on Donal Lamont) were the most distinguished.

These were turbulent years in the complex history of Europe in the twentieth century. The civil war in Spain had just begun, a war that proved to be a kind of laboratory for the major powers leading up to the Great War. In Germany, National Socialism was acting against Jews in an increasingly cruel and sinister fashion. In the Netherlands, the noted Carmelite Titus Brandsma[4] added his support to a letter written by university professors against the treatment that Jews had to suffer in Germany. This letter insisted on the dignity of every human person, as a creature and child of God, in the face of every kind of racial discrimination, including what was being proposed by the Nazi ideologues at that time.[5] Pope Pius XI, published a very hard-hitting encyclical against National Socialism, in which he highlighted the serious and pernicious errors of this ideology and the problems to which it could lead. The pontiff looked at the expansion of these ideologies with enormous concern, hence the title of the encyclical, *Mit brennender Sorge* ('with deep concern'). I believe that it would not be difficult to find traces of this encyclical in the later thinking of Donal Lamont and in some of his public stands against apartheid.[6]

His life in St Albert's International College, to which we referred earlier, must have also left its mark on the young Irish Carmelite. Those who wrote about Bishop Lamont and those who knew him well point out that he had a great regard for the German Carmelite, John of the Cross Brenninger. This man had an enormous influence on many other Carmelites of note from the last century – Brandsma, Bueno Couto, Urbanski, Xiberta, Esteve, etc.[7] As an expert in the area of Carmelite spirituality, Brenninger published the well-known *Spiritual Directory*, translated into many languages and used for decades in novitiates around the world.[8] This directory shows the clear influence of the Reform of Touraine, a reform which had marked the life of the Order and its spirituality over four centuries. Brenninger applied its teachings very much to his own life, with its asceticism, austerity and rigid observance.[9] All of this must have captivated the young Carmelite, already one who had an inclination towards virtues of tenacity, frankness, austerity and seriousness.[10] Many years later, when Lamont was on trial, accused of harbouring terrorists, the bishop would quote in public, words he had heard from John Dieminger. 'The Church will always have its martyrs.'[11] Undoubtedly, in his years in Rome, the young Lamont developed the character and the convictions that, though they may have been very basic and essential, would be what supported his principles and Christian commitment for the rest of his life.

In Rome Lamont obtained his degree in theology in 1937. The thesis he wrote (which is still to be found in the library of the St Albert's International Centre) dealt with the divine and spiritual motherhood of the Blessed Virgin Mary.[12] Although it stands to reason that the work suffers from the deficiencies of a pre-conciliar Mariology, with a tendency to promote a mariological excess or two, it nevertheless contains some very refined statements and draws greatly on biblical and patristic sources. Some of the statements are very interesting and show signs of a later Mariology, which makes one think that in St Albert's College (as the *Studium Generalis*) the theology that was being taught was of a very high standard. In this regard, we can see the importance that the young Lamont gave to spiritual motherhood in its ecclesiological dimension, expressed in the category of the ecclesiology of the mystical body, much in vogue at that time on account of the renewal that was underway in the school of Tubingen and in the Roman school that led to the encyclical of Pius XII, *Mystici corporis,* in 1943. Indeed one of the modern authors who is cited there is Karl Adams and some of the expressions recall likewise the ecclesiology of Bartolomé Xiberta, whose thinking must have significantly shaped the dogmatic theology that was being taught at St Albert's.[13] Some examples from Lamont's thesis might be useful in this regard:

> Our thesis is intended to be a study of these two truths, bringing together the spiritual motherhood of the Blessed Virgin, and the unity of all the redeemed under Christ the head … When therefore the Apostle insists so much on this analogy, he is not trying to propose an indefinite similarity, but much more to explain through the analogy of the human body, how, joined to the head, the mystery of the totality of Christ, or the mystery of the union of all the redeemed in a supernatural organism, with Christ at its head, the Church is united to Christ in a real and intimate union …[14]

However, Lamont's life was not heading in the direction of the academic or the professional despite the quality of his theological formation. On 11 July 1937 he was ordained to the priesthood in the eternal city and on finishing his exams he returned to Ireland where everything pointed toward him spending his life as a teacher.

Missionary in Southern Rhodesia

Indeed, on returning to Ireland he was assigned to Terenure College and there he taught English literature for a number of years. He also took care of a range of other pastoral duties, there and in the different houses of the Order in Ireland (novenas, preaching, retreats, etc.). He was Dean of Discipline for a number of years; he trained rugby teams and helped out at a hostel for the poor in the centre of Dublin. In those years he completed his studies in literature at University College Dublin and obtained a Masters in English Philology, with a thesis on the poetry of Richard Crashaw.[15]

However, at the end of the Second World War, Lamont's life was to take an entirely different direction. The Irish Province of Carmelites (which in those years oozed a very strong missionary spirit) was about to send some of its best men to a new mission in Africa, to Southern Rhodesia.[16] The first three to be chosen were Luke Flynn, Anselm Corbett and Donal Lamont.[17] Both in Ireland and in Rhodesia, enthusiasm abounded. The three Carmelites arrived in Zimbabwe with lots of hope, youthful generosity and enthusiasm for the mission. However, as Lamont would point out later on, there were lots of lacunae too, and they really had very little training for mission.[18]

Nevertheless, the mission in the eastern part of the country (on the border with present-day Mozambique) grew very rapidly.[19] That area had been evangelised first by the Marianhill Trappist missionaries (from 1895 to 1929) and then, for two decades, from 1929 to 1948, by Jesuit missionaries.[20] The Carmelites took over from the Jesuits.[21] It seems that the reason for the Carmelite presence was an invitation made by Archbishop Aston Chichester, Jesuit and first Archbishop of Salisbury (present-day Harare) to the Irish Carmelites, to take charge of the Jesuit missions in that part of the country.[22] An indication of how effective the Carmelites were may be seen in the fact that just eight years after their arrival, on 6 February 1953, the Holy See erected the Apostolic Prelature of Umtali, and soon afterwards appointed Donal Lamont as the Prefect Apostolic. He had been up to then the Regional Superior of the Irish Carmelites in Southern Rhodesia.

In those early years the mission followed the line that was common to other missions of the Order at that time: the priority was to set up a local clergy to help in the work of evangelisation and to give the people the basic services in the areas of education and healthcare. There was little emphasis on a Carmelite identity, indeed there was little thought about implanting the Carmelite Order there (this began only in the 1970s and 1980s). The intention was to serve the local Church (perhaps in a somewhat mistaken fashion, but undoubtedly with great generosity and without any self-interest).[23] It was the common approach to 'Carmelite missions' at that time. The same was true in Indonesia, Venezuela, and Bolivia, by way of just three examples.

To strengthen the mission, the Carmelite presence became international when in 1955 a number of Carmelites from Australia came to help, and in 1957, members of the North American Carmelite province of St Elias (known as the 'New York Province') joined the mission. Both provinces had been founded by the Irish province at the end of the nineteenth century. The Irish Carmelites continued to send young Carmelites with the result that the mission went from strength to strength and produced the best of fruits.[24]

Four years later, on 1 February 1961, Donal Lamont was appointed as the first Bishop of Umtali. The diocese was placed under the protection of Our Lady of Mount Carmel as its patroness. The new bishop chose as his motto (which will be significant for what we will see later) *Ut placeam Deo* ('That I may please God'). This was all good news for the Irish Carmelites in Rhodesia but it meant an enormous responsibility which Bishop Lamont took on with conviction and courage.[25]

The *Terenure College Annual* gave a very moving report of the ceremony of consecration that took place on 16 June 1957. According to the annual, more than three thousand people took part in the ceremony. The photograph of his first meeting with Pope Pius XII in Rome is also in the annual.[26]

The new bishop got to work on giving the diocese a structure.[27] He worked tirelessly for evangelisation and made sure that a variety of congregations, both of men and of women, should be part of this great pastoral and catechetical endeavour. In some cases his efforts to bring specific congregations to the diocese worked well, but in some other cases he found it difficult to convince religious superiors to send their members.[28] Perhaps it was because of their encouragement that in 1959 Bishop Lamont decided to found a diocesan congregation of sisters with a Carmelite inspiration.[29] Thus the idea of the Congregation of the Handmaids of the Blessed Virgin Mary of Mount Carmel was born.[30] This was really a landmark in the as yet almost non-existent history of Carmel in Africa. Even more, it could be said, this was the first attempt to create an African Carmel, that is, to translate, adapt or inculturate Carmelite values in the African context. This was even before the Second Vatican Council and it gave a definitive push to a new understanding of mission that would take the local culture into account.[31] The congregation continued to grow. In 1961 twelve sisters made their vows before Bishop Lamont, the founder of the congregation.[32] The growth would continue with the opening of new houses in the area of Mutare and later on in other parts of Zimbabwe. Clearly, the new congregation received not only juridical support from Bishop Lamont but also a very profound Carmelite and Marian input.[33] In a very touching letter, written from Terenure College in May, 1991, Lamont, already in retirement, explained to Sr Immaculata (then Superior General of the Congregation) why he had chosen the name 'Handmaids' for the congregation. He acknowledged that it was a name from another age and certainly out of date, but it recalled the attitude of Mary in the *Magnificat* and was a calling to the sisters to have a similar way of living, imitating the Blessed Virgin in her obedience and generosity:

When choosing a name for the Clti (congregation) I carefully chose a title which would express the kind of life which you Sisters would try to live in the great family of the Carmelite Order. I wanted you to be very special and to have a name which would very briefly tell of the kind of dedication to the service of God which you would try to give by your profession of the vows, and by faithfully fulfilling these promises in your lives.

That's why I chose 'Handmaid'. It is a word used in English for a very long time in the Gospel version of Our Lady's reply to the Archangel Gabriel's announcement that she had been chosen by God to be the mother of our Redeemer. It is in some ways an old-fashioned word, not much used in modern English. It has a very special meaning. It describes a woman servant who has been chosen by a great Lady, by a Queen for instance or a lady of noble birth, to be her most trusted helper, almost like a sister, but still a servant. She is someone who would live in daily contact with her mistress, whom the mistress would trust completely and with whom she could share her most intimate secrets, confident that the handmaid would be loyal and loving in her service; not just like any servant but very special. The word 'handmaid' also suggests that she would be almost like another 'hand' to work with, giving to the mistress extra ability, ready to do anything that had to be done and not expecting any reward …[34]

Bishop Lamont worked diligently in two major areas: education and healthcare, responding in this way to what were the most basic needs of the local population.[35] In the same way, he focused on the shape that the new diocese would take, providing it with the basic structures, both pastoral and administrative. After some years had passed, Lamont began the project of building a cathedral in Umtali. After a lot of effort and not a few interruptions, for political reasons, the cathedral was finally completed in 1972, thus taking the place of the old *Holy Rosary* church that had been in use since 1923. Bishop Lamont had the joy of performing the blessing and the opening of the new cathedral, dedicated to the Most Holy Trinity.[36] Another aim which he had was to set up a local clergy, an idea that was basic to the approach to mission adopted by the Carmelites at that time.

The work of the new diocese seemed to be running smoothly. Proof of this and something that gave great joy to the bishop was the growing number of local ordinations. However, the political situation was beginning to get more complicated.[37] In that area tension was rising. Various groups were beginning to emerge: groups with a strong desire for independence, springing up all over the continent of Africa. These were more radical groups that Lamont refers to in his writings as belonging to the category of 'Pan-Africanism', a term that was then coming into vogue. Then there were the groups of a contrary stamp, who wanted to maintain the domination of the white minority on the continent at any cost, and, as a consequence, the situation of racial segregation.[38] Incidents began to occur in Nyasaland (present-day Malawi) at the beginning of 1959, although the tension had been mounting for some years before that.[39] We should remember that Zimbabwe was a British colony since the nineteenth century as a result of the expeditions of Cecil Rhodes. From the very beginning this region attracted many Europeans who came to know about the wealth of its mines. In 1921 it was declared as the Autonomous Colony of Southern Rhodesia. Then in 1953 it became part of a kind of federation called CAF, the 'Central African Federation of Rhodesia and Nyasaland', that would include the two Rhodesias (the north, now called Malawi, and the south, now called Zimbabwe). This explains why the revolts of the Federation (Malawi) in the north would affect greatly Southern Rhodesia, where, indeed, the white minority was greater in number and more powerful.

This union was not well accepted by the black majority, especially in Nyasaland. The NAC (the Nyasaland African Congress) was founded in 1944 and represented an attempt to create an indigenous political group, organised to a greater or lesser degree, that might serve as a negotiating party with the British colonial authorities, protested against this enforced union. One of its more popular leaders, Hastings Kamuzu Banda,[40] who was residing in Gambia, was named as president of the NAC. Under his presidency the protests became even stronger, which led to his arrest in 1959.

In the face of the seriousness of the incidents and the fear that they might extend to the whole region, the government decreed a state of emergency on 26 February 1959. This introduced a cruel repression and the imprisonment of not a few local leaders, in addition to attacks against the black majority, even against the more moderate leaders and people who had no direct political involvement. The ANC (the African National Congress) was forbidden. Various laws were passed by the government, which restricted even more the already limited freedoms of the population.[41] It is in this context, no doubt a delicate, difficult and complex one, that the Pastoral Instruction, *Purchased People* emerged, the title coming from a phrase in the First Letter of St Peter (1 Pet 2:9).

PURCHASED PEOPLE

Just two years after his appointment as the first bishop of the new diocese of Umtali, Donal Lamont wrote this pastoral letter, which would be a landmark in the history of Zimbabwe and in the history of the emancipation of black Africa.[42] Curiously, the other bishops in Rhodesia refused to sign this letter and Lamont was left alone with his denunciation. Nevertheless, one by one, other bishops came on side and supported the criticisms that Lamont made of the racist regime. They came to a clear, decisive and common position in defence of human rights. *Purchased People* was, therefore, not only the beginning of a series of pastoral letters[43] and statements in opposition to the racist system in Zimbabwe, but also, and even more, a shot in the arm that led to the Church in Zimbabwe taking a firm and clear position against the injustice reigning throughout the country.

Lamont began by defending the intervention of a bishop in matters that belong (apparently) to the temporal order. Such a stance may be deduced from the teaching authority that bishops have, entrusted by the Lord to the apostles and their successors and supported by the promise of divine assistance. Even though, the ecclesiology might smack of a certain 'hierarchiological bent', the bishop's words ring out with prophetic power:

> In the fulfilment of his teaching office, a Bishop must always bear in mind that the message confided to him is not his to modify or dilute, or least of all, to silence … Preach the Bishop must; not permitting himself to be silenced by merely human fears or temporal considerations; not watering down his message for the sake of spurious peace, or loss of friendship with any worldly authority, or possibility of being deliberately misinterpreted by wicked men … No, the Church through her Bishops must speak, no matter what the fears, what the opposition, what the criticism.[44]

Lamont goes on to speak about what he considers to be the 'fundamental problem', which is nothing other than the neglect of God and his moral law. 'God has been banished politely from public life.' He says that 'His eternal law has been quietly set aside', and that all other ills have their root in this. By losing the Christian sense of life, by turning God into some kind of distant being that has nothing to do with real life, and turning Christ into a merely historical figure, all understanding of justice and universal fraternity falters and every individual makes the law do whatever is convenient for him.

When there is no reference to God, the Father of all, people lose the idea of a universal fraternity, a family of nations, and then war, racial tension, and self-centred confrontation begin. Even more, where Christianity is concerned, all human beings are united not only by the idea of everyone being a child of a personal God who is revealed as Father, but also by their common redemption in Christ, who has made each of us a member of his own body. Therefore, the theological starting point for Lamont is very clear. It is that all are children of the same God, all of us have been redeemed in Christ and, therefore, all human beings enjoy the same human dignity.

To support the common dignity of every member of the human race, Lamont relies on the authority of Pope Pius XII in his first encyclical entitled, *Summi Pontificatus*, published on 20 October 1939, at a most dramatic moment, when the war had just begun.[45]

It is worth noting, that right from the beginning, Lamont directed his strongest criticism towards Christians, that is to say, those people who even though they profess the Christian faith, do not believe (in their words or in their deeds) in the common dignity of the human person, or in a universal fraternity. His words are very clear.

> Yet in spite of this, in spite of this divine commandment, such is the tragedy of the world's forgetfulness of God, that men look down on, and treat with contempt and persecute and deny ordinary justice to their fellow men and continue to call themselves Christians. How far have we fallen from the primitive practice of the Church which made the heathens cry out in admiration: 'Behold these Christians, how they love one another.'[46]

Another disturbing thing (a consequence of what went before) is the neglect of the natural law that should stand, in Lamont's view and in the widespread view of the time, before all other positive human law. In the specific case of Central Africa, this turned into 'an immoral state of affairs',[47] which succeeds in placing above the human person and his inalienable dignity other values, such as race, nationalism, or the economy.

The best example of all these ills is to be found in what Lamont calls 'the clash of nationalism' which was being seen all over

Africa. Lamont begins by making clear that, on the one hand, it is logical that a certain tension should exist in the meeting of cultures that are so different and at differing stages of development. Moreover, in ordinary life, the relationships between Africans and Europeans were not bad. However, of late, movements of a certain nationalistic hue had emerged, both among Africans and among Europeans as well, that tended to reject the other and to engage in violent conflict. Lamont lists the first group under the category of 'Pan-Africanism' and he concludes that this is something that did not come from the region of Zimbabwe, but something that was brought in by certain politicians with a vested interest.

Hence, there was a need to distinguish carefully between a healthy nationalism (that would seek the recognition of an identity, a culture, traditions, and which, in the case of Africa, also meant the sincere desire not to be treated as a second-class citizen) and an exacerbated, xenophobic, violent kind that would look for conflict between races and indeed the dominance of one race over another. In this sense, Lamont condemned certain abuses that were present in the region, like, for example, the denial of rights to the aborigines.

In the face of all of this, Lamont proposed a moderate and reasonable political stance. The colonial power must respect the traditions and the rights of the native Africans, and must also foster the process that would lead to their self-governance. Lamont asks for a 'benevolent colonialism' and, in a certain way, one that is provisional: a colonialism that will seek above all the good of the country and its peoples, with proper economic, human and social development; a colonialism that clearly respects the distinguishing features of the colonised people (language, culture and traditions that do not offend the moral law). To reach those processes of proper autonomy, both the European and the African must take a good look at their point of view, and look for the common good, avoiding the kind of extremism that can lead to armed and violent conflict and to destruction.

In this regard the appeal that Lamont makes to the Africans is very interesting, when he asks them to have confidence in the

Church that will not try to take away their identity.[48] Some expressions are reminiscent of the ones that a few years later the Second Vatican Council would affirm, for example, in *Lumen Gentium*,[49] *Gaudium et Spes*,[50] or *Ad Gentes*[51] among many others.

If the call that Lamont made to African people, to be patient and to accept certain things, may smack a little of paternalism, the call to a change of mindset that he issues to the Europeans is much more direct and unyielding. He began by making a very strong criticism of those who believe that their race is somehow superior to others and who believe that the domination by the European is something natural and that it will last forever. With equally strong expressions he made fun of their presumed physical and moral superiority. Furthermore, he lamented the fact that the great majority of Europeans know nothing of the language, nor of the culture, of the local people and that they do not make even the least effort to know them, thereby demonstrating a great disdain for the native Africans.

In that same line, he called on the State to undertake necessary reforms in order that segregation and the restriction of the Africans might cease. Lamont praised the fact that some of these restrictions were already being suppressed and that the offensive 'Europeans Only' signs were disappearing from some buildings. He lamented the fact that this was happening in things that were more secondary such as access to restaurants and cinemas, while the same policy was not being applied to areas of more fundamental importance. Racial segregation is a moral evil that has no justification. Without falling into what was proposed as the forced mixing of races, an argument used by those who wished to defend the policy of apartheid, Lamont argued strongly for greater integration, that would enable the possibility of people getting to know one another, and the creation of a common society, based on peace and justice, that fosters the human development of every individual.

At the end of the letter, in a kind of postscript, Lamont explained that what he said about the African race and the European race could be applied to any race, and again, he explains very clearly that racial discrimination by its very nature is an evil that cannot be condemned enough.

The African has to have access to the land – that is, to the means of subsistence – to work and to produce food. With all of that, Lamont did not deny that white colonisation did a lot of good for the country by way of agricultural production, nor did he deny the right to private property (the doctrine of private property which is enshrined in the teaching of the Church) but he recognised that for Africans it is difficult not to give way to even violent extremes, when they find themselves in great need and see around them great spreads of land that are lying idle.

Africans must also have access to education. That is fundamental for the future of the country. Education is an area in which there has to be collaboration between the State, the family and the Church. The State must take care of these processes, without turning into an absolute State (and Lamont insisted greatly on this) that interferes in social areas that are not part of its remit.[52] The call for education for everybody is very clear and precise in the letter:

> There can be no prospect of real peace or true progress in partnership in this country until the present disparity between the educational opportunity available to the European child and that available to the African child disappears. It is futile to expect mutual understanding when in so important a matter, such a radical distinction is made between the children of both races into whose hands the future of this country is to be committed.

Only the missionaries, very often without any help, or indeed against the disapproval of the authorities, worked in this direction and set up schools and centres of education for the native people.[53]

The letter ends with a call to hope and trust in the future. Southern Rhodesia is a country that is full of possibilities and values. If the gruff inflexible paternalism of Europe, and the impatience of Africa, are overcome, the future of Rhodesia is very promising. The Church has an important mission to perform and in the process must condemn, without any fear, all the attitudes that stand in the way of the country growing sufficiently.[54]

The letter ends with a quote from the Gospel according to Matthew (25:31ff.) with an eschatological reference that is yet another indication of how ridiculous racial segregation is:

The world passes and we with it, for even birth has in itself the germ of death. In a few years we shall all be compounded with the dust and probably forgotten. There will be no privilege then, no distinction of race or of colour, and there will be no segregation. And what will decide our eternity will be simply the charity which we have shown to our fellow man in this present life.[55]

Even though, as we said previously, the other bishops did not sign this letter, some time later they wrote a joint letter (no doubt, inspired by Bishop Lamont), on issues of justice and peace.[56] This marked the beginning of a long battle by the Rhodesian episcopate against the injustices that resulted from the system of racial segregation.

HIS PART IN THE SECOND VATICAN COUNCIL

In 1986, twenty years after the conclusion of the Second Vatican Council, Alberic Stacpoole put together a work that included a number of the participants at the Council who recounted their memories and experiences. Donal Lamont was one of the bishops invited to contribute to this volume, *Vatican II: By those who were there.*[57] Thanks to this work, we have a magnificent summary of impressions and memories of the most important event in the life of the Church in the last century. It is very evident from this work that Lamont took part with great enthusiasm in the Council. The Carmelite recalled, in considerable detail, how much the pomp of the opening ceremony impressed him – the great procession of bishops, the arrival of the Pope on the *sedia gestatoria*, the enthusiasm and nervousness that was all around.[58] He also noted how many of the bishops thought that the whole thing would be over by Christmas.[59] Bishop Lamont, who took part in all the sessions of the Council, stayed all the time at St Albert's International College, where, more than likely, he would have exchanged opinions and points of view with other Carmelites who were also taking part in this great Church event: Bartolomé Xiberta, the theologian, Kilian Healy, the Prior General, and a number of bishops.[60] Even though, as he himself recognises, the missionary bishops were seen in a somewhat secondary role in the evolution of the discussions, almost without wishing it,

Lamont saw himself as one who was fully involved in the process that led to the writing of the decree, *Ad Gentes*.

Even before that, Lamont had answered a questionnaire that had been sent to bishops around the world. The two changes in the life of the Church that he suggested speak of the sensitivity of the Carmelite bishop and his pastoral and missionary bent. The first suggestion (that apparently did not go much further) made reference to the abolition of abstinence from meat on Fridays, which, he held, should be replaced by other forms of penance. Beyond the question itself (precise and concrete, and somewhat anecdotal perhaps), it seems that what Lamont wanted was a new approach to penance with new forms that would be relevant in the different cultures, where meat may be a symbol of something else and have different connotations to the ones it has in European culture. The second suggestion, no doubt of greater weight, referred to the possibility of ordaining married laymen as deacons which might prove very useful for the apostolate and missionary work of the Church. As we know, this notion would be taken up by the Council,[61] and by Church praxis later on, even though today in some countries (and not just in the mission territories) this possibility has been totally neglected or even abandoned, perhaps due to some kind of pastoral caprice or prejudices or the remnants of a clericalism that are still around.

It is worth mentioning that his contribution to the discussions was not limited to the question of the mission *Ad Gentes*. Indeed, he spoke in almost every session of the Council. In the first session, in December 1962, he submitted in writing his opinion concerning the immutability of the doctrine concerning the Church – right at the moment when the controversial scheme, *De Ecclesia*, which would eventually be withdrawn, was being discussed. By all appearances Lamont's opinion was motivated by the desire not to fall into a false kind of irenicism (to use the same word that the Council would use later on in *Unitatis redintegratio)* in ecumenical dialogue.[62] During this session Lamont visited a number of Carmelite communities in Italy. He also visited Malta and presided at the celebration of the Eucharist in the Basilica of Our Lady of Mount Carmel in Valletta on 3 November.[63] It is most likely that he was invited by Bishop

Redemptus Gauci, a Maltese Carmelite who at that time was the bishop of the Prelature of Chuquibamba in Peru, who was also taking part in the Council.[64] In fact, Lamont was one of the concelebrants at his ordination, along with Archbishop Michael Gonzi (the Principal Celebrant) and Bishop Emanuele Galea.

In the second period that began in October 1963 Lamont spoke again on an ecclesiological-type theme, and once more, in the debate on the *schema* for *De Ecclesia*. The question that was being examined was the thorny question of episcopal collegiality. Lamont took the middle position between those who insisted on the importance of the role of episcopal collegiality, and those who insisted more on the role of the papacy. His opinion was an attempt to distinguish between the sacramental power conferred on the bishops and the assistance that was promised to the whole Church. I believe that we can say, without any fear of contradiction, that the 'solution' he offered was one that was inspired by Bartolomé Xiberta, the great Carmelite theologian, who had defended this kind of position in a number of articles he had written.[65] It is very likely that in those very animated evening sessions that took place in St Albert's College, not very far from the Vatican, the Carmelite participants in the Council exchanged views and opinions, and indeed we may assume that Xiberta helped the Carmelite bishops (in the same way he did officially for the Spanish bishops).

Within this session Lamont attempted to speak on a number of occasions, but, given the abundance of requests (it was one of the most lively debates of the whole Council) it became impossible. For that reason, he offered his opinion in writing on a question that might appear to us to be merely of anecdotal interest, but which is not without significance in helping us to understand the importance Lamont gave to the laity in the life of the Church. He suggested that we should not persist in using the image of the Church as a sheepfold so much (and hence the image of lay people as the sheep) but rather replace it more with the image of Divine filiation. Thus, once again, Lamont was indicating that the document should condemn racism very firmly, since racism went directly against the truth of our common filiation. Before the session ended Lamont took part in a number of debates, adding his signature to agreed statements, or submitting his own script. However, perhaps the most important development for him, and the most unexpected, by his account,[66] was that he was elected as a member of the Secretariat for Christian Unity. Lamont's theories as to why this happened are curious. One is that because of his surname the French-speaking bishops, a large and important group in the Council, took him to be one of themselves.[67]

One year later Lamont returned to Rome to take part in the Third Session of the Council. In this session he signed the document called *Plures Patres* and he continued to be very active in his role as a member of the Secretariat for Christian Unity. He saw this as a very enriching experience, one that would leave an imprint on him for the rest of his life.[68] In the working sessions he would get to know the Methodist bishop Muzorewa and Garfield Todd with whom he would form a deep and lifelong friendship, as we shall see later on. Lamont was one of the bishops who insisted upon the need for the Secretariat to continue to work regularly after the Council was over and, as we know, that is what indeed happened.

Similarly, he took part in the debates on relationships with the Jews. In his view, these relations are a direct consequence of what was stated by the same Council on the question of religious freedom. However, there is something which is of particular interest to us, since it was a constant feature of the thinking of Bishop Lamont from the time of *Purchased People* onwards. It was that these relations are based, first of all, on the idea of one God and Father of us all, of every human being. This means that all of us are to see ourselves as brothers and sisters to one another and to everyone. Moreover, Lamont believed that it was both logical and helpful that in the context of relationships with other religions we would underline the very special bond that exists between Christians and Jews. He pointed out that to write a document on inter-religious dialogue without any reference to 'our brothers, the Jews' would be as absurd as to write a history of Europe without mentioning the Roman Empire.[69] In the same way, Lamont wanted to give a more positive tone to the text on the Jews, and to avoid that in the future anyone should think that at the time of the Council anti-Semitism was widespread in the

Church. No doubt, the topic had to be controversial. Yves Congar recounts in *Mon Journal du Concile* that Patriarch Maximus IV tried to persuade him not to make specific mention of Israel (as Lamont, Congar and others wanted to do) because that might in some way harm the Christians who were living in the Arab countries bordering Israel. Hans Küng also echoed these difficulties at various times during the Council proceedings. This resulted in Muslims being mentioned in the final version of *Nostra Aetate*.[70]

The highlight of Lamont's participation in the Council, and probably his greatest contribution to it, however, came when the 'Scheme of Propositions on Missionary Activity' was being discussed. The draft of what was to be the Council's document on the missions, was badly received by the Council Fathers right from the beginning. Various African bishops gave public expression to their unhappiness with the document and very soon the controversy began. Indeed, the situation that was generated in the process of development of this document was similar to the one that existed in the case of *Lumen Gentium* (without neglecting the differences and distinctions) and indeed that of other council documents as well. Briefly put, a draft had been offered that did not satisfy the majority of the Council Fathers (especially the missionary bishops or those bishops that were involved in some way with the missions). It was a document that did not really take account of the importance of the mission *Ad Gentes* and which did not take on board the important changes that were emerging in the modern world and which affected enormously the regions traditionally considered mission territories, in which new problems were surfacing which the Church had not yet confronted, i.e. the promotion of justice and peace, the safeguarding of human rights, inter-religious dialogue, etc. The Vatican draft, just as in the case of *Lumen Gentium*, seemed to be excessively Roman, curial and clerical, and as well as being very short and poor in its content, it did not give the proper importance to the mission of the Church in places far away from the badly named First World, or Western World.

The idea that the writers of the document had was to reduce it to a series of thirteen statements on missions. These statements (apart from the humiliation that it meant not to be either a decree or a constitution as such) were very general and very vague. The situation became even more complex when it was learned that Pope Paul VI had given his approval to the document, that others considered to be of such poor quality. The draft, from the very beginning, had attracted a lot of criticism, both veiled and open. Bishops on their own behalf and groups of Council Fathers together criticised its size and its content. Some had difficulty with its excessively juridical tone and with the concept of 'mission' that was contained in the short document: 'Mission' all directed from Rome and Propaganda Fide, without really taking into consideration the autonomy of the local churches.[71] All of these criticisms meant that some division developed within the preparatory commission itself.

Lamont was not a million miles away from these currents of criticism. As Emanuele Boaga relates,[72] a group of representatives of religious orders with serious involvement in missionary fields had formed. This group was led by Bishop Van Valenberg. Jacobus Melsen, a Carmelite, and at that time Assistant General, was also a member. It seems it was he who introduced Lamont to the group. In one of its meetings Lamont used the image of the dry bones from the prophet Ezekiel and some of the bishops (Lamont thought he remembered that it was Archbishop McCann of Cape Town[73]) urged him to repeat this idea in the *aula*.[74] Lamont then took on the task of preparing a strong intervention against the draft. He worked on this for the next few days. After a few corrections were made to the Latin style, the text of the speech was ready.[75]

The day of the assembly, 6 November 1964, the Council Fathers knew that the Pope was going to open the session with a Mass and an address in the *aula*. This was something unusual. Lamont recounted how terrorised he felt by the idea of having to read his speech (loaded with a certain amount of criticism and tongue-in-cheek) in the presence of none other than Pope Paul VI, who, it appears, had supported the document and would probably do so again in addressing the Council Fathers.[76]

Indeed, in order to lessen the criticisms and calm the spirits, the Prefect of the Congregation of Propaganda Fide, Cardinal Peter Agagianian, managed to have Pope Paul VI in person open the debate with an address in which he thanked the missionaries for their work and underlined how the whole Church must see itself as missionary. Without any pretence, the Pope praised the draft document and took it for granted that it would be passed, even though logically it would need to be touched up a bit and have some corrections made to it. This was something quite extraordinary since it was the only occasion in the whole Council in which the Pope took part personally in one of the working sessions. This amazed some and upset others among the Fathers and commentators at the Council.[77] Thus, for example, Yves Congar, describing this difficult session, offers a very severe criticism of the Pope and goes on to make the case for a more collegial and synodal way of working:

> The next time the Pope comes to a general congregation, let him be sure to bring the Gospel! Is it impossible that the Pope could come as a member of the Council and take part in the normal way in one of the working sessions? Does his status as a 'caput' isolate him so much that he has always to be on the outside? The Pope, in fact, did not take part in the assembly. He made a 'gesture'. He did not get inside, and it seems that he cannot do that …[78]

The Pope's address surprised Bishop Lamont greatly and likewise the other missionary bishops who wondered who was behind this defence of a document that was flat and had no life. The Pope's intervention seemed to be at variance with his particular style and with his obviously open and missionary approach.

Shortly after his address, Pope Paul VI left the hall and the work of the Council continued in the normal way in accordance with the roster of interventions already decided. Despite the fact that the Pope was no longer in the hall, Lamont recalls how worried he was as he listened to those who went before him in the list of speakers, since he really did not want to have to publicly contradict what the Pope had said shortly before. He tried to make a few last-minute changes to soften the criticism. In the end, as Lamont recalls with some degree of humour, he was 'saved by the bell'. The session ended and work would begin again the next day. That gave Lamont some time to touch up his speech. On the one hand he could not create a head-on collision with the Pope. On the other hand, he could not contradict what he had written in the summary that he had given to the secretary beforehand.

The following day the session, with Cardinal Julius Dopner presiding, began with the interventions of various bishops who in subtle ways and with due moderation either criticised or praised the document. Then Lamont's turn came. With a certain sense of humour he commented that he was the seventh bishop to speak. The date was 7 November and the session was the 117th of the Council, all of which he thought was a good omen.[79] Even though he had softened what he was going to say and had devised a strategy for the way he would present it within the ten minutes allowed, Lamont had no intention of stepping backwards. Indeed, he was one of the bishops who spoke most strongly against the official draft. With a definite vehemence and the kind of clarity that is rare in this kind of assembly, Lamont spoke on that day in November on behalf of the African, English-speaking bishops. What he said may be read in the *Acta Synodalia*.[80]

Lamont began by suggesting that the short document as presented did not inspire enthusiasm, and did not really provide encouragement for the missionary activity of the Church. It contained a series of rather weak statements and vacuous generalities. Then he used the image of the light cable. The propositions could serve as lamp posts to support a richer document.[81] By doing this Lamont wanted to show that the document had value and thus avoid a direct confrontation with what Pope Paul had said and put at ease the minds of the bishops who wanted to retain the document at all costs. With some astuteness he expressed his gratitude for the presence of the Pope at the beginning of the session of the previous day, and this was given a hearty round of applause in the auditorium. Later on, Lamont used in his speech the image of the dry bones taken from the prophet Ezekiel (Ez 37) and spoke of the 'thirteen dry bones' referring to the thirteen statements in the short document that had been presented.[82] The most tense moment in his intervention came when Lamont asked the Council Fathers, rhetorically, using the words of Ezekiel, *Putasne vivent ossa ista?* ('Can these bones come to life?') Many of the Fathers, not bothering about the fact that it was a rhetorical question, shouted out their response: No, No!

His devastating intervention[83] was interrupted more than once by applause from the assembly and it was decisive in the replacement of the original document (with the famous thirteen statements) by what would turn out to be, with some adjustments, the decree *Ad Gentes*. Some of his expressions were really very hard-hitting. As well as the image of the dry bones, Lamont went on to say,

> From the Council we hoped to get a Pentecostal light and all we are offered is a penny candle: we hoped to get modern arms and all we are offered are bows and arrows; we asked for bread and what we get is, not stones, but a few propositions out of an ecclesiology manual …[84]

Lamont ended his speech with the words, *Haec spes mea, ecce labor noster. Dixi* ('This is my hope, here is our work. That's all I have to say').

The impact of the speech by Bishop Lamont was enormous. Some of the bishops congratulated him straightaway when he returned to his place. Others waited for him at the exit. The moderator of the session, Cardinal Julius Dopner, demanded somewhat angrily that interventions should be very concrete and avoid rhetorical expressions![85]

In his *Speech from the Dock*, Lamont acknowledged that his speech was not the most theologically profound, and could in no way be compared to the great addresses of Cardinal Suenens, or indeed other great Council Fathers. What he wanted, with the use of sincerity and good humour, was to move the hearts of the Council Fathers and move them to reject the draft document that contributed nothing to the world of the missions, and replace it with a more worthy document on this theme.[86] The document was withdrawn almost immediately and some days later Bishop Lamont returned to Zimbabwe.

Lamont still had to take part in the fourth session of the Council which took place in 1965. On 12 October, when the document on missions was being discussed again and the new draft was being examined (presented by Cardinal Agagianian and the Superior General of the Divine Word Missionaries) Lamont intervened with a more positive and conciliatory address. He believed that the new draft was much better than the previous one and he urged that, no matter what the final redaction was like, the document should be truly a recognition of the missionary endeavour of so many religious and a strong impulse for the continuation of that work. On this occasion, Lamont ended with words that give a good indication of his missionary thrust: *Nulla gens tam fera est ut Christi Evangelii capax non sit, neque tam culta ut Evangelio non indigeat* ('No one is so savage as not to be able to receive the Gospel of Christ, or so well formed as not to need it').

Various bishops spoke in positive terms about the draft.[87] Thus, after some discussion and some adjustments, the new draft was approved by a very large majority (2,394 in favour, 5 against) and it became the Council Decree, *Ad Gentes*, on the missionary activity of the Church. This document would be the subject of some very positive criticism by theologians and experts in missiology. One example, among many, is Karl Barth, the celebrated Calvinist theologian who on a visit to Rome some months after the Council,[88] indicated to Congar that for him the best document of the council was the decree on the mission of the Church, the decree *Ad Gentes*.[89] Lamont also signed the declaration on the relation of the church to Non-Christian religions, *Nostra Aetate*.

We might think that the very radical position that Lamont took in relation to the draft offered by the preparatory commission might have created some ill feeling in the higher ranks in Rome, or indeed in Pope Paul VI, given his approval of the draft that Bishop Lamont demolished by his intervention a little later. In fact, an authoritative commentator of the stature of Yves Congar, pointed out that the Pope seemed indeed to be offended by the rejection of *De missionibus* and that he wanted people to know that he had not lost his authority. In the minds of some, the proclamation of Mary as *Mater Ecclesiae*, was his way of showing that his personal teaching authority was still intact.[90]

Hans Küng seems to suggest this when he criticises decisions that Pope Paul took on his own in the last session of the Council.

Two examples were the encyclical, *Mysterium Fidei* on the Eucharist, which contained a rejection of what was being said in the *aula* about priestly celibacy, and the setting up of the Bishops' Council with the *motu proprio 'Apostolica Sollicitudo'*. These were decisions that would have contributed (in the opinion of Küng) to a strengthening of the role of the Pope, in the face of the new trends.[91]

For all of that, it meant a great deal to Lamont that he was invited to concelebrate with the Pope at the Mass on 28 October 1965 as part of the seventh public session – a lovely example of the goodness of Paul VI.[92] This would always be a 'badge of honour', to crown his contribution to this extraordinary Church event.

Later Activities

As we have seen one of the most important moments in Lamont's participation in the Council was his election, as soon as the Council began, in 1962, as a member of the recently formed Secretariat for Christian Unity. He would remain a member until 1975. Even though Lamont manifested some doubts in this regard, out of a certain humility,[93] his election has some notable features. First, it provided a shot in the arm to the idea of missionary ecumenism, or ecumenical mission, that people began to talk about in the years after the council. Ecumenism could not be limited to the theological and doctrinal but must also take in missionary praxis, in which Christians of different confessions can work together and support one another. Secondly, given the place of his birth, Northern Ireland, his appointment signified a reaching out, a sign, a call to understanding and concord in this area that traditionally was seen as both difficult and complex, where ecumenism had become a political and crucial question.

Christopher O'Donnell, a Carmelite confrère who knew Donal Lamont very well, points out that in the question of ecumenism Bishop Lamont was fearful and cautious in the extreme. Despite the fact that he had a good solid theological training, Lamont was not a theologian, strictly or professionally speaking, and his theological foundation did not include the theological advances that Vatican II saw in other areas of theology that might have helped to produce an ecumenical dialogue that would lead to effective progress (ecclesiology, theology of revelation, theology of ordained ministry).

Nevertheless, Lamont viewed sympathetically all the progress that was being made in ecumenism and supported on more than a few occasions the decisions and positions adopted in this direction, both in Africa and in Ireland.

In addition, Lamont kept up long-lasting friendships with leaders of other Christian traditions, such as the Methodist bishop Muzorewa and the pastor, Garfield Todd, of the Church of Christ, who was prime minister of Rhodesia from 1953 to 1958,[94] and later became an opponent of white minority rule in that country.

Similarly, we should mention Lamont's work as a bishop, his long period as a representative of the Rhodesian bishops and his two years (1970–2) as President of the Zimbabwean Bishops' Conference. In that period a number of pastoral letters were issued. Some of these were of great importance and relevance, such as the one on the theme of peace in 1965, shortly after Ian Smith's government made a unilateral declaration of independence (UDI).[95] In that letter the bishops of Zimbabwe, ostensibly led by Bishop Lamont, indicated that the majority of the people were against the declaration of independence, and, what was more, they were against the idea that this declaration could be intended to safeguard Christian civilisation. The new constitution that the government was in the process of writing had nothing to do with Christian values and, indeed, it was, in Lamont's view, openly contrary to such values. Lamont found this identification of Christianity with white power and supremacy to be particularly odious. He condemned it strongly and frequently throughout his life, as we have seen.[96]

We should point out (as various authors and analysts have done) that in his episcopal teaching during those years, Lamont does not try in any way to make himself a liberation theologian. His theological background was predominantly traditional, without wishing to oversimplify the matter. As Tim Sheehy points out, in the prologue to *Speech from the Dock* (included in this volume) Lamont never cited the European theologians of the so-called radical school or political school. It would be difficult to see him as the African Camilo Torres. He himself was very clear that he had never engaged in politics and that he did not even know the principal African leaders in Zimbabwe at the time. Three ideas are repeated and hammered home in his pastoral letters and press interviews: The first is that racial segregation is contrary to the moral law and therefore is to be condemned outright. The second is that the greatest perversion consists in presenting the state of things and the regime as an example of Christian, western, civilisation. This was an excuse that the government used to justify its worst abuses.[97] By doing this, and this is Bishop Lamont's third concern, the government was making Christianity something repulsive and repugnant to the African, a religious justification for an unjust social and political order, which meant that people were being pushed towards Communism and all its propagandistic rhetoric. Lamont, and here we see the contradiction of the accusation that was made against him later, was clearly and radically opposed to Communism, which he thought of as an imported system that was alien to the African mentality, a dictatorial system that was alien to the freedom of the individual and a totalitarian system that was to be totally rejected, as it reminded the bishop of the totalitarian systems which the people in Europe had to suffer in the years leading up to the Second World War and the Mexican system at the beginning of the twentieth century.

We should also point out that Bishop Lamont took part in three Synods of Bishops: 1969, 1971 and 1974. Similarly he was President of the Commission for Justice and Peace of the Zimbabwean Bishops' Conference for many years, an office in which he was extremely active, the main fruit of which was his opposition to the government and his imprisonment – to which we will now turn our attention.

THE 1976 CRISIS AND DEPORTATION

The situation in the country was getting increasingly tense. From 1972 onwards various guerrilla forces were moving predominantly in the eastern section of the country, where the diocese of Umtali was located. Once more Bishop Lamont's life would run into complications because of the political situation. In 1965 there was a unilateral declaration of independence from the United Kingdom, the colonising power. It was an independence that was in the hands of the white minority, as their way of holding onto power. They made use of racist legislation and showed a great desire to ensure that the minority would control all the offices of power, from the political to the economic, and including education, the press and so on.

From the beginning, the Bishops' Conference, led by Donal Lamont, made it known that it did not agree with the declaration of independence and with the fact that this was said to be in the interest of safeguarding Christian civilisation. The Carmelite bishop's criticisms of the racist system of government of the white minority were getting sharper, more open and more explicit as time went on. At the same time, according to the newspapers of the time, Lamont was being subjected to constant persecution. His post, his telephone calls, his friends and acquaintances and the sisters were all under surveillance. Because of the attention the international press was giving to it, the situation was getting very tense. Civil war broke out in 1972. The religious in Lamont's diocese became involved in direct confrontations. For example, in July 1975, the army cordoned off the Carmelite mission of Regina Coeli in an effort to prevent young people going over to Mozambique, and getting tied up with the guerrillas. Some did succeed, which prompted the soldiers to enter the classrooms. The Carmelites managed to convince the soldiers that, in line with the present government's policy, school activity was to continue in the normal way, despite the war.[98]

The most serious confrontation between Bishop Lamont and the government happened in 1976. In August of that year, Bishop Lamont wrote an open letter to Ian Smith and his government. The letter was crystal clear and very direct. In it, once again, he criticised racial discrimination, and the hardening of measures taken against the black majority (with the excuse of the risk of war), and called on the government to abandon its stubbornness and its opposition to every kind of change. Furthermore, and this seems to be what annoyed the government most, he maintained that these injustices were the reason for the violence and the civil war that this African country was having to endure.

Then, on 23 March 1976, the news reached the international teletype that the Irish Carmelite bishop had been arrested by the government of Ian Smith in accordance with the Law and Order Maintenance Act. He was accused of offering medical assistance to the guerrilla terrorists, through the sisters in his diocese, and, what was even more serious, he was accused of not reporting these activities to the proper authorities. The situation for the bishop was both grave and dangerous.

Lamont, in his twenty years as bishop, had done a lot of work in the area of health. His was an effort to offer a minimum of help to masses of people who were without any proper medical assistance. Various congregations, including the one he founded, stood out for the way they offered this kind of service to the Zimbabwean people. In the *Speech from the Dock*, Lamont told the story of what happened, with no shortage of detail.[99] Briefly, what happened was that the bishop allowed (that is, he did not stand in the way of) the sisters in charge of the hospital of one of the missions to give medicines to a group of rebels. Lamont justified this in terms of the safety of the sisters (at times groups of rebels, out of control, caused veritable havoc as they went around) and also on humanitarian grounds. On various occasions Lamont said that he respected the government, despite its dubious legitimacy (questioned by a number of international bodies). He underlined the fact that he was neither a Communist nor an anarchist. He rejected the use of violent means, even though, in like fashion, he believed that the reason many had recourse to these means was the tremendous repression that the white minority was wreaking on the people. In fact, while he recognised the government, he believed that the Church could not be silent in the face of certain actions and measures and would have to raise its voice in protest against such abuses.[100]

During his trial, which had lots of repercussions, even internationally, Bishop Lamont defended the moral and legal correctness of his position and stated that the instructions he gave to the sisters were perfectly ethical. The bishop's arguments did not convince the judges. In October 1976 they sentenced him to ten years hard labour. The sentence was reduced almost immediately to a sentence of deportation and expulsion from the country. He was stripped of his Rhodesian citizenship and declared a *persona non grata*. In March 1977 Bishop Lamont left Zimbabwe and returned to his native Ireland.

From that time onwards Bishop Lamont became very popular but in a somewhat controversial way. In the eyes of some he was a traitor to the white minority and to the country that welcomed him many years previously, a subversive and a Communist.[101] For others he was a true human rights hero. He was to receive a number of recognitions, including honorary doctorates and nominations for prestigious international awards,[102] most notably a nomination for the Nobel Peace Prize. He received numerous telegrams of support that included one from the President of the United States of America, Jimmy Carter. The government of Kenya struck a postage stamp with his picture on it in 1978. That made Lamont an icon of the fight for racial equality on the black continent. Let us not forget that in those years there were still a number of governments and countries that maintained (not in theory but in practical social affairs) a system of racial segregation, to a greater or lesser extent.

Shortly after his deportation, Lamont paid a visit to Rome. On 1 April 1977 he was received by Pope Paul VI who was very encouraging in his support for Lamont's stand in defence of human rights. This is significant given the tension that existed in the third session of the Council around the draft document on mission. Somewhat as a slight on those who accused him of being a Communist or a revolutionary, and something that must have given him great personal satisfaction, the Irish bishop won the personal support of the Pope who received him in the Vatican and referred to him as 'a valiant son of the Church and of the Holy See'. He was also received at the General Curia of the Carmelite Order, where he was interviewed along with the Prior General, Fr Falco Thuis, O.Carm. and the Vice-Prior General, Fr Carlo Cicconetti, O.Carm.[103] On 3 April, Palm Sunday, he celebrated the Eucharist in the Carmelite parish of Santa Maria Regina Mundi in Torrespaccata in the suburbs of Rome. When his trial was in full swing, the children and young people from this parish had sent him a message of love and support. Even though Lamont had already responded to the message through the parish priest with a letter of his own,[104] he wanted to do it also by meeting them and sharing the Eucharist with them on that Sunday, with a word of encouragement to them to be courageous in their living of the Gospel. The young people in turn sang a song for him. The song they sang was, *What colour is God's skin?* made famous by *Viva la Gente*. Bishop Lamont and all the people listened in total silence, in an atmosphere charged with emotion.[105]

In 1980, when the civil war ended Bishop Lamont returned to Africa. The country had changed its name from Rhodesia to Zimbabwe. A new and fascinating chapter was opening. He still continued as bishop of Umtali (present-day Mutare), up to 1982 when he was replaced by the first native bishop, Alexio Muchabaiwa.[106] This period in its history was relatively calm. The new President, Robert Mugabe, spoke about Bishop Lamont and praised him publicly on various occasions. He also expressed his gratitude to the Carmelite Order for its work, especially in the eastern province. Indeed, on an official visit to Ireland in April 1992 Mugabe visited the Carmelite house of Gort Muire on the outskirts of Dublin where he met the Prior Provincial of the time and the community, and thanked them.

Bishop Lamont, wisely, left the diocese on the election of his successor and returned to Ireland. Indeed, he said that even before his trial and deportation, he had offered his resignation twice to the Pope. His principle reason was that he did not speak the Shona language all that well and that he was very aware that in the new understanding of mission arising from Vatican II, and in the context of all that was happening in Africa, it was totally necessary to be able to speak to the people in their own language.[107] He spent his last years in Terenure College, the place where his Carmelite life had begun. He worked hard in those years and was more than happy to be invited by bishops in different dioceses to celebrate the Sacrament of Confirmation or to engage in some other pastoral activity.

He gave numerous talks on the situation in Africa and on his experience there. From the literary and oratorical point of view he was very gifted, with a style of English that reflected his extensive reading and studies in English philology. He quoted his favourite authors generously. He was accustomed to quote the English classics which he had read assiduously.

In his advancing years he stayed fully abreast of what was happening in the Church and in the world. He was a regular reader of *The Tablet* and of the *L'Osservatore Romano*, and, in his preaching, would often refer to what he had read in them.

BY WAY OF PERSONAL EPILOGUE

I met Bishop Lamont on a number of occasions. In one of these meetings the idea of translating *Purchased People* into Spanish came up. He was quite enthused. He gave me a folder full of documentation, newspaper cuttings, and other papers, and even some letters that I have found very useful in writing this introduction. When the bell from the local parish rang he invited me to pray the Angelus with him and then he said goodbye, ever so courteously.

The last time I saw him was in 2001. We were holding the General Chapter of the Order in Sassone, outside Rome. On Wednesday, 12 September we were to have an audience with the Pope in which we planned to mark the 750th anniversary of the vision of the scapular given to St Simon Stock. Along with all the members of the Chapter, other members of the Carmelite Family and pilgrims from all over the world we gathered in St Peter's Square on that morning. However, what was planned as a joyous celebration turned out to be something like a top-level press conference, because it was the day after the 11 September attack on the Twin Towers in New York. All singing and clapping and every sign of festivity was suspended as a mark of respect for the victims of the tragic events of the previous day. Bishop Lamont was there, seated in a wheelchair, clad in his white cloak and brown habit. He greeted us effusively. I made a comment on the terrible events. His concern was evident. He commented on the limitless capacity for evil that is in the human person. He may well have been speaking from his own personal experience.

Ut placeam Deo:
'That I May Please God'

THE COMMITMENT OF BISHOP DONAL LAMONT IN THE
BATTLE AGAINST RACISM

'Can the government of a Christian country survive the challenging opposition of its Churches?' This is the disturbing question with which *Time* magazine began one of its reports on a springlike Monday in the month of April 1970.[1] The news jumped out at the international press when it was known that the four catholic bishops of Southern Rhodesia had just published a pastoral letter with the title, *A Crisis of Conscience.* In it they declared their intention not to comply with certain racial laws that they believed were 'contrary to Christian faith'. That came as something unusual in a country whose politicians gloried in their defence of western Christian civilisation and who had declared independence in the 'name of God'. Behind the text of this polemical statement the hand of the bishop of Umtali, the Carmelite Donal Lamont, could be clearly recognised. For many people, Lamont had turned into a herald for human rights, a promoter of social justice in Southern Rhodesia. Others, on the contrary, saw in him a dangerous and pro-Communist agitator, who had just confirmed their worst prejudices about the kind of conflictive temperament with which every Irish person seems to be gifted.

The countries of the southern part of the African continent were, at that time, a genuine political hotbed. Northern Rhodesia, changed to Zambia, had obtained independence in 1964, and two years after that Nyasaland did the same, now to be called Malawi. The third colony, that up to 1963 had made up the Federation of Rhodesia and Nyasaland, Southern Rhodesia, remained in the hands of the white colonisers who in 1965 made a unilateral declaration of its independence from Great Britain. Namibia, converted after the First World War into a South African trust, fought for independence, which the United Nations decreed in 1966, thus ending the trust, which, however, South Africa was not willing to concede. Mozambique was a tinderbox ever since the assassination the previous year of the leader of their liberation movement, Eduardo Mondlane. Meanwhile, South Africa still applied its particular policy of apartheid, or 'separate development', as its ideologues liked to call it, by means of a legislative body that imposed racial segregation with an iron hand in all areas of society, with the connivance of the Dutch Reform Church. African nationalism was flourishing in every corner, giving rise to a generation of young people who, feeling discouraged in the face of the failure of the integrationist postures of their predecessors, and convinced that non-violent means had proved ineffective, were advocating a more radical approach and had organised into armed bands who performed acts of sabotage. The armed wing of the African National Congress (ANC), called Umkhonto we Sizwe ('The Nation's Lance'), was joined by other groups such as SWAPO of Namibia and FRELIMO of Mozambique. Bits of news of their activities reached the solitary prison on Robben Island with considerable difficulty. That little island from where on the horizon there is a view of the beautiful mountains that surround Cape Town had become the prison of the leaders of the ANC. Here, there was a concentration, in great part, of the black political activism of the south of the continent, imprisoned for their illegal activities. There, prisoner number 466, nicknamed Madiba, in the solitude of his cold cell, was developing into one of the most significant political leaders of the twentieth century, the future President of South Africa, Nelson Rolihlahla Mandela.

Almost a quarter of a century had gone by since the young Carmelite, Donal Lamont, arrived for the first time in Africa. In those almost twenty-five years he had lived through one of the most turbulent and also stimulating periods on the African continent. He arrived having left the cold of Ireland, and encountered an Africa full of hope as it rebuilt after the effects of the Second World War. Under his sharp eye he saw the crumbling of the colonial system and the gradual emergence of a new Africa. He contemplated with some concern the triumph of Afrikaner nationalism in the neighbouring South Africa, and the ascent of every kind of African nationalism. He followed with great interest and concern the evolution of political events in a Southern Rhodesia whose government's behaviour was looking more and more like that of the neighbouring South Africa. Yet worse was still to come: his trial, condemnation and deportation, which would catapult him decisively to international notoriety.

When the bishops of Southern Rhodesia wrote *A Crisis of Conscience* the Catholic Church's stance had changed considerably. The decidedly racist policy that was being imposed by the government of Ian Smith had pushed the Church into moving from diplomacy to confrontation. With differing nuances, the Church in the surrounding countries had adopted similar positions. However, when in 1959 Lamont published his first Pastoral Letter entitled *Purchased People*, things were different. Then the question was no longer, 'Could the State survive without the support of the Church?' but rather, 'Could the Church survive and carry out its mission if it clashed with the State?' In the face of a government that appeared to ignore the legitimate aspirations of the African people and deny even their most basic rights, should the Church come out in the open even though that would suppose a confrontation with the State, or might it be more convenient to opt for prudence and caution? This was the difficult dilemma the Church had to resolve at that time.

Up until then the Catholic Church had lived in peaceful harmony with the State. The publication of *Purchased People* marked a clear change of direction in the relations between the Church and the government of Southern Rhodesia, a change with which not all the bishops were in agreement. This change however, as time went on, became the only means of witnessing to Christian faith and maintaining the credibility of the Church in those very difficult social and political circumstances. Here we see the importance of this document. In it we find a list of all the crucial questions with which the Church would have to deal in the years to follow: nationalism, education, the problem of the ownership of the land and the working conditions of the African workers, the dangerous rise of Communism and Church–State relations. On all these issues Lamont's opinion is expressed with frankness and clarity. Later on he himself would acknowledge that his opinion matured because of the two experiences that most decisively marked his service as a bishop: the Second Vatican Council and the Synod of Bishops in 1971. The first of these opened him to an international dimension that gave him a new perspective on the situation in Rhodesia, and led to a revision of his positions in the crucible of the council teaching.[2]

Referring to what it meant to him to belong to the Secretariat for Christian Unity he wrote,

> Here again the seminal ideas of religious liberty and racism, with their correlative problems of the relationship between Church and State and the rights of racial groups and religious and political minorities, matured in my mind and much influenced my thinking in relation to Rhodesia.[3]

In the Synod of Bishops of 1971, he coined his notorious description of Rhodesia as a 'political absurdity, a State without a nation',[4] giving shape to one of his deepest held convictions: that the work for justice is a constitutive dimension of the preaching of the Gospel. Despite this evolution, however, we have to recognise that we are dealing with a man of great intellectual coherence and vitality. Formulated sometimes in the categories of a pre-conciliar ecclesiology and expressed in a language that at times appears inadequate to us today, the theological fabric that lies beneath that first Pastoral Letter persists with extraordinary continuity throughout the whole of his life.

A grasp of the ecclesial, political and social coordinates within which Lamont carried out his ministry as a bishop is essential to get inside this vital and intellectual approach to life. Therefore, in looking at the ecclesial and theological significance of *Purchased People*, we should not lose sight of the fact that the person of Donal Lamont did not emerge in isolation. It has to be seen in the context of church leaders who questioned, with the Gospel in their hands, the unjust racist policies of some colonial regimes. In the neighbouring South Africa, Bishop Denis Hurley symbolised the more committed face of the Catholic Church in the fight against racial discrimination imposed by the system of apartheid.[5] Hurley took up the baton from Francis Hennemann, the only bishop who beforehand had shown his opposition to the segregationist policies of the South African government.[6] Along with these two, there were others, such as the Anglicans Trevor Hudleston and Michael Scott and within a short time along came the young bishop called Desmond Mpilo Tutu.[7] These were at the head of a long list of Christians who, convinced by the incompatibility between racism and Christian faith, engaged in a struggle to bring about a Gospel vision of human coexistence. Without doubt Hurley and Lamont represented more than any the commitment of the Catholic Church in the fight against racism. We might say that what Hurley was to South Africa, Lamont was to Zimbabwe. Against both of them there was the accusation of politicising the Church. However, as Lamont would say, quoting ironically his old professors of philosophy, there would be much to say about that (*disputatur inter auctores*).[8] A closer look at his reflections and his behaviour will allow us to see that behind his episcopal teaching, there was nothing other than the deepest apostolic commitment of a pastor who was capable of bringing that commitment to serve the Church to its ultimate extreme.

THE IMPERIAL DREAM OF CECIL RHODES AND THE ORIGINS OF THE CATHOLIC CHURCH IN SOUTHERN RHODESIA

When the young Carmelite missionary, Donal Lamont, arrived in Southern Rhodesia in November 1946, he found a church in the thick of a process of transformation, to which he would contribute in no small measure. In its little more than half century of existence, Catholicism in this country had acquired an interesting past. The result was a Catholic Church that was predominantly British. The Jesuits were the dominant force. There was a very clear division between the city and the rural areas and its origins were merged with the origins of the Nation. The beginnings went back to the last two decades of the nineteenth century. It was the time of the confrontation, to the south of the Limpopo river, between the Boers and the British. Just like what happened in neighbouring South Africa, the discovery of gold and diamonds had kindled the anti-annexationist anxieties of Great Britain and the greed of the British magnate Cecil Rhodes, who at that time had succeeded in gaining control of the diamond mines in Kimberley, in the Orange republic, founded by the Boers. Having become prime minister of the Colony of the Cape, and wanting to fulfil his great imperialist dream of constructing one vast colonial empire that would extend from the Cape of Good Hope to Cairo, he invested his large fortune in the dream. With a mixture of greed, energy and romantic notions that were the backbone of Victorian capitalism and of which Rhodes was a perfect example, he projected in 1890 an expedition of two hundred Europeans who would penetrate to the north of the Limpopo river. That pioneering column would procure a colony for the British, at a price that was cheap, and give them an important imperial ballast against the growing power of the Boers republics in the South, with whom the Empire had a very tense relationship which would be resolved afterwards in the tragic Boer War (1899–1902),[9] and for him it would render some very generous benefits, since with questionable cleverness he had managed to get from the Ndebele King Lobengula the mining rights on the territory of the Machonas and Matabeles, and from England, the permission to take over the government in the vast territory that extended from north of the river Limpopo as far as the great lakes of Central Africa. Strangely this son of a pastor of the Church of England chose a small group of Jesuits as his companions on the expedition, which would amount to the third attempt by the disciples of St Ignatius of Loyola to evangelise the region.[10] Even though the previous two had ended in total failure, Rhodes had to confess a deep admiration for that group of twelve intrepid missionaries who a few years before that had carried out their missionary work with such tenacity that neither the death of ten of them for a lack of quinine, nor the disappointment of not getting even one conversion made them draw back from their intent. The great feats of those British Jesuits were seen, by one with the grit and temperament of Rhodes, as of such magnitude that their story had become his best loved bedtime reading. Only thus can we explain that there was no one better than the Jesuits, for whom Rhodes had such an enormous regard, to accompany the expedition.

In this very singular way the story of the Catholic Church in Southern Rhodesia began, thanks to the work of the Jesuits and as part of the transplantation by Rhodes of the capitalist model of society to the territories north of the Limpopo. This fact marked the future of a Catholic Church that did not take long to consolidate its position as the Church of the establishment, not very far behind the Anglican Church. Catholicism had reached Southern Rhodesia, coming from the colony of the Cape, but it did so in circumstances that were much more advantageous than what it had to endure in South Africa. There, the Catholic Church was forbidden up to 1837, and after that it could develop only in a very hostile Protestant environment.[11] With a non-English speaking clergy, its liturgy in Latin, and rites that were alien to the Protestant world, the Catholic Church continued to be considered as a foreign church. Hence the assertion of Ian Linden, 'The territory of Zimbabwe was in some way the clerical frontier of the counter-reform.'[12]

Those first Jesuits saw the coming of reinforcements with the arrival of the priests of Marianhill in 1896. This religious Order was an offshoot of the Trappist monastery of Marianhill on the East Cape.[13] As these latter concentrated on the rural missions, the followers of St Ignatius remained in the capital where they opened St George, a school for European children, the aim of which was defined as follows: 'to establish in this corner of the Empire the traditions that form an English gentleman so dear to Mister Rhodes'.[14] The Jesuits counted on being able to have an influence on Rhodesia through the education of white children, convinced as they were that the Christianisation of the country would come about through the government by white paternalists who would use the power of the State against the excessive demands of the immoral colonisers.

The new directives laid out in the apostolic letter, *Maximum Illud* (1919) and the encyclical *Rerum Ecclesiae* (1926) calling for the training of indigenous clergy and the creation of new vicariates and prelatures brought about an acceleration of the missionary endeavour. The apostolic letter *Congregatio Missionarum* established Bulawayo as an independent mission entrusted to the Marianhill Fathers and *Compertum Habemus* converted the remaining part of the Zambesi mission into the apostolic vicariate of Salisbury which remained in the care of the British Jesuit Ashton Chichester who in 1934 founded the seminary of Chishawasha for the formation of native clergy.

In the meantime, in the political sphere, Rhodesia was trying to resolve the question of whether to become part of the South

African Union that had been set up in 1910 or opt for self-government. Wanting to distance themselves from, as they thought, the retrograde Boers and wanting to be free of the control of the British Company, the European colonisers were seen to be in favour of self-government in the referendum of 1922. Southern Rhodesia was annexed by Great Britain, with a *sui generis* status of 'colonial self-government', in which the British Government reserved to itself control of the appointment of the Commissioner for Native Affairs and the right to veto the passing of discriminatory laws. In addition, through a tribunal of imperial appeal, it provided missionaries with an instrument with which to try to moderate the kind of policies that were designed to favour exclusively the interests of the colonisers.

One of Chichester's greatest achievements was the recruitment of missionaries from abroad. The Bethlehem Fathers from Switzerland were the first. They were joined by a group from Burgos belonging to the Spanish Institute for Foreign Missions (El Instituto Español de Misiones Extranjeras – IEME),[15] and the first Carmelites, among whom was Donal Lamont. Their arrival coincided with the first three ordinations of African priests trained in the seminary of Chishawasha. That first missionary sap changed, in no small measure, the profile of the Church, letting it become a pluralist society that had no natural reason to want to give uncritical support to the 'English way of life' that was determining the values that dominated the country. Two qualities meant that Lamont would soon be seen as the most relevant personality in the new ecclesial setting. The first was that he had a deep and critical knowledge of British culture that gave him the ability to take care of himself in the environment of the British Jesuit hegemony, at the same time that it allowed him to identify the less friendly aspects of the British hegemony. His studies in English literature were a great help in this regard. The second quality was that he had strong moral courage, backed up by an imposing physical presence. All of this meant that he was a man who would be hard to intimidate, a mark, no doubt, that his time in Terenure College would have left upon his character, which would come to the fore when necessity called.[16]

A British Gentleman facing an Irish Bishop.
The Church between the Prudence of Aston Chichester
and the Forthrightness of Donal Lamont.

If anybody symbolised what the Catholic Church in Southern
Rhodesia in the first half-century of its existence was like, it was
without doubt the British Jesuit Aston Chichester. Under his
stewardship the evolution that Ian Linden portrays as the
transition from a mission of the Society of Jesus to a British Jesuit
Church was consolidated.[17] Described as a gentleman and a true
Englishman, a typical product of the English province of the
Society of Jesus and a likely candidate for bishop from the
moment of his conception, Chichester had governed the Church
with a style that was very different to what would be seen in
Lamont.[18] In his twenty-five years in charge of what was first
the Vicariate and then the diocese of Salisbury (1931–1956) he
vigorously defended the position of the Church against the
State. He always did that, however, with the characteristic
British *savoir faire*, overcoming obstacles through private personal
conversations with the secretary or with the minister in charge at
that time. Chichester liked to go to the Salisbury Club and rub
shoulders with the people that counted in colonial society,
convinced, as a good British gentleman, that diplomacy is always
the best strategy.[19] Not without reason, when offering his New
Year greetings in 1935 to the German Provincial he recommended
that the German Jesuits who were about to head for Rhodesia
should spend time in England first:

> For your Fathers to merely speak English is not sufficient; they
> have to understand the English mind. Hence I believe a sojourn
> in England for some little time would add to the fruits of their
> apostolate … for successful work among the natives the
> sympathetic consideration and the cooperation of the English
> officials are a great help.[20]

When, in the course of one of the sessions of the Second Vatican
Council, he died suddenly on the steps of St Peter's, Lamont in
his funeral eulogy praised him by saying, 'the best blood of old
Catholic England ran in his veins'.[21]

Chichester's British diplomacy had very little in common with the direct and forthright temperament of Donal Lamont. A story that Ian Linden tells illustrates their very different pastoral styles. While Chichester to begin a speech would joke about his disagreements with the government, praise the Land Husbandry Act and add an admonition saying that all properly understood authority comes from God, Lamont would begin in a way that would mark him out as a rebel, by saying, 'Seeing as every Irishman is opposed to whatever kind of government there is …' and thereby distance himself completely from his audience.[22] Chichester was the epitome of paternalistic language. The last years of his episcopate were marked by a considerable degree of harmony between Church and State, due mostly to the change in the government ideology that had moved from one of so-called racialism to one of partnership between the races.

The idea of publishing a joint pastoral letter on civil rights did not go down well with either Archbishop Markall who succeeded Chichester as Archbishop of Salisbury, or with the Apostolic Delegate. Markall followed the line taken by Chichester, not to put pressure on questions relating to racial relations (or not bulldozing in matters of race relations). The bishops of Southern Rhodesia, who had close relations with their counterparts in South Africa were aware of the difficulties of developing the work of evangelisation, under the suspicious eye of the government. Not without reason the South African President, Daniel F. Malan, with an eye to the Catholic Church, had approved the Statement to Parliament, declaring that 'it would not recognise the rights of those groups that would question the principles of apartheid, and would preach equality, or foreign ideologies'.[23] The so-called 'Roman danger' (*Die Roomse gevaar*) along with the 'black danger' and the 'Communist danger' formed the triplet of declared enemies of the South African government. A comparison with what was happening in neighbouring South Africa led Markall to a very positive appreciation of the relevant position and respect that the Catholic Church held among the white population in Rhodesia, and on that basis the Church could exercise a considerable influence, thanks to which the work of the apostolate could be seen as being greatly unhindered. As Markall had said to the Apostolic Delegate, any attack on the State could 'weaken the Church's credibility'. Credibility is the soul of diplomacy.[24]

What Archbishop Markall probably did not see were the inevitable negative consequences of continuing to maintain close relationships with the government and the risk that the Church, in the context of growing African nationalism, might be seen as an integral part of the imperial hegemony that was so seriously being brought into question. To hold on to such an attitude could have disastrous consequences for the missionary work of the Church among the Africans. Things had changed greatly in the last number of years. The missionary strategy devised by Chichester that had given such positive results in the years before the Second World War could now prove to be counter-productive. In the African community a very strong nationalistic spirit was rising that was demanding a greater share in political structures and an improvement in economic and social conditions.

The first paragraphs of the pastoral instruction reveal the tension between the two options. Lamont seemed determined:

> Preach the Bishop must; not permitting himself to be silenced by merely human fears or temporal considerations; not watering down his message for the sake of spurious peace, or loss of friendship with any worldly authority, or possibility of being deliberately misinterpreted by wicked men.[25]

It is not difficult to detect here a veiled rebuke of the British-minded Church that opts for caution, and the Apostolic Delegate, described by Linden as, 'the Church of silence that was centred in Salisbury and Pretoria'.[26]

The words of Lamont reflect his very clear awareness of the transcendental change of context that was taking shape in Rhodesian society. He had a very clear perception of the new world order that was emerging, based on the principle of multiracialism. In the pastoral letter there is a reference to 'the challenge of a changing world in which the barriers of space and time have so rapidly been broken down that men of different nations and of different racial origins are brought more quickly and more closely together than ever before'.[27] He goes on to illustrate his vision of the situation in Rhodesia in which the future was being prepared for an interracial community: 'Times have changed. The gruff inflexible paternalism which the European has exercised over the African for so long, must be modified and relaxed. It was useful while it lasted, but it has had its day.'[28] Lamont suggests what in the language of the time was called a 'benevolent paternalism'. Beginning with the pre-supposition of seeing African people as 'minors' in terms of age, but bearing in mind their legitimate desire for independence, this approach is characterised by gentle and kindly guidance by the white minority, which would allow the African community to reach adulthood.

African Nationalism and the Communist Threat

Purchased People was written in the complex environment of a growing African nationalism and the fear of Communist infiltration. We are on the threshold of the explosion of independence movements in Africa. As Lamont recalls, 'the first notable signs of nationalism began to appear at the end of the Second World War'.[29] One of the effects of the war on the African continent was the speeding up of the expansion of anti-colonialist feeling. In the new environment that emerged after the conflict, the allied powers debated the future of Africa. The US thought that an imprudent continuation of the colonial regime could end up throwing Africa into the arms of Communism as had already happened in South East Asia. The President of the United States of America, Franklin D. Roosevelt, had already insisted, when in 1941 he met secretly with Winston Churchill to agree the Atlantic Treaty, on including among the objectives of the Treaty, the commitment to guarantee self-determination to all the colonial territories. Winston Churchill, clever as ever, did not fail to notice that behind the American enthusiasm for self-determination there lay, in the best of cases, the economic interest of a country that was experiencing an extraordinary development in terms of technology, industry, and finance, and in the worst case, the secret hope of finally doing away with the British Empire. On his return to England, Churchill put it to the House that the application of that clause had to be restricted to the European nations that were under the yoke of Nazism, but in no way should it apply to the British colonies. These declarations, however, proved to be counter-productive. Without any desire to do so, they gave new energy to the anti-colonial movements. As J. Reader affirms, 'Churchill, unwittingly, had given a common cause to the emerging African political organisations.'[30] At that time it was becoming very clear that the days of imperial power in Africa were numbered, since Britain's two principal allies, the US and Russia, had already decided, though their political philosophies were diametrically opposed, to end colonialism on the continent.

The century, indeed, had begun with an energetic cultural and political movement of African renaissance on both sides of the Atlantic. The African continent was aflame with a new desire for identity and firm opposition to the vision for Africa that the West had developed during the colonial era. The Senegalese poet, Leopold Senghor had coined the term, 'négritude', reclaiming the black man's history and traditions. In the English-speaking world, and by way of parallel with the French-speaking culture of négritude put out by Senghor and Aimé Cesaire, the concept of African personality was surfacing. Further adding to these two movements, we find the Pan-African inspiration of William E. Du Bois, Frederick Douglas or Booker T. Washington. Pan-Africanism had arisen in the Afro-American world at the beginning of the twentieth century as a primarily cultural movement which offered a response to the imperialistic dream of Cecil Rhodes with a vision of something like a United States of Africa.

The first expressions of nascent African nationalism in the southern part of the continent appeared early in the process. In 1912 the South African National Congress was founded in South Africa. In time this would become the African National Congress (ANC). The organisation came into being as a reaction to the exclusion of the Africans from the recently formed South African Union, which denied them the right to vote. Coinciding with the Paris Peace Conference in 1919, a Pan-African Congress was held in Paris in which the participants expressed their desire for greater participation in African affairs. The idea of self-government had been in the air ever since the victorious regimes of the First World War had set up the 'trusts' in the Treaty of Versailles.

In that first stage African nationalism opted for an assimilation approach, with the aim of gaining greater representation for blacks in the parliamentary system. To a great extent the germ of their political aspirations of equality lay in the Christian values they had learned at the mission schools, which later became the driving force behind their non-violent resistance that was founded on a Christian ethic. As the South African theologian J. de Gruchy wrote, the principles adopted by the African National Congress were an affirmation of the Christian liberal values that were taught in the mission schools.[31] Not without reason, among the leaders the names of fervent Christians appear.[32] Still, in 1959 the nationalist movement was largely Christian in terms of its leadership and inspiration.

However, a second generation was developing. The failure of the non-violent approach and the conviction that the white community would never consent to the much desired integration of the black population inspired a young generation of black militants, that included the promising young South African lawyer Nelson Mandela, to change the direction of African nationalism towards a more radical form of militancy. In the event, a new era for African nationalism began, as the era of the nationalism of the masses. The most radical form of Pan-Africanism began to gain new followers. Just two months before the publication of *Purchased People* the foundation of the South African Pan-African Congress had taken place under the leadership of Robert Sobukve.

Under the name 'African Nationalism' there were two distinct currents. The more extreme, inspired by Marcus Garvey, had as its motto, 'Africa for the Africans'. This group advocated a racial exclusivism expressed in the battle cry, 'Throw the whites into the sea'. The more moderate group worked for a multiracialism of the kind that was formulated in the famous 'Letter of Freedom'. With regard to his own position, when the African National Congress Youth League was set up in 1944, Nelson Mandela recalled,

> There were people who said that a nationalism that would be capable of including white people who were supportive of the cause would be the more desirable choice. Others, and I was

among them, countered by saying, if the Africans were offered a multiracial form of campaign they would still be overshadowed by the whites because of feeling inferior. At that time I was truly opposed to the inclusion of whites and Communists in the League ... I believed that what would get freedom for us was a pure form of African Nationalism, not Marxism and not a multiracial movement.[33]

In Southern Rhodesia the growing discontent of both rural and urban populations led in 1955 to the creation of the Southern Rhodesian African National Congress. In nearby Nyasaland (present-day Malawi) the African National Congress reached the not inconsiderable figure of one hundred and fifty thousand militants. The reaction of the white community was divided between the liberals who maintained the need for urgent reforms and those who saw a potential danger in the advance of the Africans. At the time when Donal Lamont wrote his letter, a new electoral law was being debated. The reluctance of the white community to extend the right to vote to the African community clashed with the feeling in the black population, captured in the cry, 'We want freedom NOW'. The conflict was a sign of a complicated political future in Southern Rhodesia.

As Ian Linden stated, even the missionary living in isolation could not but be aware of the dramatic changes that were taking place on the continent. Nationalism could no longer be considered a fleeting aberration.[34] The Church maintained a position of support for multiracialism and this became stronger as time went on. For the majority of whites however, multi-racialism was a dangerous road, with a veneer of Gospel, promoted by people with not a whole lot of common sense. Against this background and in the face of an episcopate that was reluctant to make open pronouncements and show its cards in public, Bishop Lamont gave a clear indication of his courage by revealing sincerely and clearly his opinion regarding the controversial African Nationalist Movement at that time. As a young man Lamont came to know the legitimate desire of a people to achieve independence. As he himself wrote, 'The establishment of the Irish Free State meant a turning point for the lives of many of us who supported the nationalist cause.'[35] Ireland was the first British colony and the one that was treated more harshly than any other. This gave Lamont his understanding of what it meant to be colonised and this broke through in his theological thinking when he came to talk about the questions of Rhodesia.[36] However, as we noted earlier, his contact with Nazism had given him a sense of the excesses to which nationalist feelings can lead. That would help him to hold a balanced position between the recognition of the legitimate aspirations of the African population and the rejection of every kind of exclusive nationalism that would only foment racial hatred under whatever sign it might appear. Regarding his statements in *Purchased People* concerning African Nationalism, Lamont said some time later, 'I wrote that twenty years ago. It seems still appropriate today.'[37] Two decades had passed and African Nationalism had evolved considerably, but his arguments, he maintained, were still as valid as ever.

A new element complicated even more the panorama of African Nationalism: its link with the so-called 'Communist threat'. The emergence and consolidation of the movements that campaigned for independence coincided in terms of time with the growth of the Soviet Union as a world power. As J. Reader notes, it was inevitable that these two movements would interact in some way and that one would strengthen the other, at least in theory. On the one hand, for the Soviet bloc, Africa offered a fertile ground for the expansion of Communism. On the other hand, the expansion of Marxist thinking and Communist praxis gave an intellectual impulse to anti-colonialism at a time when the Soviet Union appeared as the great example of the dismantling of an oppressive regime.[38] The Cold War had found in the African setting an attractive ground in which to carry on its battles.

The threat of Communist hegemony spread like a shadow over many countries on the African continent. Nevertheless Communism was not the kind of ideology that would be immediately attractive to the African population. Nelson Mandela expressed very roundly in his memoirs: 'We distrust Communism very much.'[39] As we saw in the words of Mandela quoted earlier, the African National Congress rejected an ideology it considered foreign and inadequate in terms of resolving the situation of the African people. They did not trust a white left wing that, in their eyes, could divert them from the main problem in hand – racial discrimination. Furthermore, as United Nations research in Africa concluded, 'every time that there was competition and confrontation between ethnicity and class consciousness, ethnicity invariably won out in Africa'.[40]

The white community mostly shared the view that African nationalism was nothing more than Communist ideology dressed up as something else. The worry of the Catholic Church was that the Communists would exploit any racial conflict there might be in the Federation. Lamont expressed, on this point, the same idea that was held by his counterparts in South Africa: firstly, a very definite rejection of Communist ideology, secondly, the conviction that the best way to combat Communism was to create more just working conditions and social conditions for the non-white population. If anything else were to happen, it would provide a breeding ground for the movement of the black population towards Communist ideology. Here we encounter one of the fundamental theological points that lies behind the document, that is, taking God out of public life leads to a dangerous distortion of social relations, meaning that they may no longer be governed by the most basic principles of justice. In other words, secularisation was the root of the ills and the danger that affected society in Southern Rhodesia.

'UT PLACEAM DEO'
PLEASING GOD UNDER THE YOKE OF RACIALISM

In the complex transition from the colonial system to the new African nations the Carmelite Lamont chose the expression, *Ut placeam Deo* as his episcopal motto. He had entered the episcopate fortified by three valuable tools that allowed him to carry out his firm intention to please God rather than people; his knowledge of what was happening, the result of nearly a decade of working as a missionary; his background in social ethics; and his experience of the darker face of the racist ideology in the face of Nazism. It wasn't the first time therefore that Lamont had to confront the problem of racism. As Fernando Millán reminded us in his address, one of the experiences that marked the life of the young Carmelite very clearly was his experience when still a student in Rome (1933–9) of the dramatic rise of Nazism and of Fascism. Talking about the impact this had on his life he said that it 'warned me for the rest of my life against the danger of State worship or the worship of political leaders'.[41]

The defence of freedom of conscience and the rights of the human person before the State was one of the convictions, formed in the crucible of advancing Nazi ideology, that would be with him for the whole of his life and one that he would apply to what was happening in Southern Rhodesia:

> I had experienced in my young manhood the tragedies of State absolutism, of blind following of political figures. I was convinced that the old moral and paternalistic concept of the State should be replaced by a juridical and constitutional one in which the true subject of politics is the human person, the citizen.[42]

These words reflect what he had learned from his German director during his time in Rome: that the centre of the teaching of the Catholic Church is the human person with all his rights, and this is the key to the understanding of the social and political rights of every human person.[43] The proclamation of the freedom of the Church and the centrality of the person as the nucleus and hearer of the Gospel message constituted a reaction to the German theology of *Volkskirche* (people's Church) that talked about the people (*Volk*) as the recipients of the Christian mission, linking faith to ethnic heritage and to the bonds of blood, and which so dangerously had been brought into South Africa by the reformed theologians of the Dutch Reformed church and used as a theological basis for the justification of apartheid.

His knowledge of social ethics also became evident in the document. Beginning from the compendium of Catholic social teaching of the Austrian neo-Thomist, Johannes Messner,[44] Lamont argued from the scholastic distinction between fundamental rights and secondary, contingent or derivative rights. The bishops of South Africa in their *Statement on Race Relations* in 1952 held the same line by affirming the existence of fundamental and inviolable rights, which include the following:

the right to life, dignity, subsistence, the exercise of religious beliefs, integrity, the use and exercise of the faculties of the individual, work and its produce, private property and well-being, freedom of permanence and freedom of movement, marriage, the protection and education of offspring, and freedom of association.[45]

Along with these there is another set of rights that are considered to be secondary and less essential that spring from the social nature of the human person. Among these we find the right to vote, to receive state aid for education and the right to a pension. The State cannot refuse to recognise the essential rights of the human person nor arbitrarily limit the rights of a citizen. Its mission, rather, is to create and maintain the most favourable conditions for the exercise of human rights. The State must provide for the African population the possibility of gaining access gradually to full and effective participation in the political, social and economic life of their own country. This is the logic that lies behind Lamont's argument.

The third tool that helped the Irish Carmelite in his work as a bishop was his pastoral experience over a period of ten years. It made him aware of the hardness of the people's life, always having to deal with the reigning racism of the white population in Rhodesia. The problem became even more serious when it became apparent that this same racism had got inside the Catholic Church. Despite the fact of its official multiracial stance, Lamont expresses his surprise and sadness at finding how ecclesiastical segregation was a common practice in the white Catholic community.[46] That posed a difficult question for him: the problem of church segregation which was a clear denial of Church unity. In other words, racism was now a theological and ecclesiological problem.

The great legacy of the theologian Yves Congar includes a small work, written in 1953, as a response to a request by UNESCO, dealing with the Church and the racial question.[47] It was one of the very few occasions in which a Catholic theologian had written ahead of time a theological study of racism, against a background in which the social teaching of the Church stuck closely to the directives of the social teaching of Leo XIII and focused almost exclusively on the social and intellectual effects of liberal capitalism, and reactions to it, by studying questions such as working conditions for workers and the right to private property, with its individual and social aspects.[48] Two years afterwards the *L'Osservatore Romano* published an article denouncing the racial policy of the South African government as unjust and immoral. Something was changing in the Catholic mindset even though secularisation was still one of the biggest worries for the Church at that time. The Catholic vision in relation to nationalism and racialism found its most complete expression in the response of Pius XI to Nazism, written in his encyclical, *Mit brennender Sorge* (1937). We would have to wait for the Second Vatican Council for the Church to take up the question of racism again, in the new framework of relations between the Church and the Modern World, established by the pastoral constitution, *Gaudium et Spes*.[49]

As Lamont was preparing to write his first pastoral letter, racism was not among the chief theological concerns of the time. The attention that was given to the problem was indeed minor, apart from the concerns raised by the Nazi question. In that sense the publication of *Purchased People* was a milestone in the response of the Catholic Church to the racial question.[50] The first theological analysis of racism may be attributed to the pen of one of the pioneers of the ecumenical movement, the Briton, J.H. Oldham who in 1924 published a work with the title, *Christianity and the Race Problem*.[51] This work was an indication of the interest this question provoked even at the early stages of the ecumenical movement. However, it was the deep Church crisis brought on by the triumph of National Socialism that forced the Church to look at the problem of racism from the point of view of its deeper theological and ecclesiological dimensions.

National Socialism had put forward an ecclesiology of some depth: for the world it is fundamental to have a community that is universal in its essential nature and that overcomes all differences of race and nationality. The Church had to be seen to be above nationality and above race. The new movements committed to creating a new order reminded the Church of its prophetic mission in the world. In the Protestant world, the theological dialectic, led by Karl Barth, had reacted strongly to the theology of the *Volkskirche* that placed the Gospel message at the service of the ethnic values of a people, and had warned about the dangers of seeing National Socialism as a structuring element of the life of the Church. Pope Pius XI, for his part, had proclaimed that by reducing the great Christian principles to racial categories, Christianity was greatly diminished.

Lamont, who had first-hand knowledge of the rise of Nazism, no doubt took account of what that had taught him when he set about confronting the ruling racism in Southern Rhodesia. His thinking in this regard is original: his interpretation of racism in the framework of secularisation. In his vision, racism has to be analysed as part of a deeper problem: the secularisation of society. Taking God out of society means organising society in a way that ignores the fundamental teachings of Christian faith and is oblivious to the ideal of a social order based on the Christian principles of justice and charity.

Against the privatising view of religion proposed by the liberal wing, and in the face of those who would like to confine the activities of the Church to the limits of the sacristy, Lamont makes a claim for the right of the Church to intervene in political matters, to the extent that such matters affect the spiritual order of salvation. Identifying the sins of injustice, and among them the sin of racism, is part of the mission of the Church. That must mean, on occasions, getting involved in political, economic and social questions. This interpretation was sometimes questioned by a section of the white community who rallied under the banner of, 'Keep Religion out of Politics', and accused anyone who got involved in political matters of politicising the Church. The Anglican Bishop, Desmond Tutu, against whom the accusation was often made, had this to say about the incoherence of that kind of argument:

> There is a commentary that is heard so often that it has become like a nursery rhyme, 'Do not mix religion and politics'. But this kind of observation is not normally heard because a politician has included in his political manifesto some element of religion or morality. No, almost always, we hear it when some concrete action in social, economic or political life is criticised for being

counter to the Gospel of Jesus Christ. You will hear the politicians utter this cry, for example, when someone says that it is against Christian faith to neglect the development of the rural areas.[52]

An anecdote in Lamont's biography illustrates his deep conviction regarding the freedom of the Church in the face of any kind of external interference. When his prison sentence was commuted to deportation he appealed the sentence stating before the judge that he had been appointed by the Holy See to take care of the spiritual needs of the people of the diocese of Umtali and that in conscience he felt obliged to continue exercising that spiritual jurisdiction until the supreme authority of the Church and no other should take that responsibility from him. The freedom of the Church could not be put in question.

In addition to a serious ecclesiological problem, racism constituted for Lamont a theological problem of the first order. He is very firm on this point: Segregation has to be denounced because it denies our common origin and our common redemption.[53] This is the core of his theological argumentation in relation to racism. In his own words: 'This belief in our common membership of God's family, involves a daily and vivid realisation of the natural dignity of the human person.'[54] The doctrine of human fraternity under the fatherhood of God demands the recognition of the dignity of every human being and a brotherly and sisterly behaviour among all those who through the same baptism have become brothers and sisters in Christ.

LAND AND EDUCATION: THE LONGING OF EVERY AFRICAN
Without doubt, the almost ten years he spent in Southern Rhodesia up to then gave a man with the wit of Lamont a very clear perception of what was happening in Africa, which is evidence that no one knew the situation of the African people like the missionaries. Under the two headings *land* and *education*, the new bishop of Umtali summed up the deepest longings of every African, man or woman: 'Anyone who really knows the African and who seriously examines the cause of the present discontent, will always return to these essential needs, land and education.'[55]

The Work of the Church in Education

Education was one of the areas in which the growing tension between Church and State was becoming clearly evident. At the time of writing *Purchased People*, Lamont was at odds with the Secretary for African Education regarding the new Decree on Native Education, which set the State up as the only holder of authority regarding education. It was only the beginning of a conflict that was not only destined to last for a long time but also to become even more tense. This was no minor matter for the Church. The mission schools were not merely optional appendages to the work of the mission, but rather the cornerstone of all evangelisation strategy in the South of the African continent.[56] Denis Hurley was very clear about this: Catholic schools were a question of life and death.[57] The missionaries had discovered that in Africa the school is the most effective means of evangelisation. In fact, almost every Catholic in Rhodesia came from one of those schools.

In the 1920s Catholic missionaries had some one hundred primary schools. In the 1930s the Kutame Secondary School was opened and was run by the Marist Brothers. Following the common model in all the territories under British rule, where there was cooperation between Church and State, in the field of education the Church built the schools and recruited and trained the teachers while the State paid the salaries. The Church provided the people and the State provided the money in a project whose purpose was to transform society through school education and the creation of an African middle class through Catholic education. With State subsidies, the expansion of missionary work began to depend on government help. The government financed the mission schools but that implied an acceptance of government control. The colonial State did not show any sign of wanting to relinquish control of an education system that it broadly maintained. Reading the description that Lamont gave of the Church, reduced in the education mission 'to the condition of an emaciated and etiolated prisoner of the State',[58] there is something very prophetic in the words of the Jesuit, H. Colingridge in 1930, stating that in educational matters, the Church was turning into a financial prisoner of the State.[59]

South Africa had known a situation similar to that of Southern Rhodesia with the promulgation in 1953 of the Bantu Education Act. The new law of the South African government established that the control of black education, which was conducted at that time mainly in mission schools, was now to pass to the State and specifically to the Department of Native Affairs, responsible for racial policies. The Christian churches were aware that this promulgation responded to the interest of maintaining the social structure of apartheid. It was a question really of making education a tool of white supremacy, making sure that the black population would be identified with the roles assigned to them by apartheid, putting an end to education being delivered in mission schools, based on the premise that education is intended to prepare people in accordance with their opportunities in life and the sphere in which they find themselves, without creating false expectations. In reality, behind the passing of the law lay the old conflict that the Afrikaner community kept up with British missionaries who, in their eyes, taught their pupils dangerous values of justice and equality, aimed, not at 'separate development', but at the integrationist ideal so much in vogue among white liberals. However, taking on the government might mean the loss of all schools, since, by virtue of the new law, the Churches who decided to remain in control of their own schools would lose all government subsidies. This would place these schools in a very difficult economic situation that would threaten their survival.

Lamont was one of the bishops who was present at the meeting that the South African Bishops' Conference held in the spring of 1954 for the purpose of deciding on what strategy to follow. As Denis Hurley recalls, there was no agreement among the bishops on what to say and how to say it. The bishops were divided between those who, like him, believed that the Church should be seen to be more openly opposed to the government, and those who were proud of the traditional moderation the bishops always demonstrated in these matters. Aware of a more than predictable failure of negotiations with the government, Hurley came down on the side of not postponing a direct confrontation with the government, which was bound to happen sooner or later. Under the slogan, 'the sooner we clash, the better', Hurley argued that it was better to confront, while the moral standing of the Church was still intact. It is particularly significant that at that meeting, Lamont supported Hurley's position without reserve.[60] In the end Hurley's position held sway and the Catholic bishops, as distinct from the Anglican bishops, the majority of whom had caved in, chose to hold on to the control of their schools, thereby losing their State subsidies, and relying on the possible funding that they might receive from abroad. In 1959, when he wrote *Purchased People*, Bishop Lamont's South African counterparts were engaged in a genuine crusade in defence of the mission schools orchestrated by the semi-official newspaper of the Bishops' Conference, *The Southern Cross*. This newspaper had no doubt about portraying the campaign as an 'unprecedented example of interracial charity in a world that looked upon South Africa as the last bastion of racial discrimination'.[61]

The school was one of the places where the Church expressed more visibly and more concisely its racial understanding. Its option for what were called the 'native schools' had signified from the time of the arrival of the first catholic missionaries to the coast of Southern Africa the commitment of the Church to the African people. Education was also the key to testing the real commitment of the government to the African people. The distance between our comprehension of what was then called the 'racial question' and what was true at the time Lamont wrote *Purchased People*, requires a brief explanation, but not without first noting that the vision that our bishop presents coincides with what the South African bishops had said in the *Statement on Race Relations* of 1952, to which we alluded earlier. From the point of view that today has been superseded, and strongly questioned by cultural anthropology, *Purchased People* speaks about people of 'differing cultures', or about 'two races at different points of development', or they are referred to as 'children', that have not yet reached maturity. It is that situation of inequality in the levels of development that justifies that some of the 'secondary' rights were not granted automatically.

However, natural law imposes the obligation to behave within the parameters, as we noted already, of what in the language of the time was known as 'benevolent colonialism', which exercises a caring power that favours the development of people and allows for their progressive incorporation into economic and political life. Lamont quotes the words of Pius XII claiming that people cannot be denied proper political freedom, and neither can any obstacle be put in its way. Lamont was unmovable on this point: 'It is sheer deceit to talk of giving political equality to all races, if they are not given first of all, at least the educational opportunity which will enable them ultimately to qualify for the vote.'[62] He referred to the obstructionist practices of the government in hindering access to education for African children (not granting licences to open new schools, higher costs, shortage of secondary schools). The Carmelite bishop appealed to the State to exercise a distributive justice in this matter, by granting the same opportunities to the children of the European colonisers and to the African children: 'Basic justice involves equality of opportunity for all citizens, irrespective of race or colour or creed.'[63]

The education question was also one of the areas in which the Church showed very firmly the freedom of the Church in the face of government interference. This firm will on the part of the bishops to preserve the freedom of the Church in the work of evangelisation was shown in the same way in the case of South Africa. In the words of South African Archbishop, Denis Hurley:

> The decision taken by the bishops in relation to the schools was not a decision against apartheid. It was a decision against a legislation that made it extremely difficult for the Church to maintain its schools. It was more a fight for religious freedom than for human rights.[64]

Lamont showed this same reaction towards a Church whose freedom was being restricted. In the pastoral letter he denounced State interference in the educational endeavour of the Church in these terms: 'In particular, by exercising such radical control over African education, the State grievously obstructs a very important aspect of the missionary activity of the Church, and this is a most serious matter.'[65]

ACCESS TO THE LAND AND MATERIAL CONDITIONS

On the day of his ordination as a bishop, Donal Lamont surprised his audience by referring to the main reason for African discontent: hunger for land and the inhuman living conditions of the urban African population, who had been forced to leave the land and move to the cities to find paid employment. It is no wonder that it was one of the questions that received special attention in *Purchased People*.

In his excellent history of Christianity in the African continent, Charles Groves mentions the important meaning which the question of land and labour had acquired in Africa. The white colonisers were judged on the basis of their performance in these two areas because the colonial policy in no other matter could be seen so clearly for what it was than in the use that the colonial administrations made of their power over the land.[66] To the extent that Christian faith was associated with the Europeans its performance in these two questions was key to the success or otherwise of the missionary endeavour.

The question of dispossession or ownership of the land was one of the great unresolved questions of colonial Africa. In the case of countries with intense European colonisation, like Rhodesia, South Africa or Kenya, the Africans were forced to hand over their land and then end up being employed as cheap labour on the farms or in the factories. The impoverishment of the African farmers forced a great number of them to seek work far from home. One of the worst consequences of the urbanisation of African workers was the distortion and division it created in families. It wasn't easy to apply Catholic teaching on property in a context in which this question was complicated by the question about the morality of the acquisition or the legitimacy of the occupation.

In Southern Rhodesia the debate around land and labour, with all its paternalistic protection language, took on the form of opposition between policies of 'assimilation' and policies of 'segregation'. The former were equivalent to the proletarianisation of Africans, unprotected in the white economic dominion. The latter could be interpreted as the maintenance of tribal authority and the safeguarding of the Africans in reservations.

The missionaries sometimes opted for the protection that the reservations offered when they saw the awful conditions in which people lived in the urban suburbs. During their first decades of work the Jesuit missionaries had strengthened the farming area through the creation of self-sufficient Christian farming communities. Following the model of the reductions in Paraguay, a settlement was created in Chishawasha close to Salisbury that soon became a symbol of what the Church was trying to do for the Africans: an ideal society in which whites and blacks would live together in a relationship of paternal benevolence that would unite the material fruits of farming with the spiritual fruits of divine grace. Chishawasha represented, in this sense, an interesting example of the adaptation of the reduction strategy to the continent of Africa.

The Marianhill Fathers had also contributed to the agricultural development of the African people. The social teaching of Leo XIII and Pius XI inspired the formation of the Catholic African Union (CAU), founded by the Marianhill Fathers, who under the banner, 'better fields, better houses, better hearts' focused on farming through the formation of cooperatives and in facilitating access to credit for the African population.

The Decree of Land Adjudication of 1931 was the culmination of the colonisers' efforts to force the segregated occupation of the land, to deny the African people the right to acquire land outside the reservations and to prevent any kind of competition from the African farmers. The Catholic Church kept silent on that occasion even though Archbishop Chichester stated a little later in a pastoral letter, 'Catholic justice and charity do not differentiate in the smallest degree between European and Native. In the presence of God every living human soul is equal.'[67] Lamont expressed his doubts about the morality and honesty of the governing minority acquiring the most fertile land and the greater part of the land.[68]

The increase in the demand for raw materials during the Second World War had contributed to the transition from a merchant capitalism to an industrial capitalism. The manufacturing industry grew considerably as did the wage-earning population. This process was strengthened by significant increases in foreign investments which in consideration of the rise of African Nationalism in 1948 in South Africa, began to be invested in Southern Rhodesia. The economic boom attracted a wave of European immigration and again pushed the African population into the townships or into the over-populated and over-exploited reservation lands. The Land Husbandry Act of 1951, designed with the aim of alleviating conditions, was received with indignation – being seen as just a continuation of colonial policy. Hundreds of thousands were being forced to move into protected villages that were not very different from the *bantustans* of the neighbouring South Africa. In *Purchased People* Bishop Lamont described the reality of the poor land in over-populated reservations and criticised the speculation on the ownership of the land by landowners who put their own economic interests ahead of the common good. Bearing in mind that 'land-hunger has always been the most effective motivating force in nationalist movements for independence',[69] he insisted on the need to establish a more equitable distribution of land.

By Way of Conclusion

More than a half-century ago in a small town in Alabama, a young black seamstress with a calm disposition called Rosa Parks, with the provocative idea of not giving up her seat on the bus to a white person began one of the greatest revolutions in the history of the twentieth century, leading to the fight for the recognition of civil rights for the Afro-American community. A Christian pastor, Martin Luther King, was the one who became the clearest expression of the struggle. His face quickly became an icon for the power of a message. Its affirmation of the human brotherhood that could transcend all racial divisions sprang from the deepest convictions of the Gospel. With one more small gesture, this time in the form of a pastoral letter, the explicit stand of the Catholic Church against racism began in the far away colony of Southern Rhodesia. That short pastoral letter with the title *Purchased People,* that an Irish Carmelite bishop wrote when Martin Luther King was marching through the dusty streets of Alabama demanding the integration of black people in the United

States of America, is a very important document for all who wish to learn the history of the Catholic Church and the racial question.

Although little known, *Purchased People* is of enormous value: it is one of the rare but extremely important statements by the Catholic Church against racism in the period before the Second Vatican Council.

Notes

DONAL LAMONT
– THE MAN AND HIS WORK

1   The title takes its inspiration from the 'Speech from the Dock' of
    Robert Emmet, the Irish patriot who was executed in Dublin in 1803.
    The later *Speech from the Dock* was published by Kevin Mayhew in
    cooperation with the Catholic Institute for International Relations in
    1977.

2   Donal Lamont, *Pueblo adquirido Discurso desde el banquillo de los
    acusados*, eds F. Millán and C. Márquez, Ediciones Carmelitanas,
    Madrid, 2011, 9–46.

3   This college, founded in 1860 was the first Carmelite college in
    modern times. It has just celebrated its 150th anniversary. The
    celebrations included a number of important events, including visits
    by the President of Ireland, Mary McAleese and the Archbishop of
    Dublin, Diarmuid Martin. In addition an important history of
    Terenure College was published, written by Prof. Fergus D'Arcy,
    Terenure College 1860–2010, A History, Dublin, 2010.

4   Many years later, in his *Speech from the Dock*, Bishop Lamont said that
    Titus Brandsma 'has been my hero', 68 in this volume.

5   Titus Brandsma's action did not go unnoticed by the German author-
    ities and the circles close to Nazism in the Netherlands, who strongly
    criticised the group of professors. It was one of the first run-ins with
    Nazism that would end up with him being sent to the concentration
    camp in Dachau, where he died in 1942. Cf. L. Glueckert, *Titus
    Brandsma: Friar against Racism*, Darien, Illinois, 1985; F. Millán Romeral,
    'Tito Brandsma y el nazismo; notas sobre un enfrentamiento', *XX
    Siglos* 57, 2007, 158–69.

6   Even though the word 'apartheid' is used mostly in reference to
    South Africa, we use it here in the general meaning that it has
    acquired as synonymous with racial segregation.

7   He explained in his *Speech from the Dock* how he was influenced by the
    people he came to know in St Albert's, and by the unfolding of
    international events. For information about the history and atmosphere
    at the centre in those years, see E. Boaga, 'Il Collegio Internazionale S.
    Alberto di Roma: 100 anni di storia e di servizio', *Analecta Ordinis
    Carmelitarum*, 50 (1999), 236–361.

8   John of the Cross Brenninger, *The Carmelite Directory of the Spiritual
    Life*, Chicago, The Carmelite Press, 1951.

9 Regarding the importance of Brenninger see, among others, E. Boaga, 'P. Giovanni della Croce Brenninger: La persona e l'opera', *Analecta Ordinis Carmelitarum*, 47 (1996), 268–78. J.M. Guarch, *El P. Juan Brenninger visto por los que le trataron de cerca*, Madrid, 1950.

10 See the remarks made by Fr Christopher O'Donnell in his homily delivered at the funeral of Bishop Lamont, in Terenure College, which can be read in *Causa Nostrae Letitiae*, Spring 2004, 35–9, and in the *Terenure College Annual*, Dublin, 2004, 22–4.

11 He revealed this in an interview given to the review, *La Madonna del Carmine*, 31 (4–5/1977), 16–20. I was prepared for this because I could remember the words of Fr Brenninger that I quoted during the trial: 'The Church will always have its martyrs.'

12 D.R. Lamont, O.Carm., *Espositio relationis Divinam inter et spiritualem Beatae Mariae Virginis Maternitatem*, Apud Collegium S. Alberti, Romae, 1938.

13 This is a subject which would need further study, but it would not be out of place to think, given the quality of some of the professors of that time, that in this international centre a very solid theological formation was given, despite the scarcity of qualified people in some areas of theology. One might suggest that it reflected a certain theological current, more vital and spiritual than juridical, that would have a significant effect on different disciplines within the *corpus theologicum*, as it was taught in St Albert's.

14 Theoio nostra studium harum duarum veritatum scilicet, Maternitatis spiritualis B. Virginis, et unitatis omnium redemptorum sub Christo Capite, optime coniungit … Cum proinde Apostolus adeo insistat in hac analogia adhibenda, evidens omnino est, eum non ita velle similitudinem indefinitam proponere, sed potius quod pro eo analogia corporis humani, coiunctio capitis cum membris, modo aliis clariore, mysterium totius Christi, mysterium unionis vitalis omnium redemptorum in organismo supernaturali cuius Christus est caput, naturam intimam ecclesiae realemque cum Christo unionem exponit … (Ibid., 35).

15 A baroque poet, interpreter and orator, born in London around 1613. He was one of the so-called 'metaphysical poets'. In his poetry religious and mystical themes abound. He even wrote an ode to St Teresa of Avila entitled *The Flaming Heart*. He died in Loreto in 1649.

16 See the excellent collection of articles (including some by Donal Lamont) entitled, *Celts among the Shona*, edited by M. Hender, Dublin, 2002. The volume contains some very interesting anecdotes about the first years of this mission in what is now called Zimbabwe.

17 Concerning the first steps on this mission see A. Corbett, 'The First Year: 1946' in *Celts among the Shona*, 7–12. See also J. Smet, *The*

Carmelites, vol. V and G. Toelle, 'Carmelite Foundations (1946–9) in Southern Rhodesia' in *The Sword* 14 (1950–1), 164–9.

[18] This is told by J. Galvin in: *Carmeletter*, 'Diamond Jubilee 1946–2006', May 2007, 5: 'How ill-equipped we were to go into the mission-field ...how foolish, even arrogant, we were during those early days ...'

[19] Lamont, in a '*Letter from the Mission*', made an appeal for help for the mission, explaining the multitude of tasks and challenges that life in this part of Rhodesia presented (reprinted in *Celts among the Shona*, 165–70).

[20] Regarding the missionary work of the Trappists and the Jesuits, see *The Catholic Church in Manicaland*, 7–16.

[21] Lamont, in an open letter addressed to his successor and written from Dublin in 1996, on the occasion of the celebration of the centenary of evangelisation in that area, expressed his gratitude for the wonderful missionary work of both. 'Especially important is the history of the heroic work of the first Jesuits and Trappists who came up through the uncharted and fever-ridden lowlands around the Lundi and the Sabi rivers, and made their way on foot up to the hills of Inyanga to Nyamaropa, Katerere and beyond. Their dedication and courage so impressed the local people that the missionaries who succeeded them were welcomed and their work was made easy by comparison ...', Quoted from: *The Catholic Church in Manicaland*, 5.

[22] See *The Catholic Church in Manicaland*, 17–18. Some years earlier (in 1934) Chichester had set up the Chishawasha Seminary, for the training of local clergy. In relation to the difference in style between Chichester (diplomatic, moderately critical but always observing the proper customs needed to stay on good terms with the white minority) and Lamont (frank, direct and openly critical) see the article by Carmen Marquez Beunza in this volume. When Chichester died unexpectedly on the steps of St Peter's Basilica in 1962, Lamont said of him that, 'the best of the old Catholic England ran in his veins': I. Linden, *The Catholic Church and the Struggle for Zimbabwe*, London, 1980, 43.

[23] A Carmelite from Zimbabwe highlighted this in a magazine commemorating the sixtieth anniversary of Carmelite mission in the country. 'But if we continue on this path our people will get little or nothing of our spirituality', Carmeletter, *Diamond Jubilee 1946–2006*, May 2007, 23–4. See also: *The Catholic Church in Manicaland*, 26–8.

[24] See *The Catholic Church in Manicaland*, 20.

[25] *Celts among the Shona*, 31–4. The news appeared in the official bulletin of the Order, *Analecta Ordinis Carmelitarum*, 20, 1956–7, 165–6 (which reproduced the text of the erection of the new diocese in the metropolitan see of Salisbury, with its seat in Umtali, known as

Mutare today); 167–8 (where we find the text of the appointment taken from the *Acta Apostolicae Sedis* along with the letter that was addressed to the new bishop), 188–90 (with news and commentary on the creation of the new diocese of Umtali and Lamont's appointment).

26 The *Terenure College Annual*, 1957, 40–2. There is no doubt, Lamont could have enjoyed a relatively comfortable position among the colonial authorities, with material comfort and prestige, if he had not taken the pastoral line that he did take and if he had decided to keep up a discrete and formal relationship with the colonial authorities. In this regard, see, for example, the sermon preached on the occasion of the death of George VI in February 1952 at the request of the mayor and the local authority in Umtali, published recently in the review, *Causa Nostrae Letitiae*, spring–summer (2011), 38–9.

27 These words of one who was not a Carmelite are valuable. Mons. D. J. Hatton, the representative of Propaganda Fidei for this section of Africa: 'Mutare's first Bishop, Mgr Donal Lamont, O.Carm. is probably the best known personage in Zimbabwe, and his priests have the affection of Catholic and non-Catholic alike. The Church is making great strides in the Mutare diocese where the zeal of her missionaries is second to none …' (*Celts among the Shona*, 107).

28 The possible confusion between what is diocesan and what belongs to the Carmelite Order, combined with the rather strong personality of Lamont, may explain some of the differences between him and the local Carmelite superiors in the years that followed.

29 See the list of male and female congregations that Christopher O' Donnell includes in his homily, quoted above, note no. 10.

30 The official date of the foundation is 2 February 1959 and its affiliation to the Carmelite Order happened just a few days later on 14 February 1959.

31 The Congregation, that has celebrated its first fifty years, now has 111 professed members, according to the latest edition of the *Status ordinis*. See also *The Catholic Church in Manicaland*, 41–3.

32 To this work, and to many others, both social and religious, the Carmelites have devoted themselves for more than sixty years in Zimbabwe. It is very moving to see the graves of many of them in the cemetery in Triashill Mission.

33 *Celts among the Shona*, 108–9.

34 The letter is preserved in the archive of the Congregation in Mutare and is one of the few expressions by Lamont that are extant and that deal with the foundation of the sisters. It was made available to us very kindly by the Superior General, Sister Evelyn Kadzere. It was published in part in *The Catholic Church in Manicaland*, 42–3.

[35] See *The Catholic Church in Manicaland*, 21.

[36] Ibid., 23–5. It would seem that for this reason Lamont asked the author Hilda Richards to write a brief history of the diocese. This book was never published. See *Carmeletter*, 'Diamond Jubilee 1946–2006', May 2007, 5.

[37] Bishop Lamont, at the beginning of *Purchased People*, alludes to things that were happening in the area. Some of the later editions include an introduction that explains the existing situation.

[38] Years later, Lamont would indicate that the fact that the government would place restrictions on the black population, even in Churches, caused him great difficulty.

[39] *The Catholic Church in Manicaland*, 47–56.

[40] He was a medical doctor who had studied in Europe. When the protests began he was working as a doctor in Ghana. Banda returned to Nyasaland in 1958 and headed the rebel movement. He would end up becoming the prime minister and first president of Malawi, and he governed the country somewhat like a dictator from 1966 till his death in South Africa in 1997, having amassed an immense personal fortune.

[41] Three in particular, approved together on 15 May 1959: The Unlawful Organisation Act, which destroyed any attempt to create a political organisation or association, The Preventive Detention Act, which in practice gave the government the freedom to detain local leaders without any kind of guarantee, and the Public Order Amendment Act, which under the pretext of preserving public order, gave the government lots of room to manoeuvre.

[42] I will limit myself to a brief outline of the letter. For a full analysis of the document I refer you to the work of Carmen Márquez Beunza in this same volume. The original English text can be found in an edition put together by the Catholic Mission Press, Gwelo, 1959, or in the recent edition published in *Analecta Ordinis Carmelitarum*, 61, 2010, 117–47, on the occasion of the fiftieth anniversary of the Pastoral Letter.

[43] The full list can be seen in *The Catholic Church in Manicaland*, 47–8.

[44] *Purchased People*, 16 (in *Rhodesia – the Moral Issue*, 'Pastoral Letters of the Catholic Bishops', Gwelo: Mambo Press, 1968).

[45] Original text in *Acta Apostolicae Sedis*, XXXI, 1939, 427–8.

[46] See *Purchased People* in this volume, 19.

[47] Ibid.

[48] Lamont invites them not to be taken in by Communism ('the devil the African does not know'), an important point, when dealing with the accusations that were made against Lamont later on in the midst of the conflict in 1976.

49 By its work, the Church ensures that the good that has been placed in the mind and in the heart of the human person, in the rites and cultures of these peoples, will not only not disappear, but will gain strength and be raised up and perfected for the glory of God, the confusion of the evil one and the happiness of the human person. (*LG* 17)

50 Faithful to its own tradition, and conscious of the universality of its mission (the Church) is able to enter into communion with different forms of culture, a communion that will enrich the Church, and the different cultures at the same time. (*GS* 58)

51 'And so, whatever good is found to be sown in the hearts and minds of people, or in the rites and cultures peculiar to various peoples, not only is not lost, but is healed, uplifted, and perfected for the glory of God, the shame of the demon, and the bliss of people.' (*AG* 9)

52 Once more, the position of the Carmelite bishop distances him from the propaganda of sectors close to Communism which, we must not forget, were beginning to exercise more and more pressure in certain parts of Africa. See note 31.

53 The Carmelites have been working since 1985 in Kriste Mambo (Christ the King) College, that earlier had been run by religious from the Netherlands, the Dutch Sisters of Mercy, and has offered a very high standard of education to local girls.

54 Here Lamont proposes the example of the bishops of the countries behind the iron curtain who paid the price of a loss of freedom for their mission of announcing the truth without fear or deceit. It is a further example of the opposition to Communism that is evident in the letter (see notes 31 and 35) and a denial of the accusations that were made against him at a later date.

55 See *Purchased People* in this volume, 23.

56 *Peace through Justice*, Pastoral Instruction of the Catholic Bishops of Southern Rhodesia (1961). It was a hard-hitting letter in which the bishops again denounced the evil of racial discrimination and pointed out that without social justice and without fundamental moral values, African society will not find any kind of true and lasting peace.

57 Donal Lamont, 'Ad Gentes: a Missionary Bishop Remembers' in AA.VV., *Vatican II: By Those Who Were There*, ed., A. Stacpoole, London 1986, 270–82. See also the work by E. Boaga, 'Mons. Donal Raymond Lamont al Concilio Vaticano II', *Analecta Ordinis Carmelitarum* 54 (2003) 207–20.

58 Y. Congar recounts in *Mon Journal du Concile* (Du Cerf, Paris 2002), that he felt a little disillusioned by the pomp of the opening ceremony, while at the same time noting a certain nervousness and joy about being there at that historical moment.

[59] D. Lamont, 'Ad Gentes: A Missionary Bishop Remembers', 272.

[60] A photo that appeared in a number of newspapers and Carmelite magazines of the time shows all the Carmelite participants of the Council on the patio of St Albert's. Very soon *Edizioni Carmelitane* will publish a collection of articles by Fr Redemptus M. Valabek first published in *Carmel in the World*, during the years of the Council and the period immediately after, in which the part Carmelites played in the work of the council can be clearly seen.

[61] 'Since, however, the laws and customs of the Latin Church in force today in many areas render it difficult to fulfil these functions, which are so extremely necessary for the life of the Church, it will be possible in the future to restore the diaconate as a proper and permanent rank of the hierarchy' (LG 29). The topic was developed further in later pontifical documents such as the apostolic letter *Sacrum diaconatus ordinem*, 18 June 1967, in which the corresponding canonical norms are given; in the apostolic Constitution, *Pontificalis romanis recognitio*, 17 June 1968, in which the new rite was established; or the Motu proprio, *Ad Pascendum*, 15 August 1972, among others.

[62] See 'E. Boaga, Mons. Donal Raymond Lamont', 210. See also *Unitatis redintegratio* (UR), no. 11.

[63] A record of this visit appears with a photograph in the programme for the festivities at the Basilica, published in the review, *Madonna Tal-Karmnu*, Lulju, 1995, 39, 47.

[64] John XXIII appointed him in June 1962 as the first Prelate of Chuquibamba in Peru. He was ordained a bishop on 30 April 1967 and died in Malta on 10 February 1978.

[65] See Xiberta's excellent study of this theme in S. Madrigal Terrazas, 'Primado y episcopado, la solucion xibertiana', in AA.VV. *Cerni essentia veritatis*. Miscelánea homenaje al P. Xiberta de la Región Iberica Carmelita, F. Millán Romeral, ed., Claret, Barcelona, 1999, 189–217. There is also a reference to this question in a wider ecclesiological study in, 'El servicio de Pedro en il siglo XXI' in AA.VV., *Ser cristiano en el siglo XXI*, Salamanca, 2001, 299. Recently a thesis was defended at the Pontifical Gregorian University in Rome, directed by Salvador Pié Ninot, on the ecclesiology of Xiberta in which special attention was given to this theme. See J. M. Manresa Lamarca, *La eclesiología del P. B. Xiberta (1897–1967). El «Redescubrimiento» de la Iglesia como «la obra de Cristo»* (Roma, 2011).

[66] 'I shall never understand how my name came to be proposed as a candidate for the newly created Secretariat for the Promotion of the Christian Unity', Donal Lamont, *Ad Gentes: A Missionary Bishop Remembers*, 272.

[67] Ibid.

68 'Simply to be a member of the Secretariat, to attend the regular and hard working meetings, to have one's mind sharpened by men such as Bea, Willebrands, de Smedt, Congar, Deprey, Pavan, Courtney Murray, Barnabas Ahern and others was an education *sans pareil*, a formation for life and for this Council in particular. Who could have associated with such men without something rubbing off?' Donal Lamont, *Ad Gentes: A Missionary Bishop Remembers*, 273.

69 See E. Boaga, *Mons. Donal Raymond Lamont*, 213. See also *G. Caprile, Il Concilio Vaticano II*, vol. IV, Roma, 1966–8, 88.

70 See the interesting references to this question that S. Madrigal makes in *Memoria del Concilio. Diez evocaciones del Vaticano II*, Madrid/Bilbao, 2005, 46, 154–5.

71 As Congar pointed out in his diary, in relation to another moment in the Council, the *ecclesia* was putting the Curia in its place (S. Madrigal, *Memoria del Concilio*, 47).

72 E. Boaga, 'Mons. Donal Raymond Lamont', 215–16.

73 D. Lamont, *Ad Gentes: A Missionary Bishop Remembers*, 274.

74 Regarding this period before the discussion on the draft, see N. Tanner, 'The Church in the World (*Ecclesia ad extra*)', in AA.VV., *History of the II Vatican Council II, IV*, ed. G. Alberigo, 331–45.

75 E. Boaga, 'Mons. Donal Raymond Lamont', 216. Lamont made a reference to an Italian Carmelite colleague, D. Lamont, *Ad Gentes: A Missionary Bishops Remembers*, 275. Boaga names him as Stefano Pozzanzini, O.Carm. Some Irish Carmelites point out that Lamont also spoke about the help received from Aloysius Ryan, O.Carm. for the Latin version of his speech.

76 D. Lamont, *Ad Gentes: A Missionary Bishop Remembers*, 275.

77 Tanner points out: This was the only working session of the Council – as distinct from solemn sessions to open or conclude the Council – that either John XXIII or Paul VI attended. Indeed, inasmuch as Pius IX and the popes of the time did not attend the working sessions of Vatican I and Trent, it was the first time that a pope had attended such a session of an ecumenical or general council since the Middle Ages …, N. Tanner, *The Church in the World*, 333.

78 *Mon Journal du Concile II*, Du Cerf, Paris, 2002, 243.

79 'It was a good omen. Seven is my lucky number – so superstitious are the bishops!', D. Lamont, *Ad Gentes: A Missionary Bishop Remembers*, 277.

80 See *Acta Synodalia*, III–6, 373, 392.

81 Lamont commented with some humour that because some words in the simile were hard to find in Latin they caught the attention of many of the Fathers who were listening with a lot of curiosity. This helped to relax the atmosphere. *Ad Gentes: A Missionary Bishop Remembers*, 278.

[82] As seemed most appropriate, this was the reading chosen for Bishop Lamont's funeral at Terenure College in Dublin, 2003.

[83] C. O'Donnell commented in his funeral homily 'In his speech Bishop Lamont spoke with irony and barely controlled anger ...' (See note 10).

[84] *Acta Synodalia*, III–6, 392.

[85] The recollections of D. Hurley, Archbishop of Durban (South Africa) are very interesting in this regard. In his *Memories of Vatican II: Keeping the Dream Alive*, Pierermaritzburg 2005, he wrote: 'It is possible that out of respect for the Holy Father's favourable view of the schema, these speakers toned down their criticisms.' Then he went on to refer to the intervention of Cardinal Frings and of two bishops as the most memorable, the well-known Fulton Sheen and Donal Lamont, about whom he says, 'Bishop Lamont made heavy calls on his not inconsiderable endowments in the line of histrionics and humour and produced a side-splitting lament over the emaciated condition of the schema. In glowing language he described what members of the Council had been expecting and contrasted that with what they actually found in the schema, borrowing the image of a field of dry bones from the Prophet Ezechiel. Pausing for effect, he brought out two words with devastating emphasis: "*ossa arida*". The Council was convulsed but the Bishop received an admonition from the Moderator, Cardinal Dopfner, who did not seem to appreciate the "oratory". When Bishop Lamont got back to his seat he found a note waiting for him. It read as follows: "Your mission subsidy has been cut by 50%, signed, Cardinal Agagianian." The culprit was Bishop Ernest Green of Port Elizabeth, South Africa. Bishop Lamont later described how while he was listening to the words of commendation pronounced by the Holy Father, he had felt the text of his intervention burning a hole in his pocket,' 112.

[86] Lamont, summed up his intervention by saying: 'Man's innate sense of humour seemed to have been touched, and hard cerebral attitudes melted. The Holy Spirit acts that way. Thoroughly mature and integrated men cannot remain too serious for too long. The Council began to be a happy place ...', D. Lamont, *Ad Gentes: A Missionary Bishop Remembers*, 279.

[87] D. Hurley, in his *Memories of Vatican II: Keeping the Dream Alive*, Pietermaritzburg, 2005, comments on the radical change that this second draft meant with respect to the 'dry bones' of the first draft: 'This schema, characterised as "dry bones" in the now historical speech of Bishop Lamont of Umtali, had been rejected by the Council in the third session. It had come back filled out with flesh and blood,' 136.

[88] Barth was invited as an observer to the last two sessions of the Council, but could not attend for reasons of poor health.

89 Congar mentions this in *Mon Journal du Concile II*, 533. Congar also pointed out in his diary, that he had written the first chapter of the Decree with some help from J. Ratzinger. See cf. S. Madrigal, *Memoria del Concilio*, 65, 283–4.

90 S. Madrigal, *Memoria del Concilio*, 57–9.

91 Ibid., 154.

92 Some years later, indeed, Paul VI would firmly support him when he was in conflict with the government of Ian Smith. This conflict led to the expulsion of Lamont from Zimbabwe.

93 See note 66.

94 Originally from New Zealand, he got very involved in the political scene in Zimbabwe and in the defence of the black majority. This cost both him and his family. They had to suffer a number of different repressive measures, even imprisonment. In the last years of his life, he confronted the Mugabe government and criticised the dictatorial steps he and his government were taking. On account of this, he was stripped of his Zimbabwean citizenship. He died in 2002.

95 *A Plea for Peace*, 1965. See also *The Catholic Church in Manicaland*, 49.

96 He wrote, for example, the following: 'However, it is no surprise that many people say, That's what Christian civilisation is like! That's Christianity! The protection of the few and the rich and the abandonment of the many who have nothing! They also say, It's like as if the missionaries, exponents of Christianity, have deceived us. They came here just to prepare the way for the racist state where we will always be the ones who do all the hard work and where a few privileged people will be able to control and delay our development indefinitely.' The government tried to suppress this paragraph in the Chisora and Ndebele translations of the letter. Many years later, Lamont would point out that his expulsion from the country would help in the process of purification of the Church in Zimbabwe since many were of the opinion that the Church would never be able to stand up to the white minority. See *La Madonna del Carmine*, 31 (4–5/1977), 19.

97 In *Speech from the Dock,* he stated: 'The same racist ethic that is the source of all our present discriminatory legislation, that informs the minds of the electorate and determines the customs of the privileged governing class, is completely alien to the mind of Christ.'

98 M. Hender, *Our 1970s in Zimbabwe*, Harare 2011, 8–11.

99 *Speech from the Dock*, 114ff. See also T. Sheehy and E. Sudwort, 'Bishop Donal Lamont of Umtali', *The Sword* 63 (2003), 61–72.

100 It would be interesting to compare this argument with what Titus Brandsma used in his declaration before Sergeant Hardegen in 1942. There are a number of interesting similarities.

[101] One example was the review *Cambio 16* in Spain. In it there is a report with the title, 'Lamont, Red Bishop', *Cambio 16*, 251, 27 November 1976, 51–2. Among other reviews that wrote about him we might pick out one that had the title, 'He wanted to be found guilty', in *Nigrizia*, 95, 1977, 20–4; likewise, 'Rhodesia's Bishop Lamont in exile; U.S. Speech', *Origins*, 8, 1978, 296–9; 'Conscience compels me: the witness of Bishop Lamont', *St Anthony's Messenger*, 85, July 1977, 12–22.

[102] In the General Archive of the Order in Rome, the correspondence that he kept up with Fr Louis Rogge, of the Province of the Most Pure Heart of Mary (PCM), and this latter's correspondence with Fr P. Raymond C. Baumhart, SJ, President of Loyola University of Chicago, with the idea that Lamont might accept a doctorate *honoris causa* from that university. In the end it was never bestowed because Lamont was not able to travel to the United States.

[103] Fr Falco Thuis, Prior General of the Carmelite Order, had sent him a message as his trial approached saying: 'The General Curia and all your Carmelite Confreres send a message of comfort to you in these difficult days.' The telegram is preserved in the General Archive of the Order.

[104] 'Your affection and solidarity has helped me greatly in these difficult days' is what Bishop Lamont wrote. His message is preserved in the archive of the parish. The parish priest Fr Lucio Zappatore very graciously showed it to us.

[105] Regarding the time he spent in Rome in April 1977, see *La Madonna del Carmine*, 31 (4–5/1977), 1, 16–19.

[106] In the letter from May 1991 that we mentioned earlier (see note 26), to the Superior General, Sr Immaculata, and the other sisters, Lamont, now in Dublin, expressed his concern for the health of Bishop Alexio, who by all accounts was in very poor health at that time and he concluded: 'Please, convey my great and prayerful sympathy to the diocese. Pray for me too that I may do God's will in everything. You probably remember that that was the motto I chose as a Bishop, *Ut placeam Deo*, that I may please God …'

[107] 'Two years ago, I offered my letter of resignation as Bishop of Umtali to the Holy Father, because I could never speak the native language all that well and because I believe that it is necessary and indispensable to proclaim the Gospel in the normal way that the people can understand,' interview in *La Madonna del Carmine*, 31 (4–5/1977), 17.

Ut placeam Deo:
'That I May Please God'

1   The article was published in *Time* magazine, on 13 April 1970.
2   This is how Lamont himself expresses it: 'Once again the experience of four years working in an international atmosphere, meeting intelligent and disciplined men from every corner of the globe, influenced my understanding of world affairs, and made me realise there was emerging in history a planetary unity of mankind and a notion of international community. The contrast with the parochial, morally primitive and racist existence of Rhodesia, provided a revelation and a shock from which I have never recovered.' D. Lamont, *Speech from the Dock* in this volume, 79.
3   Ibid., 80.
4   Ibid., 82.
5   This member of the Congregation of the Oblates of Mary Immaculate (OMI) was born in Cape Town and gloried in the fact that he grew up on Robben Island before it became a prison that housed the prisoner Mandela. He was appointed Bishop of Durban at the age of thirty-one. In 1951 he was elected the first President of the South African Bishops' Conference, having been for many years the most outstanding of the South African bishops. He died in February 2004, at the time he was writing his memoirs, that were thus interrupted just when he had concluded the part on the second Vatican Council. They have been published in two volumes: P. Kearney was the editor. *Memories: The Memories of the Archbishop Denis E. Hurley OMI*, Pietermaritzburg, 2006; D. Hurley, *Memories of Vatican II: Keeping the Dream Alive*, Pietermaritzburg, 2005.
6   In 1939, as apostolic vicar in Cape Town, Hennemann wrote a pastoral letter in which, breaking with the tradition of episcopal silence, he stated that segregation constituted a grave danger as it would incite hatred and confrontation. In line with Christian morality, he condemned all attempts at racial segregation. The rise to power of the Afrikaner nationalists in 1948 gave rise to the publication of another letter, this time to the clergy of his vicariate, with the title *Crisis in the life of the Nation.*
7   Regarding the work of the Anglican Church in South Africa at the time of apartheid, see T. Huddleston, *Naught for your Comfort*, London, 1956; M. Worsnip, *Between the Two Fires: The Anglican Church*

and Apartheid, 1948–1957, Pietermaritzburg, 1991; A. Paton, *Apartheid and the Archbishop: the Life and Times of Geoffrey Clayton*, London, 1974.

8   See *Speech from the Dock* in this volume, 74.

9   At that time, South Africa was divided into four territories – two under British rule: the Cape and Natal; and in the north, the two republics governed by the Boers: the Free Orange State and the Republic of the Transvaal. The discovery of diamonds (1867) and gold (1886) in the 'highlands' of the Boers sparked British interest, seeing here the opportunity to prop up financially an empire that was beginning to flag. Hence the convenience of gaining the territories to the north of the Boer republics. The British expansionist policy however met with the resistance of the Boers. The situation was resolved by victory for the British in the British–Boer war.

10 The first attempt goes back to the beginning of the seventeenth century. The second took place in 1879, at the instigation of the Vicar Apostolic of the East Cape, who sent a dozen Jesuits to follow the trail of Livingstone, and evangelise present-day Malawi and the country of the Ndebele.

11 Both in the time of the government of the Dutch East Indies Company (1652–1795) and in the short period of British rule (1795–1803), Catholicism was prohibited. Only in the short period of the Batavian Republic (1804–06) was religious freedom granted to Catholics. The first Vicar Apostolic for the Cape, appointed by Pope Pius VII in 1818, who never managed to set foot in Africa, had to set up his residence on the island of Mauritius. The same thing happened to his successor, who also had to lead the Catholic community from that beautiful island. The Irish Dominican, Raymond Griffith, third Vicar Apostolic, had more luck. Under new legislation, he was allowed to have his residence in South Africa and, in 1837, he was appointed bishop of the Cape. With him the official history of the Catholic Church in South Africa began.

12 I. Linden, *The Catholic Church and the Struggle for Zimbabwe*, London, 1980, 7.

13 The amazing history of this Trappist monastery, which, with two hundred and eighty-five monks, became, at the end of the nineteenth century, the largest Trappist monastery in the world, and which had acquired the largest amount of lands, deserves to be recorded. Behind its development there is the figure of the Austrian Trappist Franz Pfanner, who responded to the invitation from the bishop of the East Cape colony to set up a community that would serve as a model of agricultural management. The difficulties of combining missionary work with the norms regarding silence and the disciplines of Trappist life gave reason to separate from the Trappists and the foundation

of a new congregation, the Marianhill Missionaries. When the separation occurred in 1909, the monastery was attending to the more than fifty churches in the twenty-five missions that they had founded, and they had converted some twenty thousand Africans. Regarding the history of the Congregation of the Marianhill Missionaries see this monograph: R. Kneipp (et. al.) *Marianhill and Its Apostolate: Origin and Growth of the Congregation of the Marianhill Missionaries.* Reimligen, 1964.

14 Quoted in I. Linden, op. cit., 19.

15 The origins of this organisation go back to 1899, when the priest Gerardo Villota founded the *Colegio de Ultramar y Propaganda Fidei* that, at the instigation of Pope Benedict XV, in 1920 became the National Seminary for the Missions. In 1947 it became the Instituto Español de Misiones Extranjeras and came under the Congregation of Propaganda Fide.

16 See I. Linden, op. cit., 43–5.

17 Ibid., 28.

18 Ibid., 32.

19 The Salisbury Catholic Social Club, to which Lamont sometimes makes reference, was a society of business and professional men, under the patronage of the bishop of Salisbury. In 1959, the Archbishop, Markall, who succeeded Chichester at the head of the archdiocese, tried to convert it into a multiracial club, by reforming its statutes to allow the admission of black members. His attempt failed and he withdrew his patronage.

20 Quoted in I. Linden, op. cit., 31.

21 Ibid., 43.

22 Ibid., 46.

23 We must remember that for Afrikaner nationalism, that was a fervent profession of Calvinism, Catholicism was considered to be 'a danger to the soul of the nation'. It was a foreign ideology, with a foreign world vision, and a multiracialism and universalism that were contrary to Afrikaner nationalism and which furthermore constituted a danger to genuine Christian faith. See J. de Gruchy, 'Catholics in a Calvinistic Country', in A. Prior, ed., *Catholics in Apartheid Society*, Cape Town, 1982, 67–81.

24 See I. Linden, op. cit., 51.

25 See *Purchased People* in this volume, 18.

26 I. Linden, op. cit., 52. With Salisbury and Pretoria, Linden is alluding to the respective seats of Markall and the Apostolic Delegate.

27 See *Purchased People* in this volume, 33.

28 Ibid., 45.

29 Ibid., 45.

[30]   J. Reader, *Africa, Biography of a Continent*, New York, 1997, 640.

[31]   J. de Gruchy, 'Christianity in South Africa' in M. Porzesky and J. de Gruchy, eds, *Living Faith in South Africa*, New York, 1995, 87.

[32]   Among the most notable, there was the Anglican priest, James Calata, who was the General Secretary of the organisation from 1936 to 1949, and the congregational lay preacher, Albert Lutuli, joint recipient of the Nobel Peace Prize in 1961.

[33]   N. Mandela, *Long Walk to Freedom*, Little Brown, 2008.

[34]   See I. Linden, op. cit., 58. In fact in Southern Rhodesia, the efforts by the government to put an end to the nationalist movement proved to be entirely fruitless in the face of an organisation that unceasingly reproduced itself, like an octopus. After the outlawing of the African National Congress, a new group emerged, the National Democratic Party which in turn was reborn in the Zimbabwe African People's Union.

[35]   See *Speech from the Dock* in this volume, 66.

[36]   See I. Linden, op. cit., 26.

[37]   See *Speech from the Dock* in this volume, 78.

[38]   See J. Reader, *Africa, A Biography of a Continent*, 629.

[39]   See N. Mandela, op. cit., 110–18.

[40]   See J. Reader, op. cit., 623.

[41]   See *Speech from the Dock* in this volume, 69.

[42]   Ibid., 83.

[43]   Cf. ibid., 67.

[44]   J. Messner, *Naturrecht: Handbuch der Gesellschaftethik, Staatsethik und Wirtschaftsethik*, Berlin, 1950.

[45]   The document may be consulted in A. Prior, ed., *Catholics in Apartheid Society*, Cape Town, 1982, 167–9.

[46]   By way of an example, Lamont's complaint about the very meagre number of Africans who were invited to the Mass that was celebrated for the election of Pope John XXIII.

[47]   Y. Congar, *L'Eglise Catholique devan la question raciale*, Paris, 1953.

[48]   An interesting analysis of the social teaching of the magisterium and its application to the racial question may be seen in D. Hurley, 'Catholic Social Teaching and Ideology', in A. Prior, ed., *Catholics in Apartheid Society*, 22–4.

[49]   Bishop Lamont recognised how he revised his own views on this question in the light of the council teaching.

[50]   In the vision that D. Hurley presents, *Purchased People* is situated at a time when the problem was in a stage of fermentation and attracted the attention of the local hierarchies in countries like South Africa, Zimbabwe and the USA where racism was particularly serious. All

of those reflections contributed to the position taken by Pope Paul VI in *Populorum progressio*, see D. Hurley, op. cit., 41.

51 J. H. Oldham, *Christianity and the Race Problem*, London, 1924.

52 D. Tutu, *Hope and Suffering*, Grand Rapids, 1984, 36.

53 See *Purchased People* in this volume, 43.

54 Ibid., 22.

55 Ibid., 35.

56 The centrality of education can be seen in the words of Arthur Hinsley, Apostolic Visitator of Catholic missions in the British colonies in Africa, who, in 1928 warned the missionaries to make sure that education was their first priority. Having urged them to work in close collaboration with the respective governments he went on: 'Collaborate with all your power and where it is impossible for you to carry on both the immediate task of evangelisation and your educational work, neglect your churches in order to perfect your schools', C. Groves, *The Planting of Christianity in Africa*, vol. IV, Cambridge, 2002, 119.

57 P. Kearney, ed., *Memories: The Memories of the Archbishop Denis E. Hurley*, 57.

58 See *Purchased People* in this volume, 42.

59 See I. Linden, op. cit., 47.

60 See P. Kearney, op. cit., 103.

61 *The Southern Cross* was the semi-official publication of the South African Conference of Bishops.

62 See *Purchased People* in this volume, 38.

63 Ibid., 45.

64 P Kearney, ed., *Memories: The Memories of the Archbishop Denis E. Hurley*, 118. Hurley recognised, at that time the very forceful response of the Church when it saw its rights being threatened became a more cautious and vacillating reaction when human rights were at stake.

65 See *Purchased People* in this volume, 39.

66 See C. Groves, *The Planting of Christianity in Africa*, vol. IV, Cambridge, 1958, 91.

67 Quoted in I. Linden, op. cit., 31.

68 See *Purchased People* in this volume, 36–9.

69 Ibid., 35.